Mindlessness

Mindlessness

The Corruption of Mindfulness in a Culture of Narcissism

THOMAS JOINER, PhD

OXFORD
UNIVERSITY PRESS

Oxford University Press is a department of the University of Oxford. It furthers
the University's objective of excellence in research, scholarship, and education
by publishing worldwide. Oxford is a registered trade mark of Oxford University
Press in the UK and certain other countries.

Published in the United States of America by Oxford University Press
198 Madison Avenue, New York, NY 10016, United States of America.

Library of Congress Cataloging-in-Publication Data
Names: Joiner, Thomas, Jr., author.
Title: Mindlessness : the corruption of mindfulness in a culture
of narcissism / Thomas Joiner.
Description: 1 Edition. | New York : Oxford University Press, 2017. |
Includes bibliographical references and index.
Identifiers: LCCN 2017006335 (print) | LCCN 2017020685 (ebook) |
ISBN 9780190200633 (updf) | ISBN 9780190200640 (epub) |
ISBN 9780190200626 (hardback)
Subjects: LCSH: Mindfulness (Psychology) | Attention. | Narcissism. |
Self-interest. | BISAC: PSYCHOLOGY / Clinical Psychology.
Classification: LCC BF637.M56 (ebook) | LCC BF637.M56 J65 2017 (print) |
DDC 158.1—dc23
LC record available at https://lccn.loc.gov/2017006335

9 8 7 6 5 4 3 2 1

Printed by Sheridan Books, Inc., United States of America

Contents

Introduction
Favor the Penguin and Fear the "Selfie"

THE TALE TO BE TOLD IN THESE PAGES IS OF A NOBLE AND useful idea—mindfulness—sullied by a culture of superficiality, mediocrity, and especially, selfishness. Although there are various definitions of mindfulness,[1] a workable one is the nonjudgmental awareness of the richness, subtlety, and variety of the present moment—importantly, *all* of the present moment, not just the self. It is not the same thing as meditation, though meditative activities and exercises are often deployed in its cultivation. Neither is it the emptying of the mind; far from it, as the emphasis is on full awareness. Mindfulness is a currently popular notion, and trends suggest that this is unlikely to change any time soon. One reason for the popularity of mindfulness is that there is both a nobility and a humility inherent in this approach to life. It is noble in the sense that it recognizes every instant of existence, even those of great misery, as teeming and sundry. It is humble in the sense that it places the self in its proper, miniscule place within each moment's infinitude. Another reason for mindfulness' popularity is that it represents a potentially effective solution to problems in living as diverse as performance anxiety during standardized testing, poor decision-making, mild cognitive impairment, and major depressive disorder.

There is much to admire in this version of mindfulness, the form, it should be emphasized, which was and remains the original and undiluted version. The critique contained within the following pages is aimed *not* at this genuine, authentic version of mindfulness. This original version, however, is not completely beyond criticism, and indeed a part of what follows points out limitations and problems that are inherent to even the original version of mindfulness. But this book is mostly not about mindfulness as just described; instead it acknowledges the utility and refinement of the authentic original as it protests the adulteration of mindfulness into something altogether different.

To get a sense of the difference between these two versions of mindfulness, consider the views of a psychiatrist of my acquaintance, who has few rivals in terms of the extent of his erudition, the range of his reading, and the richness of his decades-long experience with the mental health landscape. His understanding of mindfulness was that it directed people to gaze inward, and his thorough familiarity with the folly of doing so made him very skeptical of mindfulness, which he understood as "chronic undifferentiated narcissistic self-preoccupation." Another psychiatrist of my acquaintance, also widely read and insightful, viewed what he had seen of mindfulness circles as "condescending and inflexible," two of the last descriptors for which genuine mindfulness advocates would strive. My wise friends have misunderstood what mindfulness was originally meant to be, but they have very clearly understood what it has been defiled into, at least in some quarters.

From within the mental health field, and certainly from within certain subspecialties of it (e.g., nonacademically oriented clinicians), the spread and ubiquity of mindfulness-related ideas is approaching a full saturation point. It is worth remembering, however, that this is not nearly as much the case as one moves from these subspecialties to groups removed from them. I have already mentioned my psychiatrist friends, who had heard of mindfulness, or rather of the ersatz version of it. I recently had the pleasure of a dinner with the parents of my best friend from childhood. My friend and I are now around 50; his parents one generation older, of course. These are educated and cultured people, who, when they asked me what book I was writing and I told them, could not have been nicer in their encouragement nor clearer that they had never heard of mindfulness (they are not mental health professionals). Indeed, in a survey of more than 2,000 British adults, the organization YouGov reported that only 11% believed they had a good understanding of what mindfulness is, and it is an open question as to just how good of an understanding these 11% really have.[2]

A preoccupation of this book is the effects of mindfulness and kin concepts on the general culture and vice versa. It would be an exaggeration to view mindfulness as the main driver or even a main driver of unfortunate cultural trends (trends to be identified throughout the book). A more realistic view perhaps, and nevertheless a worrisome one, is that "faux" mindfulness is one of many voices in a chorus, a chorus which, if not encouraging trends like egoism is compatible with them, and which in turn could have significant negative effects on a species that is already inherently pretty self-concerned, but that needs a vibrant polity and society to survive and prosper.

The book thus needs to manage two realities: Overall, even deplorably distorted versions of mindfulness are a drop in the cultural bucket; and, depending on the drop (cf. a lit match) and on what else is in the bucket (cf. kerosene), one drop can make a difference and even be disastrous. True mindfulness is being usurped by an impostor, and the impostor is loud and strutting enough that it has replaced the original in the general understanding of what "mindfulness" is, at least for many people. And not just in the general understanding, but even in the understanding of specialists, even those with awe-inspiring perspicacity, like my psychiatrist friends. This represents one drop in the cultural bucket, and this book asks whether it is a bad enough drop to make a difference or even be ruinous.

Just as an earthquake can transform an architectural wonder into a pile of rubble, and just as the viability of a spacecraft can change from complete to disastrous with the smallest of breaches, so mindfulness has been transformed into its creepy, self-obsessed doppelgänger. However, when a building is obliterated or spacecraft destroyed, they are gone, and the rubble is no longer called "a building," the debris no longer called "a spacecraft." By contrast, mindfulness—the original, unsullied version—is not gone; it still exists with its imperfections, nobility, humility, and utility intact, for now. What also exists side by side with genuine mindfulness is an ersatz version of it, one that has exploited the original version's weaknesses and one that in my view encourages narcissism, spawns a circuit of workshop peddlers, trumpets its own glories (even though there are none), and misunderstands human nature, while in reality containing none of the nobility, humility, and utility of the true original. A dilemma, and an impetus for this book, is that both things are called "mindfulness". One truly is, and the other certainly is not, leading to confusion and to the possibility of the imposter version transcending and choking out the genuine article.

The story to be told in these pages is thus of the rise and fall of a constructive if imperfect idea—authentic mindfulness. Derailed by a culture of self-importance, authentic mindfulness has lost its way and its doppelgänger has appeared, a vehicle for solipsism. Troublingly, this denatured version of mindfulness has proliferated. The cover article of the February 4, 2013, issue of *Time* magazine observes "we're in the midst of a popular obsession with mindfulness as *the secret* to health and happiness" (italics added). We have heard many such "secrets" already and seem to have trouble learning from the inevitable disappointments of naive belief in the absurd. Indeed, in 2003 the same magazine ran a similar cover story, but about meditation instead of mindfulness. In both instances and perhaps tellingly, a blond-haired quite beautiful white woman, in white flowing garb, was depicted on the cover rapturously engaging in the wondrous activity du jour. At the annual meeting of the American Psychiatric Association in 2016, attendees were reminded in the conference materials to "take a Zen moment" by stopping in at "the new meditation zone . . . bring your own yoga mat . . ." This advice was accompanied by a picture of an attractive and youthful white female with blond hair doing yoga. *Time* told us in 2003 of meditation's potential. If there was potential, it is as yet unrealized, however, as we will see, there are claims to the contrary.

Recent books on the topic are numerous (e.g., *Mindful Parenting, Mindful Eating, Mindful Teaching, Mindful Politics, Mindful Therapy, Mindful Leadership, A Mindful Nation, Mindful Recovery, The Power of Mindful Learning, The Mindful Brain, The Mindful Way through Depression,* and *The Mindful Path to Self-Compassion*). There is a Center for Mindfulness and Justice, a Center for Mindfulness and Empathy Education, a Center for Compassion Focused Therapy and Mindfulness, and so many centers for mindfulness that an accurate tally is a challenge. "Dancing Mindfulness" is a thing that exists. There is a new monthly magazine called *Mindful* and an academic journal called *Mindfulness*. Mindfulness even has its own month (it's May).

I know yet another psychiatrist, also talented and experienced, who was developing a book project on the understanding and management of bipolar disorder. Part of the reviewer feedback he received boiled down to "less lithium, more mindfulness" (despite the fact, with which the psychiatrist had deep familiarity, that "less lithium" can and repeatedly has led to more death by suicide in patients with bipolar disorder).

Approximately 500 employees of General Mills have gone through mindfulness classes, and in every building of the company's Minneapolis campus, there is a meditation room. General Motors and Target have similar programs. The World Economic Forum begins its day, every day, with meditation sessions. At the meeting of the International Association for Suicide Prevention in Norway, there was a gathering on top of the Oslo opera house early in the morning for everyone to practice mindfulness. One of the first times I ever used the camera on my phone (after first grappling with it to get it off its inevitable "selfie" default setting) was in the Amsterdam airport. The photo is of a sign the designers of which apparently intended to convey very basic and essential information: Directions to emergency exits; directions to first aid stations; and directions to the nearest meditation room. A highly similar sign in San Francisco's airport lacks reference to a meditation room but includes directions to the yoga room. I pointed out yet another such sign to my graduate students as we were on our way to a conference in Chicago; they were amused by my observation as well as bemused that they had never really noticed such signs before, an indication of cultural saturation. Another clear signal of cultural spread is whatever is now being taught at children's martial arts classes, and sure enough, along with actual martial arts, and their centuries of thought, practice, and refinement in the making, there are now mindfulness classes, the McMansion on the block. Speaking of which, another sure sign of cultural saturation is that one can now have "a more mindful burger" (at Epic

Burger in Chicago). I believed I had taken a picture of the slogan as I walked by the restaurant, but this was before I had figured the camera out in Amsterdam, and thus the picture is of me.

Reader, take note. This last anecdote is fairly representative of this book's tone and content. These are largely my own idiosyncratic musings and intellectual wanderings, and beyond their being these, little merit is claimed for them. Indeed, to claim any particular merit for them would flatly contradict my own view of authentic mindfulness, which, among other things, counsels humility. The material here is not free of rigorous scholarly content, but its goal is not limited to scholarship. Rather, the aim is to articulate my personal observations of the mindfulness movement and of tendencies that have cropped up around it, many of which I see as nefarious. In doing this, I attempt to balance the personal and the empirical, and I reiterate that my target is the defiled version of mindfulness, not the authentic original.

This book describes the genuine virtues of authentic mindfulness; documents how this sound idea was perverted into an excuse for self-indulgence; shows the baleful consequences for many sectors of society (e.g., mental health, education, politics); ponders what if anything can be salvaged from the original, useful concept; and suggests ways to free ourselves from a cultural mindset that not only counsels recursive and unmoored self-regard, but that also profoundly misunderstands human nature.

The faux version of mindfulness thus operates in much the same way as do brood parasites, for example, like some species of the cuckoo. Just as some cuckoos lay their eggs in the nests of other birds, some strands of our culture—the self-esteem movement and the rise in narcissism being two examples—have deposited "cuckoo" ideas into the nest of true mindfulness. Drawing out this comparison further, just as cuckoo chicks hatch earlier than the host's own eggs and then evict and thus kill the eggs or baby birds of the host, it is an ominous possibility that faux mindfulness may evict true mindfulness from its rightful place in the nest of ideas. A goal of this book is to contribute to the prevention of that intellectual travesty.

This will be no small feat, because the imposter ideas are alluring and durable, promising health and spiritual purity with trendiness thrown in for the bargain. Furthermore, they mimic the genuine ideas effectively enough that growing numbers of people, including mental health professionals, are not properly equipped to discern genuine from adulterated mindfulness. Here too, the comparison to cuckoo birds is apt: Cuckoo eggs are durable (they are double-layered so as not to break when dropped into nests), and cuckoo eggs are effective mimics, having evolved to resemble the host's eggs.

But cuckoo and host eggs *are* discernible, as are genuine and ersatz mindfulness, and a purpose of this book is to serve as a guidebook in telling the difference. Some host species of birds mob cuckoos to drive them out of their territory. This book attempts a similar mobbing of fake forms of mindfulness.

Cuckoos fight back. Some, for example, will completely destroy the nests of hosts that dare to reject their eggs. I too expect a fight. The faux forms of mindfulness represent a burgeoning industry of books, consultants, and seminars, which this book intends to undermine. Furthermore, these forms of fake mindfulness have infiltrated the culture, in part because they provide an easy, faddish, and seemingly high-minded and spiritual excuse for self-regard and self-indulgence. Further still, and understandably enough, adherents of true mindfulness may keep to their own rather sheltered and insular enclaves, and thus may not fully appreciate the significance or even the existence of the growing menace. This in turn both deters them from the fray and disposes them to view any critique of mindfulness with reflexive suspicion as a possible heresy, even critiques with which, on reflection, they would agree. In what follows, I attempt to demonstrate why the original nest of genuine mindfulness, despite imperfections, merits vigorous defending, and why the eggs of faux mindfulness need rejecting.

I suppose it is conceivable that the distorting of mindfulness, decried in these pages, will be to the ultimate good. This in fact happens in the example of cuckoos' brood parasitism: There is one species, a kind of crow, which can benefit from a cuckoo laying eggs in its nest because the cuckoo chicks secrete a repellent substance that deters predation on the nest. This may be an apt metaphor for the invasion of authentic mindfulness by what has been referred to as "McMindfulness." "McMindfulness" is repellent—at least that is the view articulated in this book—and perhaps occasionally helpful to some individuals. However, just as the cuckoo's parasitism is helpful to only a few species, only in particular seasons, and usually is a bane on host species' existence, so I will argue is "McMindfulness" a troublesome parasite on authentic mindfulness, on mental health practice, and on the larger culture.

A professor sits in a trendy coffee shop, and on the table before him is a coffee, ordered so exactingly that you (perhaps) and I (certainly), had we been observing, would have felt a mixture of confusion, irritation, and intimidation, as well as harbored a gnawing suspicion that a full 45 seconds was just spent ordering what actually amounts to coffee with some milk in it. Suspicion is allayed, however, by the professor's air of tranquil certainty tinged with self-satisfaction, aided, no doubt, by the session of yoga that preceded his visit to the coffee shop. On the table next to the coffee is his laptop—MacBook, needless to say. Later that evening, out to dinner with friends, the care that goes into the selection of a bottle of wine makes the coffee shop's deliberations seem shallow.

There is a kind of discernment—one might even say mindfulness—in the decisions and actions of this individual. Not just coffee with milk, but something much more thoughtful and sophisticated; not just exercise, but something unique and even spiritual; not just any computer, but one with special features and supposedly exuding certain values; and not just any bottle of wine, but one that satisfies specific esoteric criteria, many of which the average person has never even heard. In all of this, the professor is not merely particular. Rather, he is particular in ways that are both self-promoting and self-involved.

That this individual displays discernment, at least of a kind, is plain. But is there anything substantive, and even if so, is there anything admirable, in this attitude? My answer to both questions and an animating principle for this book is "no."

If you imagine, incidentally, that you know just the professor of whom I am thinking, I have two responses: (1) This is impossible, as this is an amalgam over many years of at least a dozen academics across fields (granted they are usually certain fields). And (2) that I have described a hypothetical that seems quite real to many suggests that it may be a valid type (examples of which are numerous); in other words, we may have a cultural problem on our hands. Reference to this type appeared in a CNN article written by Richard Galant and posted on their website on March 15, 2014. The article was about Andy Weir, a computer programmer by day and science fiction writer at night. Chapter by chapter, Weir posted to his website an absorbing novel about an astronaut stranded on Mars. The book gained an enthusiastic following, and Weir may write a second book (the first one has been made into a movie starring Matt Damon). He stated, "I'm working on a pitch for my next novel right now, and if I get an advance, I'm going to quit and be a full time writer, which is the culmination of my dream coming true. I think I have to go sit in a coffee shop when I do that. And wear a neckerchief."

Back to our hypothetical professor, now (thanks to Weir) neckercheifed, who sips his coffee and works on his MacBook, citing Derrida, Foucault, and the latter's notion of "subjugated knowledges" (yes plural), confidently writing that there is no real knowledge, untroubled by the implications thereof for things like his own air travel and his MacBook's functioning, never mind for the contribution to knowledge he is currently attempting to make. As this placid and comfortable coffee-shop activity is proceeding, emperor penguins in Antarctica begin their annual trek from the sea to their ancient, ancestral breeding grounds. In the process, these animals endure intense hardship, including extreme cold and howling winds. The females each lay a single egg and leave it with the males to incubate for the ensuing 4 months, during which time the males' only sustenance is water from falling snow. The males lose fully half their body weight during these 4 months; the sole focus of their entire existence for this time is protecting the egg from the elements. Meanwhile, the mothers trek back to the sea, which is now even farther away because of the accumulating ice. The mothers do this so that they can feed themselves and their young, which they do after an arduous return journey back to the breeding grounds, where the males stand around in the snow, serving as living incubators and very little more. Once the mothers have returned, it is the fathers' turn to sojourn to the sea, the distance now the equivalent of almost three marathons, and this through bitter cold and endless wind, and after not having eaten for months, "every one of them," wrote Jonathan Franzen, "as heroic as Shackleton."[3]

In this ancient, annual process, the penguins are single-minded; there is little in their comportment that reflects discernment or mindfulness. One spot of snowy ice is about as good as any other for the males to stand on for weeks on end. When they finally arrive back to the sea, the ravenous penguin mothers reflect very minimally on the type or quality of their prey. Same with the fathers once their 4-month fast is broken. Nuance does not enter into it; neither do "subjugated knowledges;" neither does discernment; and neither does mindfulness.

A point of this book is that there is much to recommend the attitude of the penguins over that of the professor. Unlike the latter, the penguins are not self-regarding. The penguins do not appear to view themselves as particularly unique—one is a penguin just as another is—whereas the professor knows he is special, deep in his soul (the lack of evidence for which does not trouble him, because in the professor's mind, things like evidence and truth either are relative or do not exist). Both the professor and the penguins are self-focused, but motivated, in the former case, by posturing, and in the latter, by posterity. The penguins are living examples, full embodiments of virtues like sacrifice and persistence; the professor, ironically and in violation of a sacred trust, often has little of either. In the clash of ideas inherent in the demeanor of the penguins and the professor, I favor the penguins.

I wish I could report that I got on the trail of mindless mindfulness in the heart of an august library, poring over scholarly journal articles, the gorgeous scent of open books piled around me serving as inspiration. I have gotten on other trails like that and look back with deeply fond nostalgia on the work involved, as hard as it sometimes was (and I also grieve a little about how unlikely it is for my sons and students to have that book scent experience). But no, I may never have noticed the depths to which mindfulness has sunk were it not for checking Facebook and the like a couple of times a day for the last few years.

It was not the direct discussion of mindfulness on various social media platforms that caught my attention (though such discussions do of course take place there); rather, several posts, comments, and so forth—at first seemingly unrelated—kept flashing across the screen. Of the hundreds of people with whom I am "friends" or otherwise see on Facebook, one seemed extremely interested in mindfulness, loudly so (if Facebook can be called loud, as I think it can), and yet was breathtakingly self-absorbed, often in the very same posts. And by "breathtakingly self-absorbed," I do not mean merely self-focused. As we will see in a later chapter, mere self-focus has become the new norm, the new cool, to all our detriment. No, by "breath-takingly self-absorbed," I mean problematically narcissistic, the kind of malignant and blinding self-regard that makes even adherents of the new "self-focus is cool" ethos remark, "That guy needs to tone it down."

How can it be, I wondered, that someone who touts the benefits of a mindset, which properly understood, demotes the importance of self, reveal himself in the same breath to be Narcissus arisen from the depths? (In this last sentence, how many readers will mistake "demotes the importance of self" for its semantic opposite "denotes the importance of self," as I myself did in rereading the sentence? For you dear reader, like me, are steeped in a culture of narcissism, which drips away only slowly, with the danger, to be guarded against with vigor, of a stalagmitic residue of self-regard being left behind.) Mildly interesting questions, I supposed, and ones over which I did not linger unduly. Until, regarding the "mindful" Narcissus, it happened again and again and again, not only with regard to the one Narcissus in question, but also with regard to his confreres. This produced in me the distressing dual realization that Narcissus shook off the waters and roosted in 21st-century souls with some regularity, and that in so doing, he often targeted souls who extolled the virtues of mindfulness.

At about this same time, an eminent and widely admired academic psychologist died, having suffered from a condition that he and others knew would soon kill him. When it did, the expected nature of his death did not seem to quell the genuine outpouring of grief, much of it apparent on social media. The sentiments were touching, so much so that I was able to temporarily put aside my doubts about the propriety of death announcements on Facebook and just read them for what they were: sincere expressions of admiration for a man now lost to us. These expressions were not just moving; they were also numerous enough that, for a time, there was little else in my Facebook feed.

But there *was* something else in the feed: Scattered in among the testaments and tributes to a great man now fallen were the self-absorptions of the Narcissi. There were reflections (if they can be called that) on the virtues of things like first-class air travel, the theme of which was not "here are some dispassionately described features of first-class versus coach travel" (as questionable a theme as that is), but rather "hey, look at me, I'm in first class!" This is a sentiment that cries out for advice about finding yourself in the end zone after having scored a touchdown (usually attributed to Vince Lombardi): "Act like you've been there before." But the voice of Lombardi was absent, as I wish were the actual replies—vapidities, rather—encouraging the Narcissus to continue to be a "rock star." There were actual reflections (and they can definitely be called that), in the form of "selfie" photographs. (I am, I understand, hopelessly out of cultural tune in more ways than one when I acknowledge that for a grown man to take an unironic picture just of himself—any part of himself it unfortunately must be said—is very difficult for me to understand. To then compound the act by arranging for that same picture to be broadcast in a public way is, to my perhaps peculiar mind, unfathomable. But that's just me, who squirms at the thought of a picture of a freckle being retained in my dermatologist's records.) To make matters worse and the difference even more stark, the Narcissi were posting *only* about their self-absorptions and were silent on the question of tributes; everyone else, only or mostly posting about tributes, silent on the topic of self-exaltation. In my reckoning, the Narcissi are exemplars not of authentic mindfulness, but of its deterioration.

The contrast of the reverent tributes to an accomplished and now deceased scholar with the self-promotional detritus of the Narcissi struck me as so discordant as to approach the grotesque. This same contrast struck me many months later in the days after the spring 2015 Nepal earthquake. Sincere expressions of shock and grief, along with links to aid organizations, dominated the feed, sullied by the same exact Narcissi posting on the same exact themes (e.g., first class travel, luxury hotel experiences). The quote occurred to me, "O, that you could turn your eyes toward the napes of your necks and make but an interior survey of your good selves! O, that you could!"[4] And the question recurred to me, How can an outlook that places the self in its rightful, infinitesimally small place coexist with self-importance so vaunting, like that of the "mindful" Narcissi, that it approaches the obscene? How can the Narcissi so frequently post about authentic mindfulness and within a few more clicks miss its entire point?

Relatively few people have fixed their gaze on the original, sensible (and yet still, in my view, inherently problematic) definition of mindfulness, which is the moment-to-moment and nonjudgmental awareness of the totality of subjective experience. Instead, many have become distracted, magpie-like, by a diluted and devolved version emphasizing the positive, significant, and mystical in individual self-awareness. A related implication of this book is that there is nothing particularly positive or significant or mystical in individual self-awareness.

Perhaps, however, you are one of the few who have understood the original and reasonable concept of mindfulness, and therefore have formed in your mind an objection to my depictions of the professor and the penguins, which is that I have misunderstood true mindfulness; that neither the professor (because he is judgmental) nor the penguins (because they are minimally aware of their own subjectivity) are examples of true mindfulness (what I will refer to as "authentic mindfulness").

In a way, this is quite true, because what I am lampooning in the example of the professor and throughout the book is what has come to pass as mindfulness, a conceptual defilement, generated mostly by certain segments of the mental health profession and by the larger culture of boundless self-regard. But I intend to show in what follows that even the spare and down-to-earth conceptualization of authentic mindfulness—a perspective that does indeed contain utility—nevertheless was born into an ocean of problems it cannot solve, some of which are inherent to the concept.

Authentic mindfulness demands self-awareness at the same time that it requires a nonjudgmental, dispassionate attitude, *including about the self*. The focus of the true version of mindfulness is the present moment generally, which includes the self as only a small component. In the next chapter, I attempt to give authentic mindfulness its full due, both as an interesting and useful philosophical vantage point in itself, but also as an empirically supported means to address various problems in living—both substantial achievements that certainly not all intellectual efforts can claim. In a subsequent chapter I describe cultural developments involving narcissism that are not the fault or result of authentic mindfulness, but which nevertheless have intertwined with the mindfulness movement to create a Frankenstein's monster. The rest of the book chronicles the dispiriting consequences and ponders ways to mitigate if not undo them.

Some things that culminate in disaster can seem quite innocuous at first, and indeed may have remained so were it not for the coming together of unlikely and ultimately deadly strands. I will argue that faux mindfulness is one such thing, but as another example, consider the space shuttle *Challenger* as it was poised for liftoff on a cold Florida morning in January 1986. If not innocuous, the shuttle certainly did not seem ominous looking, its magisterial pose on the tarmac diminished only slightly because a successful space launch had come to seem mundane, even easy. Seventy-three seconds after liftoff, this illusion of ease was viciously shattered by the shuttle's explosion, which killed the seven astronauts on board (and very cruelly, it did not immediately kill them). That night in an address from the Oval Office, President Reagan attempted (by most lights at least partially successfully) to console and reassure a shaken nation, saying of the astronauts, "We will never forget them, nor the last time we saw them, this morning, as they prepared for their journey and waved goodbye and slipped the surly bonds of earth to touch the face of God."

Challenger had millions of parts, and the failure of just one—a seal called an O-ring, which prevents the intense explosive power of the rocket booster from catastrophically igniting the external fuel tank—was a strand that ultimately led to the shuttle's destruction. But it was just one strand, one that by itself could not bring the shuttle down without the contribution of other strands of contingency. One such condition involved rare freezing temperatures in Florida, which robbed the O-ring of its pliability and thereby produced the seal's failure. This failure can be detected on video; it produced a brief puff of smoke on the right side of the vehicle immediately upon ignition and liftoff.

How can something with the vast explosive potential of a shuttle fuel tank be exposed to the fierce flame of a rocket and not immediately erupt into a massive fireball right on the tarmac? It cannot. And yet *Challenger*, with these disastrous conditions in place immediately upon liftoff, flew and operated normally for another 72 or so seconds, instead of exploding right there on the tarmac and instantiating a harrowing if temporary hell on earth.

How? Some evidence suggests that an ad hoc seal formed from melted materials and somewhat miraculously performed the functions intended for the O-ring for more than a minute, until it too failed. But why did it, in its turn, fail?

The answer to this question involves the last cruel contingency: a substantial crosswind, which placed shearing stress on all parts of the shuttle, including the ad hoc seal. There is a substantial possibility that, absent the shearing force of the crosswind, the seal would have held long enough for *Challenger* to make it into orbit, and in doing so, escape catastrophe.

The seeds of disaster sprang in part from truly innocuous sources. In and of themselves, cold temperatures and a crosswind did not represent danger. Less innocuous, but still far from boding certain doom, the O-rings were slightly flawed, but were sufficient including even in cold weather, in which they had operated well in the past (though not in temperatures as cold as it was on the morning of January 28, 1986, which was about 18 degrees Fahrenheit at their lowest). The O-rings were a genuine enough flaw—a chink in *Challenger*'s formidable armor—exploitable only under certain specific conditions and even then, potentially survivable because of factors like an ad hoc seal. The intertwining of otherwise unremarkable strands and contingencies—very cold temperatures, flawed seals, a shearing crosswind—meant, among other things, the terrible deaths of seven astronauts.

Challenger was a pinnacle of human artistry and engineering, but it had its O-rings. I doubt even the most ardent admirers of the mindfulness movement would claim that level of human innovation for their ideas—or perhaps some of them would—but in any event, authentic mindfulness *is* an achievement, as I catalog in detail in the next chapter. But does it have its O-rings? And if so, did they conspire with other contingencies to produce a disaster?

As to the O-rings of authentic mindfulness, one involves the encouragement of an inward gaze. To be sure, the original, genuine version of mindfulness emphasized dispassionate attention to the richness and variety of the present moment *generally*, not to one's own sense of self specifically. The mindful person is thus attuned, in part, to the miasma of sensation that has nothing at all to do with one's own subjectivity, but rather concerns the features of the present moment surrounding one's own mind, in its minute detail and its vastness too. And, in addition to attunement to this external moiling of sensation, one is also and simultaneously dispassionately attentive to the contents of one's own mind.

I appreciate the following definition of mindfulness, provided by a former Buddhist nun now affiliated with the University of California, Los Angeles (UCLA)'s Mindful Awareness Research Center: "Paying attention to present moment experiences with open, curious attention and a willingness to be with what is."[5] There are various versions of original mindfulness, but in my judgment the most defensible and useful version is selfless.

Notice the miles traveled between original mindfulness' perspective on an individual's particular thoughts—"they are nothing special, everyone has them, they are very often wrong, and if not wrong, very often obvious"—to mindless mindfulness' cult of individuality. Accepting one's thoughts as merely thoughts (and specks of dust at that) is very different from treasuring one's thoughts; one may as well treasure one's sweat or saliva. The cult of individuality has encouraged an emphasis on positive self-regard, and it is worth noting how *judgmental* positive self-regard is. The original movement's origin is that one need not be persuaded by negative, ruminative thoughts, which are mere mental events akin, in terms of their importance and meaning for reality, to mundane thoughts like "I like sardines." That is a useful stance. But for it to be consistent, the same view must hold for positive thoughts too. They are mere mental events, among trillions.

The goal, then, and it is a lofty one, is dispassionate awareness of everything in the present moment, not merely nonjudgmental awareness of the self. The problem with this goal (one of its O-ring–like flaws) is *not* its loftiness. Ambition is often to the good, and in any event, serious adherents of genuine mindfulness fully understand the difficulty of attaining truly complete mindfulness, which is one reason that they counsel frequent practice over many months and even years. Having tried it myself in a full-day retreat, I am convinced that it is a learnable skill that takes considerable practice. The flaw, rather, is insufficient regard for the gravitational pull of the self, and this insufficiency is detectable in both conceptual and practical domains. From a conceptual standpoint, just as all astronomical objects are not equal in their gravitational effects, neither are all the elements of any given present moment. Within any such moment, the self vacuums up attention just as a black hole feeds on all matter around it. This effect is detectable in the writings of central figures within mindfulness circles, for example, consider the following definition of mindfulness: "Mindfulness comprises two facets—present moment awareness and nonjudgmental acceptance of emotions and thoughts."[6] Does this definition not allow the interpretation that mindfulness is largely self-focused, given the emphasis on one's own thoughts?

A knowledgeable mindfulness adherent may counter that this is precisely why so much practice is needed. To resist the pull of self-focus and attend to *all* of the current moment is a high-level skill. To which I respond—and this brings us to the practical domain—then why are so many mindfulness exercises self-focused?

In the daylong mindfulness practice retreat in which I participated in late 2013, we took off our shoes and sat in a circle (from my perspective, an inauspicious beginning to what proved to be a mildly enjoyable and edifying day). We spent approximately 90% of our time focusing inward. It is important to add that we were mostly focusing not on ourselves but on our sensations—the coolness of our breath as it hit the back of our throats, the minute muscular changes as we engaged in very slowed-down walking (called "mindful walking"), the stretching and strain points in our muscles and joints as we engaged in different bodily poses ("mindful stretching"), and so on. These exercises did not encourage self-focus in the sense of excessive self-regard; far from it, their point was moment-to-moment awareness of bodily sensation qua bodily sensation, without any elaboration of the sensations into judgments, interpretations, or thoughts. Someone fully in this state of mind has no room in his or her mind for ruminations about his or her self-esteem; in this mindset, the urge to take a "selfie" tends not to occur. Relatedly, though I sensed that many of my fellow participants possessed temperaments and outlooks quite different from my own, there was a quiet esprit de corps, a feeling that sandpapered the rougher edges of my own views on mindfulness and thus of this book. To their credit, the retreat participants produced an atmosphere in which I—a temperamentally somewhat reserved outsider and skeptic—felt comfortable engaging in, to take one example, extreme slow-motion walking in public. Furthermore, as a capstone to the day, the retreat leader exhorted us to remember the selflessness of genuine mindfulness and not to "fetishize" it into a cultish solution for self-enhancement or for the affluent's petty aggrievements. I thought this was one of the most attuned and appropriate wrap-ups to a workshop that I have ever witnessed. It echoed a similar point by Jon Kabat-Zinn, a credentialed leader of the mindfulness movement, who advised people from going on and on about their mindfulness practice to their friends and families, because doing so will dissipate the energy needed for the actual practice itself. "The risk is that pretty soon you won't have any time to meditate anymore; you will have become more involved with the story of your meditation practice than with the ongoing experience of meditating."[7]

But still, in the retreat I attended, there is no escaping the fact that we looked inward for 90% of the time and outward for the rest. One may counter that an inward focus, as opposed to an outer one, is needed to deter pernicious thoughts that arise from within, to which I have a few replies. First, to privilege negative inner thoughts over other ones is to empower them, and second, it is to be judgmental about them in that privileging is a form of judgment. Third, the retreat I attended was for a general audience and not specifically for people for whom negative thinking was a concern; still we focused inward rather relentlessly. Last, those whose thoughts trend toward the negative are nevertheless susceptible to egoism, as are we all.

Though my target is mostly distortions of authentic mindfulness, I believe the tendency toward self-focus can be detected even in authentic mindfulness. Consider, for example, the words of Kabat-Zinn: "Ultimately I see mindfulness as a love affair—with life, with reality and imagination, with the beauty of your own being, with your heart and body and mind, and with the world." I have learned to tune up my skepticism whenever the phrase "love affair" is used to describe anything other than an actual love affair, but putting that aside, Kabat-Zinn's sentence contains eight main nouns (life, reality, imagination, beauty of your own being, heart, body, mind, world). Half of these (beauty of your own being, heart, body, mind) are explicitly about the self, and in the case of "beauty of your own being," floridly so. How many of his readers will view the other four things through the lens of the self, taking "life" to mean "*my* life," "reality" to mean "*my* reality," and so on?

I believe many will, because of the phrasing that occurs throughout Kabat-Zinn's book and the rest of the mindfulness oeuvre. For example, here is how a mindfulness-based technique is described in a press release regarding a University of Wisconsin study to be conducted in 9- and 10-year-olds in Madison public schools: "To practice mindfulness-based stress reduction, students and teachers are trained through a variety of practices to focus on the present moment, including bringing attention to their breathing. They are also taught to be attuned to their bodies and aware of their emotions, to 'drop in' on their present state."[8] Notice how 100% of this is self-focused (and to reiterate, being taught to kids). By the way, if you are an American taxpayer, you are paying for this. The project is funded by a $1.5 million grant from the U.S. Department of Education.

Or consider the following description of mindfulness from Kabat-Zinn's book (*Mindfulness for Beginners: Reclaiming the Present Moment—and Your Life*), which is representative of the issue: "an ongoing adventure of inquiry and discovery about the nature of your mind and heart and how you might live with greater presence, open-heartedness, and authenticity—not merely for yourself, but for your interconnected embeddedness with those you love, with all beings, and with the world itself." It is to his credit that Kabat-Zinn balances the self-focused opening of the sentence with references to "all beings" and "the world itself," and that is only as it should be as Kabat-Zinn is within the core group of mindfulness advocates with credibility. As one drifts farther and farther from this core, the emphasis on the self grows dramatically.

Further to his credit, Kabat-Zinn warns readers against "selfing," by which he means the knee-jerk tendency to cling to the "I," "me," and "mine" of things. But in a later passage from the same book, he writes of his book and of mindfulness more generally, "You can think of this volume as the front door to a magnificent edifice, like, say, the Louvre. Only the edifice is yourself and your life and your potential as a human being."

A few pages back I characterized the National Aeronautics and Space Administration (NASA)'s space shuttles as pinnacles of human artistry and engineering, and I wondered whether mindfulness advocates would claim that level of human innovation for their ideas, and I now have an answer: Mindfulness is comparable to the centuries of awe-inspiring art in room after room of the Louvre. Authentic mindfulness *is* an achievement, and mindfulness advocates would do better to leave it at that. Moreover, in the preceding passage from Kabat-Zinn, mindfulness is equated with one's self, life, and potential. The solipsism—ironically the "selfing"—inherent in even credible versions of mindfulness is a real phenomenon and one of its primary flaws.

Intriguingly, there is a version of mindfulness that emphasizes moment-to-moment attention to *external* stimuli, as well as openness to creative engagement with them. The existence of this version is counter to the assertion that there is something necessarily inward-looking about mindfulness. This perspective has been advanced since the 1970s by the psychologist Ellen Langer, and although it has many similarities to mindfulness as described by Kabat-Zinn and others, there are differences. A key difference is the emphasis in Kabat-Zinn and others' version on introspection, an inward-looking stance.[9] The two versions were developed at about the same time, and a point I hope to make is that it is no coincidence, given the current culture of the self, that the inward-looking version has captured the popular imagination and the therapeutic workshop circuit more so than Langer's outward-focused version. It is also peculiar, but at least in my experience quite true, that Langer is rarely if ever acknowledged in the work of current mindfulness proponents. In developing this book, I have attended several presentations by current mindfulness advocates, and I have never heard her mentioned. Her name does not appear in Kabat-Zinn's *Mindfulness for Beginners* or in other mindfulness-friendly books (e.g., Dufrene & Wilson's *The Wisdom to Know the Difference*). This is so despite the fact that a case can be made (at least based on year of publications) that Langer's work on mindfulness preceded that of Kabat-Zinn and others.

I view the inward-gazing aspect of non-Langerian mindfulness as a doubly mistaken emphasis. First, for the purposes of the daylong retreat itself, I found the inward-looking exercises a mixed bag in that some clicked and many were tedious. Conversely, I found the outward-focused exercises (e.g., noticing the facets of the room's ambient light and sound) to be the day's highlight. There are relatively few things that can be said to be simultaneously relaxing and stimulating, but I found these outward-looking activities to be just that. They were relaxing because we put aside the burden of selfhood and just were, just existed, much as do bacteria and galaxies. They were stimulating because of the novelty, variety, and nuance that existed in moment after moment of basic ambient experience. Moreover, the outward-focused activities facilitated later inward-looking ones, whereas the reverse was not as true. That is, having focused on minute ambient sounds and light, moment after moment, trying to take them simply as they were, with no further elaboration of judgment or interpretation, we were well positioned to take precisely the same attitude toward the products of our own minds.

A counterpoint perhaps is that I was a mere mindfulness novice, and had I been more versed, I would not have needed to have my hand held, as it were, on the journey from outward to inward. That I was a novice is beyond dispute. Indeed, in what I viewed as one of his few mistakes during the day, the group leader asked which of us had never meditated. The mistake here is the possibility that only one person (of 50 or so) would raise his or her hand and would thus feel insecure throughout the rest of the day. In fact, only one person did raise his hand, and that person was me, though I did not feel insecure throughout the day, a credit to the leader and to the group (and as we will see, some people do have distinctly negative and sometimes lasting experiences in response to such retreats).

I was the least experienced of the group, but I confess to moments in which I suspected I might be the *most* mindful ... not perhaps in the sense that my fellow retreat participants might mean, but in another sense that I suggest is at least as important. I am referring specifically to the ability to hold in mind multiple ideas and opinions simultaneously, even ones rather alien to one's own, and to pay at least as much attention to the ones that feel foreign or disagreeable as to the ones that do not. This ability, essential in the university-based life of the mind and elsewhere, encourages listening more than it does talking, and more precisely, it encourages close attention to what someone is saying while simultaneously not paying much mind to one's own thoughts. In conversation, this skill facilitates an actual *exchange* of ideas and perspectives, as opposed to—and alas I fear this is very much the norm—each party remaining immersed in his or her own thoughts, putting voice to them whenever others stop talking (and often before that). In this regard, my conversations at the mindfulness retreat were unfortunately no better than those I have had otherwise (and no worse I should add), which I found mildly

ironic and disappointing. Shouldn't mindfulness enthusiasts be particularly adept at moment-to-moment awareness of experience, and
shouldn't the latter definitely include what someone else is saying?

It is not that I said much—I didn't because I was there to listen—
nor was it that what I did say was particularly contrarian. I was struck,
rather, by the fixation on one narrow band on the vast continuum of
intellectual ideas, the relative lack of awareness of this fixedness, and
the simultaneous, ironic, and hollow exaltation of broad-mindedness.
No one is fully exempt from this natural human foible, for example,
it is on ready display in American political life or to take another example, in many university professors. Like these latter, mindfulness
advocates should know better, by virtue of what defines them.

They frequently do not. Regarding professors, I recently served
as the outside committee member for a dissertation defense, one alas
above average in its stultifying characteristics (and that is saying
quite a lot). To pass the time, I counted the number of words I said
during the 2-hour affair (of the 27 words I spoke, six were "I have
nothing incremental to add"), and the number of times the other
professors spoke to rather than past or over each other during the
defense (two times). Disciplines vary on this latter metric in dissertation defenses, allowing me to derive the theorem, obvious once it
is stated, that the number of times professors talk past or over one
another is inversely proportional to the intellectual value of the proceedings. I wish I were superhuman enough, or many dissertation
defenses interesting enough, that I did not need coping strategies
such as counting things and the production of obvious theorems, but
wishing does not make it so.

I have experimented in numerous settings with Spartan word use,
my most extreme accomplishment to date consisting of total silence
during one phase of a NASA meeting (a phase, I should add, in which
I felt I had much to learn; during another phase in which the activity
involved brainstorming and the like, I spoke). This feat did not go unnoticed, though it did seem to go unappreciated, as if it is a violation
of cultural norms to listen instead of speak. In fact, it *is* a violation of
a cultural norm if the culture is one of narcissism. Although NASA
is still a last bastion of the Narcissi's extreme opposites, there is cultural creep even there, especially when half the room is made up of
consultants who are not full and direct NASA employees (that was
my status too).

Returning to the mindfulness retreat I experienced, I did not conceal my skepticism from my fellow attendees (neither did I go out of my way to display it), and I sensed that they somewhat dismissively viewed it as a lack of knowledge, experience, wisdom, and openness. Ironically, on this latter count, I had just agreed to allow in the clinic I direct brief mindfulness exercises to be a part of our weekly dialectical-behavior therapy (DBT) consultation meetings. Since then, I have participated genuinely and nonsarcastically (not true of everyone in attendance) and can report no salutary effects (or negative ones).

If I only practiced more, my fellow retreat attendees may have thought, I would shed my child-like naiveté and mindfully mature (although it is striking how many mindfulness advocates compare advanced mindfulness to a childlike sense of wonder). A similar reaction was described in a September 2014 *Atlantic Monthly* article. The setting is a mindfulness session led by Congressman Tim Ryan, a mindfulness enthusiast. Another enthusiast, smiling broadly, queries a newcomer regarding how he liked mindfulness. The newcomer replied "Uh, I didn't love it," to which the enthusiast counters, with great serenity, "It takes time."

To be sure, there is evidence that status as a novice matters when it comes to the practice of mindfulness. In a prominent paper, Richie Davidson and colleagues showed that Buddhist monks who, over the course of their lives had meditated for at least 10,000 hours, had brains with electroencephalogram (EEG) signatures that differed from those of novice meditators. More specifically, their EEGs showed more functional connectivity between brain areas as well as more gamma-wave activity, which is associated with high levels of alertness. While intriguing, it should be kept in mind that these expert meditators were unique in many ways, including that they averaged almost three hours of meditation per day, every day for 10 years.

Far from 10,000 hours, I had zero hours with both meditation and mindfulness at the time of the retreat, and so it is quite possible that my reactions to the material were attributable to my lack of experience. This is possible, but I think doubtful, judging from the several conversations I had with my fellow retreat attendees (none of whom, recall, raised their hands to admitting to be a novice). It seemed to me that everyone there, regardless of experience level, tended to view the outward-focused exercises more favorably.

I noted earlier that I viewed the inward emphasis as a double mistake, one aspect of which was pragmatic: The outward-looking activities were more effective. The other aspect of the mistake is conceptual and more fundamental: To encourage an inward gaze among extremely self-interested creatures is to court excess. In fact, this is one major theme to be developed throughout the rest of the book. Mindfulness adherents will protest that they are not encouraging excessive self-regard, but I think they are wrong. It is true that they do not *mean* to encourage excessive self-regard— on the contrary, they aim for the opposite—but as anyone who has thrown a football, taken a free throw, submitted a grant proposal, or taken a penalty kick can attest, aim is one thing, outcome can be quite another. This is a key point: Authentic mindfulness *intends* laudable things. My argument here, however, is not about what authentic mindfulness *intends*, rather, it is about what it has *become*, at least in some circles. To be aware of one's own subjectivity at all requires looking inward; to do so moment-by-moment, even more so. To encourage self-focus in humans seems akin to encouraging something like video games in adolescent males: Absent encouragement, it will usually happen naturally enough; with encouragement, the potential for excess is a worry. Is it wise to counsel creatures, who are already preternaturally and prenatally prepared for self-interest, to turn their gaze even more upon themselves? To instruct them to do so constantly, moment to moment?

The advice to gaze inwardly is, I argue in the pages that follow, a flaw, a chink in the armor of authentic mindfulness. The nature of this flaw warrants a moment's reflection. To ask that people gaze inward is not asking too much of them—more on that in a moment—to the contrary, it is asking too little. It is inviting them to let natural inclinations run amok, to the point of unseemly excess. In moderation, self-examination can lead to a reasonable and unobsessed awareness of one's emotional tendencies, thought patterns, impact on others, and blind spots. What is it in excess? It is the sound of a cell phone click as one takes a "selfie," and it is the sound of the button pressed as this picture is posted to social media, and it is the reverberation of this being done over and over and over again, the self glorified while the culture falls around it.

Thus one flaw of authentic mindfulness is that it asks so little from us. The other is that it asks too much. In *Light in August*, William Faulkner wrote, "Memory believes before knowing remembers." This is, characteristic of the author, a little opaque, tantalizingly thought provoking, and accurate as well. His point, since confirmed empirically many times, is that we judge *before* we deliberate, intuit *before* we reflect. It is how we are wired. Our capacities for deep thought, as prodigious as they are as reflected by things like Faulkner's sometimes hauntingly beautiful novels and perhaps even more, things like $E = mc^2$ and Darwin's masterpiece, can deceive us, because they lull us into forgetting that we are evolved creatures. We hail from the mud, as do bacteria, insects, and worms, and like them, we survived over eons in a nature famously described as "red in tooth and claw" (Hobbes, Tennyson) and "clumsy, wasteful, blundering, low and horridly cruel" (Darwin), leading lives that were "solitary, poor, nasty, brutish, and short" (Hobbes). We did all this, in part, because of thoughtless, mindless reflexes.

The observations of this truth by our most perspicacious intellects are numerous. For example, Giambattista Vico wrote, "man became all he is without understanding it," and David Hume, "The rules of morality are not the conclusions of our reason." Another, Semónides of Amórgos observed in verse in the seventh century BCE, that

> We who are human have no minds,
>   but live, from day to day, like beasts and know nothing
>   of what God plans to make happen to each of us.

E. O. Wilson made a compatible point in his book *The Social Conquest of Earth*: "Consciousness, having evolved over millions of years of life-and-death struggle, and moreover because of that struggle, was not designed for self-examination. It was designed for survival and reproduction. Conscious thought is driven by emotion; to the purpose of survival and reproduction, it is ultimately and wholly committed."[10]

In the mindfulness retreat I attended, I was perplexed by the repeated juxtaposition of two concepts, namely, a nonjudgmental mindset and one that might be termed "choicefulness." The point of the latter concept, I gathered, was to avoid doing things by rote and instead to deploy one's attention on purpose, by choice. I sensed that this did not trouble my fellow attendees, but it did me, for multiple reasons. An emphasis on personal choice can encourage a neglect of virtues like duty and obligation, characteristics that are essential to a thriving society. It can also further the tyranny of growing self-importance, a pernicious cultural force that is the focus of Chapter 3. But the main reason it bothered me is its intellectual incoherence with other mindfulness principles, for while both concepts at first glance seem consistent with a definition of mindfulness along the lines of "moment-to-moment nonjudgmental awareness, on purpose," they have at least some contradictory elements. A choice is a judgment; while one can step back from a choice and thus see it mindfully, it must ultimately be evaluative, or else it will not be a choice. Thus to emphasize "choicefulness" can be viewed as contradictory to a nonjudgmental mindset. Mindfulness proponents may go to some lengths to distinguish judgment from "choicefulness," often with appeals to the subtlety and nuance of the difference, but there simply is no categorical difference. Judgment finds its way back even in outlooks that try to banish it, just as forces like gravity have their say regardless of attempts to escape them. Judgment is inherent to life, and the attempt to negate it is an illusion.

On the first page of F. Scott Fitzgerald's masterpiece, *The Great Gatsby*, in the voice of narrator Nick Carraway, Fitzgerald writes, "I'm inclined to reserve all judgments, a habit that has opened up many curious natures to me and also made me the victim of not a few veteran bores." The trouble is that Nick Carraway is extremely judgmental throughout the novel. In fiction as in life, those who deny our judgmental natures can turn out to be among the most scathingly unaccepting.

Mindfulness advocates show some awareness of these dilemmas, including of the specific fact that we judge before we think, but I believe that they misconstrue them. In *Mindfulness for Beginners*, Kabat-Zinn writes that " 'Just hearing' includes the knowing that you are hearing. The knowing is awareness. It is available before thinking sets in."[11] Here is a major fork in the road between this book's outlook and that of the mindfulness movement: I claim that what is available before thinking sets in is mindless, emotional, preprogrammed, and reflexive; they claim it is a meditative, cultivated, and sophisticated state. Is it both? Is a rapprochement possible? I pick up this question at the end of the book when turning to solutions to the problems created by faux mindfulness.

Should you doubt our mindless and creaturely natures, I sympathize, for it is comfortable and understandably human to do so. However, to assuage your doubts, consider snakes. More specifically, consider those who work in wild settings with lots of snakes, and who regularly report the following experience. They are hiking along a path, with nothing particular in mind, when they find themselves in midair, having suddenly and in a real sense unintentionally leapt backward. They are not consciously aware of the snake until a half second or so after having been startled and having leapt backward. An excerpt from Percy Fawcett's journals, published posthumously in 1953, and cited in Lynne Isbell's book *The Fruit, the Tree, and the Serpent: Why We See So Well*,[12] described one of these experiences: "What amazed me more than anything was the warning of my subconscious mind, and the instant muscular response. [These snakes] are reputed to be lightning strikers, and they aim hip-high. I had not seen it till it flashed between my legs, but the 'inner man'— if I can call it that—not only saw it in time, but judged its striking height and distance exactly, and issued commands to the body accordingly."

This "inner man," the body-first, consciousness-later kind of reaction, may be to a degree what Faulkner had in mind when he wrote "Memory believes before knowing remembers." My colleagues and I used a similar perspective to understand what we termed the "high place" phenomenon,[13] which involves "flash in the pan" suicidal thoughts when on a high place, such as a bridge crossing, a mountain ridge, or the balcony of a high building. In these scenarios, a surprisingly high proportion of people report the impulse to jump, and a key point is that most people who have this experience are neither depressed nor suicidal at the time.

What is really happening when a person in a more-or-less normal state of mind walks across a high bridge and finds him- or herself inexplicably concerned with jumping? Many have answered with concepts combining impulsivity and a death wish: The drive for death springs from within and then is impulsively acted upon. We viewed this answer with suspicion for many reasons, including that it contradicts one of the most important ideas in history, namely evolution by natural selection, and also that it is misunderstands the role of impulsivity in suicidal behavior. On the latter point, incidentally, psychologist Michael Anestis and his colleagues[14] concluded that lethal suicidal behavior is rarely if ever impulsive, because it is too frightening and physically daunting to enact without considerable forethought as well as rehearsal and preparation in mental if not in physical forms. Instead, Anestis and coworkers argued that a history of impulsive behaviors inures impulsive people to the fear of death, and, should they develop the desire for death, are thus more capable of it.

A more plausible account of the "high place" phenomenon is similar to the one involving snakes in the wild. Just as people leap back away from a snake before they know it, people on a high place are experiencing very rapid brain reactions along the lines of "danger, back up!" Before they know it, that thought is in their head, and then, during the subsequent few seconds, they reflect on why that danger message is in their minds. The death instinct perspective provides one answer—the wrong one—and it is simply that the instinct suddenly reared its head. A more sensible answer is that the brain's "fast-fire" sending of danger messages put the thought of danger in the more reflective parts of the mind. Cerebral reflection, being slower and also prone to cultural influences like the idea of a "death instinct," mistakes a danger message for the manifestation of a death instinct, and forms the wrong conclusion.

This state of affairs has an ironic element. What is often interpreted as evidence of a death drive is in fact just the opposite: The "high place" reaction is an instinctual manifestation of the drive for self-preservation.

All the foregoing implies a mind compartmentalized into instinctive versus reflective components, a concept that mindfulness proponents tend to neglect. St. Augustine was aware of it centuries ago and struggled with it (as he did with many things, including his desires: "Grant me chastity and continence, but not yet"). In his theology on trying to understand how the compartmentalized trinity can be one, St. Augustine wrote that the compartments include, ". . . the mind itself, its knowledge . . . and thirdly love. These three are one, and one single substance."[15]

Authentic mindfulness asks too much of us when it prioritizes conscious awareness and reflection. We have evolved some systems of perception that are extremely fast and automatic, but are "dumb" in the sense that they cannot be modulated and are not subject to conscious control. In this way, we are similar to fantastically complicated machinery, like a spacecraft. In the book *Why We Believe in God(s)*, psychiatrist J. Anderson Thompson wrote, "Consider the Apollo spacecraft, a packed array of engineering devices, each dedicated to analyzing a constant stream of information and solving a particular problem, all while the astronauts are consciously aware only of a select few. We work the same way."[16] Earlier in the same passage, he wrote "Your snap judgments are millions of years in the making."

Researchers Tina Bloom and Harris Friedman reached a similar conclusion, but now regarding humans' abilities to read the emotions of dogs. Writing in the journal *Behavioral Processes* in 2013, they showed participants pictures of one specific dog (named Mal, who is a Belgian Malinois), taken in situations that provoked various reactions in Mal (i.e., happy, sad, surprised, disgusted, angry, and afraid). The people were very adept at identifying Mal's emotions, because these kinds of judgments were eons in the making, given our long partnership and co-evolution with canines. In an interesting twist, however, the researchers showed that those with less experience with dogs made more accurate determinations, and they speculated that this occurred because reading dogs' emotions is an innate human skill, rather than one that needs to be learned via experience. Those with a lot of experience, "mindful" of dogs' emotions, are likely to be highly attached to their dogs, and thus biased to see positive emotions even when they are absent. The snap judgments of the inexperienced were superior.

The situation is different in elite golfers, but nonetheless leads to the same general conclusion. These golfers are different from the rest of us, and much if not all the difference is attributable to their thousands and thousands of hours of careful and coached practicing. They are far from inexperienced. If expert and novice golfers are asked to make a series of putts for example, the difference between the two is plain to see. One thing that reduces this difference, that makes the elite golfers a little less so, is to ask them to think aloud as they putt. This disrupts their automatic "snap" movements and thus their performance, but has little effect on the novices.[17]

From dog observers and elite golfers, let's turn next to psychotherapists. Surely, of all professions, a mindful approach is likely to be the most helpful for therapists. The vast majority of mental health professionals would opine that it is, and many have done so in print (e.g., the confusingly titled book *Mindfulness for Two*; the confusion being that the "two" are patient and therapist, not a romantic couple). But believing it does not always make it so, Shakespeare's genius notwithstanding. We run a psychotherapy training clinic at Florida State University. At any given time, we have 20 or so PhD students, each seeing four or so psychotherapy patients, and each supervised by a faculty PhD psychologist. They are an enthusiastic and agreeable group, and true to character, agreed to be studied (rather than they doing the studying, which is of course the norm for PhD students). We measured each of 23 therapists' mindfulness levels (using the Mindfulness Attention Awareness Scale, which was created by two prominent contributors to the literature in this field[18]) and examined the relationship of therapist mindfulness to the psychotherapy outcomes of 144 patients, using both patient- and therapist-rated measurements of overall outcome. The following passage from the article captures the study's bottom line well: "In no case was there support for therapist mindfulness as a significant predictor of positive client outcome. On the contrary, in every case, the direction of results was such that greater therapist mindfulness was associated with worse client outcome."[19] To reiterate, not only didn't mindfulness help with regard to an essential outcome, it hurt.

In the examples of observing a dog's emotions (a natural, inborn skill, with deep roots in our co-evolutionary past with canines) and the performance of elite golfers (a learned skill), a possible bottom line is "don't think, just do." When the elite golfers thought—became mindful as it were—their performance suffered; when experienced dog lovers allowed their feelings and thoughts to enter into it—were being mindful—they made poorer decisions. We interpreted the findings from the psychotherapy study similarly: These therapists were performing a high-level, learned skill (i.e., manualized cognitive-behavioral therapy) and were expected to follow the psychotherapy protocol to a high degree of fidelity. Our team's view was that "mindless" students were better at this than mindful ones, because the latter were becoming distracted by things in the moment, when they should have been ignoring those and focusing laser-like on the protocol.

A recent study on memory and mindfulness reached compatible conclusions.[20] In comparing a group of participants who engaged in a brief bout of mindfulness meditation to a group who had not, the mindfulness participants were less able to differentiate items they had actually encountered from those they had only imagined. Specifically, all participants were asked to memorize a 15-word list; all words on the list involved the concept of trash (e.g., rubbish, waste, garbage, can, etc.). A key point is that the list did not contain the word "trash." Close to 40% of the mindfulness group members falsely recalled seeing the word "trash," as compared to around 20% of the control participants (who had been advised to think about whatever they liked during the 15-minute intervention). These findings were replicated in two additional experiments reported by these researchers. Ironically, in these experiments, being mindful meant losing awareness of details.

University of Missouri social psychologist Ken Sheldon and colleagues have investigated the effects of mindfulness on states of "flow," defined as a mental state in which one is fully absorbed in an activity with all attention focused on the activity and none on the self. Given the "present-moment" emphasis of flow, mindfulness proponents might argue that flow and mindfulness are highly positively correlated. However, Sheldon and coworkers found quite the opposite: The two are *negatively* correlated; that is, the one tends to prevent the other. The researchers explained that this is actually predictable: "After all," they wrote, "flow involves *losing* self-awareness within an activity, and mindfulness involves *maintaining* self-awareness throughout or even despite an activity."[21] Indeed, this is one of the chinks in its armor.

There is evidence that a state of mindfulness undermines motivation to engage in challenging tasks.[22] In four studies, researchers showed that various mindfulness meditation inductions led to decreased future focus and decreased arousal, which, in turn, deterred participants' desire to engage in difficult tasks. Social psychologist Roy Baumeister and colleagues have shown that a present-moment focus can be facilitative of happiness but tends to reduce the meaningfulness of one's existence, whereas the reverse is true: A focus on the integration of past, present, and future produced high levels of meaningfulness. Furthermore, happiness—which mindfulness facilitated—was associated with being a "taker" rather than a "giver," whereas meaningfulness showed the reverse pattern.[23] This is hardly the picture that many mindfulness advocates paint.

Researchers at the Université du Québec à Montréal in Canada have also shown that mindfulness can, in a sense, backfire—at least when it is explicitly rather than implicitly encouraged.[24] This team asked participants to bring to mind a very distressing past experience, and then studied the participants' reactions. Those who had consciously engaged in a mindful self-focus exercise experienced *more* negative effects (e.g., anxiety) than others. The exercise in question consisted of an 8-minute procedure, in which participants were asked to focus on 28 mindfulness-related statements (e.g., "Think, without judgment and objectively, about the physiological sensations you are experiencing now"; "take note of your thoughts and feelings without judging them"; "consciously attend to your breath for a few seconds"). Notice how these statements have the potential to turn gazes inward, which was not helpful to the participants.

By contrast, an *implicit* mindfulness activity was helpful. Generally, implicit methods involve "sneaking" things into the mind without the individual noticing. In this specific study, the procedure involved forming three-word sentences from a four-word scramble of words. For example, "awareness play hockey kids" would yield a response of "kids play hockey." The word left out is mindfulness-related (in the example, "awareness"). Notice in this technique that mindfulness is encouraged (if implicitly) without the gaze being forced inward, a point that I will return to at the end of the book where solutions are pondered.

I have decried already, and will do so again later, the tendency that mindfulness encourages an inward gaze. Mindfulness proponents might object that actually mindfulness does *not* encourage this, but rather, urges nonjudgmental, moment-to-moment awareness to all aspects of a given moment. The proponent would be correct and also would have won a pyrrhic victory, for at least three reasons. First, what proponents counsel, and what devotees actually do, may be quite different. I am arguing that they *are* different in this case as proponents counsel attention to all facets of a given moment, whereas devotees mostly take this counsel to mean to gaze inward. That is, proponents of authentic mindfulness intend one thing but may unwittingly achieve another. Second, as we have seen already and will see again, the actual writings of mindfulness proponents contain many explicit and implicit suggestions that mindfulness is primarily about looking inward. And third, the experimental results discussed earlier, which suggest that being mindful involved losing awareness of details, seem predictable when cast in the following phrasing: If someone is navel-gazing, might they miss some things happening around them? Of course they might.[25]

Snap judgments and "mindless" but superb performance are but two aspects of our basic natural endowment. "The mind is its own place," John Milton wrote in *Paradise Lost*. "And in itself can make a Heaven of Hell, a Hell of Heaven." For better or worse, right or wrong, we judge. Our nervous systems—perhaps nature's crowning achievement—evolved to discern figure from ground. To discriminate. To judge. Put aside for the moment the obvious fact that discrimination or judgment can be for better or worse and focus for now on the fact that the very nature of the system is such that it facilitates discrimination, discernment, and judgment in their broadest sense, and often on a "snap" basis. Furthermore, our neurobiology evolved to subserve love, fear, loyalty, pain, anger, and joy, themselves, without exception, discernments, and rather strong ones at that. Authentic mindfulness demands that we be nonjudgmental and dispassionate and asks us to resist our very nature, to swim against the riptide of eons of mammalian and primate evolution and to endorse Descartes' error.

Many mindfulness advocates promulgate not just awareness of the present moment, but acceptance of it, overlooking the point that acceptance *is* a judgment. Some form of judgment is unavoidable; our minds are adapted for it, just as our cardiovascular and other systems have evolved to handle gravity. NASA has countermeasures to cope with circulatory changes in microgravity, none of which the vast majority of humankind ever need (because so few are space-faring . . . to date). The blanket recommendations of some mindfulness advocates strike me similarly; they may have truth under certain conditions, but only then.

Further still, our emotional and judgmental nature is adaptive and functional in another way: It helps us to predict the future. As just one of many angles on this, consider the role of emotions in decision-making and what happens when emotion is removed from the process. How may emotions be removed? One way involves neurological insult (e.g., stroke, tumor): Lesions in the ventromedial sector of the prefrontal cortex disrupt the processing of emotional signals, but spare most basic cognitive functions. A main upshot of the loss of emotional processing is a deterioration in every aspect of decision-making.[26] "Gut level" feeling is essential to making good decisions about future courses of action.

Snap judgments and gut feelings, then, are essential to proper functioning. Is it necessarily wise to counsel inherently judgmental and emotional creatures to be mindful, especially in areas in which it is likely to undermine performance and prospection?

Such counsel may be admirable in some contexts. It may also prove possible to enact a mindful mindset much of the time for many people, and it appears that doing so can carry tangible benefits (e.g., more focus, less depression). For some individuals (e.g., those who hear voices or those whose self-talk is damning), learning specific mindful techniques can be a salvation. But to suggest that everyone gaze inward and to simply deny our prejudicial, lustful, and warlike nature, is not only to be unrealistic, it is to court cultural disaster.

It is even possible, though far from certain, that authentic mindfulness contains the seeds of its own undoing even without the conspiring force of a culture of self-regard. The advice to be self-aware and at the same time nonjudgmental and dispassionate, *including about the self*, produces philosophical questions if not problems, a point that famously occurred to Descartes. Does self-awareness not require self-judgment in order to qualify as self-awareness? If I have truly suspended judgment, how do I know who I am, if I exist, where I begin and end? I am very content, indeed relieved, to leave such questions to my friends in the Department of Philosophy and in other allied fields, but I raise them in passing only because they show that authentic mindfulness qua authentic mindfulness may itself ultimately be a road to intellectual perdition. Even if not, authentic mindfulness rendered mindless by the intertwining of its flaws with the culture of the self seems to me a sure recipe for cultural decline.

At the outset of this chapter, I championed the virtues of emperor penguins. Writing in *The New Yorker* about a trip to Antarctica, Franzen noted with admiration the behavior of a different species of penguin: "Many of the adults had retreated uphill to molt, a process that involves standing still for several weeks, itchy and hungry, while new feathers push out old feathers. The patience of the molters, their silent endurance, was impossible not to admire in human terms."[27] There is a danger, I realize, in idealizing these animals, and even if that pitfall is avoided, there is another in anthropomorphizing them. Indeed, in the months after the release of the documentary *March of the Penguins*, more than one commentator extolled the penguins for what amounted to their family values. After all, so the commentators' argument went, the penguins were not only devoted to their offspring, but to each other—they were "monogamous." What these commenters failed to appreciate is that the penguins, while undoubtedly enduring great hardship on behalf of their young, "divorced" the following spring. There was monogamy of a kind, but not the sort the commentators had in mind—it was serial monogamy, meaning that the bond between a male and a female was exclusive while it lasted, but it only lasted through that particular annual cycle, after which new pairs were formed, and so on, and so forth.

I do not hail the penguins as paragons of conservative family values, however those may be defined. But I do view them as exemplars of dogged single-mindedness, and more generally, I view them as admirable and virtuous. Further still, I am impressed by how much they accomplish and how things like mindfulness are not involved at all. The penguins are not professorly and neither do they practice authentic mindfulness. They represent a third way, in that they are not examples of the breathtaking vanity of the professor, nor of the much more credible (not to mention useful) concept of authentic mindfulness—they are too unaware for that. Rather, they represent an animal version of an ancient human virtue that I will extol at the end of this book as a potential solution to the cultural problem of unmoored, self-regarding "mindless mindfulness": stoicism (of which most have heard but which relatively few accurately and fully understand).

Yes, they're just penguins; yes, they're just following the dictates, embedded in their genes, of eons of evolutionary pressure. But that is the point—that is a more admirable thing than pretense about wine, coffee, and yoga.

Examples in nature are far from limited to Antarctica. When a leafcutter ant, designed by her genes to be a queen, does not produce offspring and thus does not retain her throne, what does she do? She just simply puts aside her crown and gets to work. She becomes just another worker ant, along with tens of thousands of her nestmates, and allows a fertile queen to take her place.

One could go on and on about examples of single-mindedness across nature. One may complain that humans may act similarly single-mindedly, selflessly, and virtuously in similar circumstances, and indeed, we will encounter such examples in the pages that follow (ones, tellingly, that rarely involve discernment about things such as coffee and wine). Furthermore, one might reply that the kind of dogged single-mindedness I am extolling is only applicable to mind-less creatures, but surely not to our supreme species.

Perhaps, but I am not so sure. Suppose humans and nonhumans were exposed to the same trying conditions, and then were followed for years and assessed for their physical health and behavioral func-tioning. This would allow some comparative insight as to just how virtuously resilient humans are. In fact, just such a comparison was possible regarding the September 11, 2001, attacks and their after-math. The comparison is between dogs who worked in the rubble and chaos of the fallen twin towers (notice, incidentally, I have already used the word "dogged" more than once), and humans, who did the same. (This example emphatically does *not* include those killed or physically injured on September 11, nor does it include those who directly witnessed atrocity as it was unfolding, nor does it include bereaved family members. Rather, the example is limited to people working in the aftermath, the vast majority of whom were diligent and laudable.) As many as half of the workers at the site have filed for compensation because of physical and/or mental health consequences of the work, whereas all of the dogs seem unfazed physically as well as behaviorally.[28] That work was mentally taxing and in many cases physically grueling, for dogs and humans alike, and thus it is unsur-prising that people would be affected ... but shouldn't the dogs be affected too?

It is not that dogs are unable to be affected by trauma. In fact, they can, as has been observed in military settings. The U.S. military now employs approximately 2,500 dogs—mostly Dutch and German shepherds, Labrador retrievers, and Belgian Malinois—and their work involves activities like patrol and bomb detection. A report by Tony Perry in the *Los Angeles Times*[29] described Cora, a Belgian Malinois very skilled at detecting buried bombs. Cora began her work in Iraq as a confident and composed dog; in the words of one of her handlers, "a very squared-away dog." But over time and with continual exposure to sharp noises, intense emotion, danger, and death, Cora changed. She became sensitive to loud noises, and reluctant to do the work that she formerly relished. She grew irritable and began to fight with other dogs. Cora developed a canine version of post-traumatic stress disorder (PTSD), and, like many humans with PTSD, responded well to a treatment regimen combining behavior therapy and medication (the same medicines that help humans, such as SSRI antidepressants).

Thus, dogs and humans alike can be lastingly traumatized by horror. But there are two crucial caveats to this truth. First, although there is to my knowledge no definitive systematic research on the point, there is suggestive evidence that dogs develop PTSD-like reactions at a lower rate than do humans. This was the case regarding the cleanup at Ground Zero, and it seems to be true as well in combat settings. Second, like dogs, humans are pretty resilient: Even in the face of considerable trauma, most people cope and adapt well, and only about a quarter or so develop PTSD.

Mammals like dogs and humans are designed to withstand a lot. How can it be otherwise after eons of evolutionary pressure? Emperor penguins, if anything, are hardier still, and other possible examples from nature are legion. Of all of these organisms, one might expect the species with access to electricity, the Internet, books, centuries of recorded history, the ability to travel into space and to ponder the nature of the shockingly vast (and probably infinite and possibly multiple) universe—*that* species—to be the toughest, the most stoic in the face of challenge, and the most virtuous in the face of hardship. But it is not necessarily so. There is much to admire in our complex, subjective awareness of things like tragedy; there is just as much to admire, I would suggest, in the hardy, stoic, and rather mindless attitude that most of the rest of nature takes toward those very same things.

Inherent to authentic mindfulness are O-ring–like chinks: the urging, even if implicit, of an inward gaze in already self-obsessed creatures and the encouragement to misunderstand our very nature. These are flaws which, if left alone, need not have culminated in anything negative at all, and certainly not in cultural decline. But immerse these flaws in the shearing crosswinds of a culture of narcissism, steep them in the freezing temperatures of a billion selves on Facebook talking past one another while "liking" their own self-image, then seals fail, a monster awakens, and the Narcissi reign.

Authentic Mindfulness

A UTHENTIC MINDFULNESS (MOMENT-TO-MOMENT NON-
judgmental awareness of one's environment and subjective
state) has lost its way, derailed by a culture of self-importance. It is
turning into a vehicle for solipsism. I have noted that there is variation
in what is meant by "authentic mindfulness." One useful distinction
is between the focused-attention and open-monitoring versions.[1] In
the former, one directs attention to a particular thing and sustains
attention on it; in the latter, one monitors all of the present-moment
experience (not just the self) in nonjudgmental fashion. In this chapter and throughout others, what I mean by "authentic mindfulness"
is largely the latter, although I hold that my critiques apply to both
versions, and both versions are susceptible to defilement into excessive self-regard. In the focused-attention version, the more the object
of attention is related to the self, the more the potential for solipsism.

The rise of the collection of ideas I term "authentic mindfulness"
is easy enough to understand. It is very helpful for many people,
especially people whose thoughts tend to include ones like "I'm hopelessly defective" or "I should kill myself" or "I should kill someone else" or "I am being monitored and reported on by the insects
living in my wall," to view those thoughts dispassionately, as mere

thoughts with the same initial standing as ones like "The paint on that wall is green" and "It is autumn now."

The vast majority of thoughts and sentiments—and I do mean vast, as in trillions of trillions—no matter how they may feel at the time, are profoundly mundane and insignificant. "Most thoughts are worth their weight in gold" is a witticism conveyed by the revered psychologist Paul Meehl.[2] And the thoughts and perceptions we do have, as trivial as they tend to be, are merely a fraction of those we could potentially have, but do not, because humans' exposure to the universe's information is so miniscule. Consider vision in this regard. "Vision is based in *Homo sapiens* on an almost infinitesimal sliver of energy, four hundred to seven hundred nanometers in the electromagnetic spectrum. The rest of the spectrum, saturating the Universe, ranges from gamma rays trillions of times shorter than the human visual segment to radio waves trillions of times longer."[3] Our hearing is no better; E. O. Wilson again: "We walk through nature ... sensing only a few vibrations, able to interpret almost nothing."[4] The truth of the matter is that we perceive a tiny fraction of the universe's data, and contained within that fraction are trillions of trivial thoughts and feelings.

Compare this emphasis on each and every one of us being almost unimaginably trivial, to these words: "Walt Whitman said, in 'Song of Myself': 'I am large! I contain multitudes!' It's actually true. We are like universes, each one of us. We are boundless." These words are from Jon Kabat-Zinn, mentioned already and to whom I am regularly referred to correct the error of my ways when I suggest that much material in the mindfulness canon includes an inherent self-focus. Far from contradicting my point, words like these—some of them the most self-celebratory lines of all of Whitman's poetry—make my point.

If this idea of our triviality seems anathema to you, that is quite understandable, for two reasons. First, it means that the overwhelming majority of your deepest sentiments and thoughts are not very important. If it helps, I am by no means singling you out; on the contrary, in this I include all 7 billion of us. Second, many of the 7 billion of us live in a culture that may be a first in human history for its views of the individual as not just valuable and important but unique. To view an individual's thoughts and feelings as similarly important to—maybe less important than—individual grains of

sand on miles of beach is to flatly contradict certainties in our current cultural mindset.

But these certainties need contradicting. This is so, even in the
context of one individual's life, never mind the context of all human
kind or the context of the cosmos. In July 2013, as is their wont, the
good people of the National Aeronautics and Space Administration
(NASA) did us the service of reminding us of our place. The images
of earth taken from Saturn by the *Cassini* satellite show us as a tiny
blue dot within an infinitude. In his latest book *The Meaning of
Human Existence*, the eminent Wilson wrote, "The tiny blue speck
we call home is proportionately no more than that, a mote of stardust
near the edge of our galaxy among a hundred billion or more galaxies in the universe . . . It would be becoming of us to speak modestly
of our status in the cosmos." We are each of us virtually invisible
smudges of organic matter dotting a piece of dust.

Just as one need not necessarily perpetrate an appalling crime as
a consequence of the mundane thought "It is autumn now," so one
need not necessarily kill in reaction to the thought "I should kill
someone." This latter thought is mundane too—or can be viewed as
such—if it is seen for what it really is. It is not a profound and ordained dictum, but a mere excretion of the mind, as much a basis for
taking another's life as other bodily excretions like sweat and saliva.

The considerable value of this insight may elude you if you are
fortunate enough to rarely have thoughts like "I should kill someone" or "I'm hopelessly defective." If you have had such thoughts,
however, you understand their peculiar power: They can feel like
indictments or pronouncements delivered from on high, so emotionally compelling that they appear self-evident, and so urgent that
they compel immediate action. The traction of these thoughts on
behavior, their leverage point, often rests on feeling. For example,
the thought "I am hopelessly defective" may lead one to self-injure
because it leads one to feel overwhelmed by shame and related painful emotions.

Hallucinations can be even more compelling a mental experience
than thoughts like "I'm hopelessly defective." To have the thought
that one is defective is painful; to hear a voice in one's head saying
that one is defective is, in addition to being painful, terrifying. Some
hallucinations are termed "command hallucinations," because they
command a certain course of action, often a nefarious one. Thoughts

can compel actions; hallucinations can command them. It can therefore be quite a relief to view such voices as nothing more than loud thoughts (or as visible thoughts, in the case of visual hallucinations). The logic in force here is that a product of the mind is merely that, and this is so regardless of whether that product is a thought, an idea, an emotion, or a hallucination. Sure, a hallucination can be vivid and jarring, but it nonetheless remains a thought, and so therefore is subject to the same kind of mindful reflection as the thought "it sure is hot today."

Thus one useful aspect of authentic mindfulness: To be dispassionate and nonjudgmental about all thoughts, including those like "I am hopelessly defective"—and even including command hallucinations—is to pause, reflect, and gain distance and perspective.

Pausing, just by itself, can be surprisingly helpful, a truism captured by the clichéd and somewhat exaggerated maxim "time heals all wounds." A more modest rendering might be "the passage of time tends to lessen the pain of some wounds." I have learned this distinction myself through the great misery that was and is my dad's death by suicide, as well as the leavening effects of more than 25 years having passed since. It is certainly not the case that the wound has been fully healed, and I am under the impression that it never will be—an impression repeatedly affirmed by conversations with others who have been bereaved by suicide. Nevertheless, the white hot agony and shock of his death have diminished very considerably and now burn more with the intensity of an ember than of a star. Some other things aided in that improvement, but the sheer passage of time was a major factor.

One need not be particularly mindful to reap the benefits of time's tincture (though authentic mindfulness exerts its salutary effects, in part, via simple delay). Consider in this regard an exercise that has become a routine part of the treatment of bulimia nervosa (and other clinical problems to boot) in the clinic I direct, as in many such clinics around the world. The syndrome is characterized by repeated binges on food, as well as by ways of purging food (e.g., self-induced vomiting, laxative abuse).

We instruct patients, in response to the urge to binge or purge, to instead sit at a desk with pencil and paper and simply graph out their minute-to-minute mood, usually for about five minutes. The horizontal axis of this graph represents the passage of time in minutes, and is numbered from 1 to 5 or so. The vertical axis of the graph represents overall negative mood, ranging from 1 at the bottom (feeling good) to 10 at the top (feeling very bad). For virtually everyone who does this exercise, and who begins the exercise at say a 9 or 10 (feeling bad, as will usually be the case for a bulimic patient who forestalls a binge or a purge), the graph will slope downward as time passes. The slope is often relatively gradual, from say a 9 or 10 down to around a 6 or 7.

In response to seeing a graph like this, the therapist is positioned to respond with something like the following: "Your rating went down from a 9 to a 6, about a 33% drop, pretty substantial. Tell me again what you did to produce that substantial of a drop in negative mood." A typical answer is, "Nothing. I just sat there for a few minutes and graphed my mood."

In the psychotherapy clinic I direct, we have recently hit on another activity that is even more mundane than mood graphing, but with similar effects on mood, and that activity is none other than brushing one's teeth. The mild but positive effects on mood may stem from the simple passage of time that toothbrushing necessitates, but I conjecture there may be at least two other operative processes. First, for someone mired in ruminative loops of self-recrimination, guilt, and apathy, an easy-to-accomplish task that demonstrably takes matters from worse to better is a balm, a noticeable one even if a very minor one, one that breaks a string of negative thoughts, feelings, and behaviors with a positive. Second, for many of the patients we see, certainly to include those with prominent mood disorders but not limited to them, defectiveness of self is a major concern. There are relatively few activities that literally clean the interior of the self, but toothbrushing is one of them, and to boot, it is one of the easiest, most pleasant, and least off-putting.

We take pains not to get carried away with the effectiveness of interventions like this, but nevertheless the lessons learned from simple activities like mood-graphing and toothbrushing, can be multiple and significant. For example, if sitting at a table for a few minutes and occasionally rating one's mood or brushing one's teeth can substantially improve one's mood, it therefore follows that (1) emotions must not be all that powerful if something so simple can so easily change them; (2) emotions pass, and do so relatively quickly and easily; and (3) regulating one's emotions need not be all that hard to do.[5]

Authentic mindfulness—including, but certainly not limited to, purposefully being aware of one's moment-to-moment mental state in a dispassionate and nonjudgmental fashion—can thus be useful in part because it induces one to pause. Pausing and mindfulness are not the same thing: There is more to mindfulness than a mere pause, and furthermore, it should be reiterated that one can pause without being especially mindful. Indeed, in the mood-rating exercise previously described, the only bit of awareness that is required is the occasional snap rating of one's mood, which is hardly the picture of deep meditation. Besides that brief snapshot of mood, people doing the exercise can think about whatever they like or not think at all.

Mindfulness, when it is authentic, not only assures the passage of time—helpful in itself as a disruption in the rapid-fire sequence from thought to feeling to destructive action—but can also facilitate reflection during those seconds the pause allows. The thought "I am hopelessly defective," if simply left in the mind for a few seconds, can morph from a reason for profound shame and immediate self-injury to a mental debate about—even a friendly consideration of—the thought's facets. A few seconds of reflection can lead to questions such as "If I am hopelessly defective, is that all I am?" and "If I am defective, how did I qualify for the status of hopelessly so?" Notice the tone and nature of these questions: They are not confrontational nor are they really even disputatious; they are not brooding.[6] Rather, they are fair, reflective, clarifying, and nonjudgmental, which is a reasonable criteria set for a mindful thought. They accomplish this, in part, by accepting, at least for the moment, a premise of the thought, namely, the matter of defectiveness.

The momentary acceptance of a thought of defectiveness does not require acceptance of defectiveness as truth, but rather, acceptance for the time being of defectiveness as a conjectural object. Unlike truth, which is foundational bedrock cemented into the ground beneath our feet by eons of relentless gravitational force, a conjecture is like a pebble: It can be picked up, handled, turned over and over, examined, held up to the light, put back down, and picked back up again. It is a very helpful insight indeed for someone with the thought "I'm hopelessly defective" or "I should kill myself" to treat the thought as an object of dispassionate scrutiny rather than as unshakeable and foundational truth. This is an extraordinarily useful idea, which is one reason that I see its deterioration into faux mindfulness as troubling.

Kabat-Zinn, for whose writing I had criticism regarding the solipsism in some of his phrasing on mindfulness, also deserves praise for his gift of explaining this aspect of authentic mindfulness with vividness. For example, he writes, "Sometimes thoughts cascade through the mind like a waterfall. We might take some delight in this image, and visualize ourselves sitting behind the torrent in a little cave or depression in the rock, aware of the ever-changing sounds, astonished by the unending roar, resting in the timelessness of the cascading mind in such an extended moment."[7]

Kabat-Zinn's fluency with such imagery is an important aspect of his appeal, and justifiably so. To be able to guide and persuade someone, who for example, is immersed in self-hatred, or is overwhelmed by desires for suicide, to view those thoughts and desires as a torrent behind which one sits with equanimity, is to relieve misery and avert potential catastrophe.

This perspective encourages the deliberate consideration of subjective mental experience as a thing, even a plaything. One has distance from and perspective on a plaything; it is not so close at hand that one cannot see it. Furthermore, what is there to fear from a plaything? The objectification and even trivialization of a thought like "I should kill myself"—treating such a thought as a mere pebble that can be tossed from hand to hand and that is merely one pebble among the myriad—puts the thought in its rightful place in the universe. Odds are quite high that the thought—any thought—is not especially important. Likewise, the thinker of the thought is not particularly important in the scheme of things. To paraphrase Charles de Gaulle, cemeteries are full of indispensable men. This sentiment is regularly invoked to be grim and can rile the modern ear, immersed as it is in a sea of self-obsession and self-importance. But the statement need not necessarily be read as grim; it can also be read as humble.

Authentic mindfulness requires humility and is largely defined by it. Viewing the mind's moment-to-moment products as of a similar standing as floating motes of dust—myriad, ephemeral, individually insignificant—takes genuine humility, a benefit of which is freedom from the tyranny of thoughts like "I'm hopelessly defective." A mote of dust with the message "I should kill myself" is still merely a mote of dust, hardly the basis for such a misery as suicide and its aftermath. This state of mind also looks outward, away from solipsism and out to the world and all it contains: motes of dust, thoughts, people and all. The loss of self-focus and self-importance, combined with authentic interest in what exists outside one's own narrow ken, represent an authentic version of mindfulness, one with centuries of actual Buddhist and other thinking behind it.

In a sense, Michelangelo's *David* and many other glories to boot are composed of motes of dust. It is not necessarily the case then that an authentic mindfulness perspective relegates all products of the human mind to a dustbin of automatic triviality. Rather, the perspective acknowledges the existence of extreme greatness, but at the same time, recognizes its extreme rarity in context of the infinitude of mundane and insignificant thoughts and sentiments that you and I produce every day—and importantly, that Michelangelo himself also produced every day. Authentic mindfulness advocates for the same humility Albert Einstein meant when discussing his views on religion: "What I see in Nature is a magnificent structure that we can comprehend only very imperfectly, and that must fill a thinking person with a feeling of humility. This is a genuinely religious feeling that has nothing to do with mysticism."[8]

The true leaders of authentic mindfulness regularly tend to show understanding of truths, such as the humility inherent in mindfulness, and that it is meant for the rough and tumble of the real world, not just for the coddled, candle-scented, and yoga-matted environs of affluent North Americans and Europeans. I have already alluded to the leader of the daylong mindfulness retreat I attended. His name is Zindel Segal. Look up his bibliometrics if you doubt he is more than just a mindfulness retreat leader. Zindel closed the day with advice that we not fetishize mindfulness but instead use it moment by moment to do real good for others. In this, he echoed the words of Kabat-Zinn, a similarly credentialed leader alluded to earlier. The following was transcribed by psychologist Ken Pope at one of Kabat-Zinn's workshops:

> The challenges we face, the choices we make, the places we go, and the work that we do all become occasions for opening to the life we are actually living and the life that is ours to live if we show up fully and pay attention. You could say life itself is the meditation teacher,

curriculum, and the gift that comes to us through showing up for life in its fullness and meeting it . . . It is life itself that is the meditation practice, the real arena of mindfulness. In that spirit, everything and every moment becomes practice and an occasion for waking up . . . Wakefulness, as best we can muster it, brought face to face with the human condition itself, this is the challenge of a life lived, and lived fully in the only time we ever get to live or learn or love: This moment, this now.[9]

Authentic mindfulness has been perverted into solipsism. However, another misunderstanding deserves attention: the notion that mindfulness involves the emptying of the mind.[10] Not only is it nonsensical to think of the emptying of the mind (just as it is nonsensical to think of emptying the body, or even of fully cleansing it, given its trillions of bacteria), it is emphatically *not* what authentic mindfulness counsels. Rather, it advises nonjudgmental awareness of the moment, including but far from limited to, awareness of the contents of the mind in the moment. It is thus possible to conceive of a continuum regarding proper self-focus in various construals of mindfulness. At one end of the spectrum resides the misunderstanding just alluded to, which is a mind emptied of all, including of the self. At the opposite end of the same spectrum is located the focus of this book, which is a mind tediously, nonjudgmentally, and in the most extreme cases, monstrously focused mostly or entirely on itself.

In between these two poles of the continuum sits authentic mindfulness, the location of which is not at the midpoint, but rather, is decidedly closer to the spectrum's self-abnegation end. As one travels from this authentic, intermediate point toward the self-obsessed end of the spectrum, the problems highlighted in this book loom larger and larger.

Regarding the self-obsessed endpoint of this spectrum, Ludwig Wittgenstein thought that it could circle back and become one with self-abnegation, a view that would change the linear dimension I just described into a circular one. He wrote that ". . . it can be seen that solipsism, when its implications are followed out strictly, coincides with pure realism. The self of solipsism shrinks to a point without extension, and there remains the reality coordinated with it." It can be hard to tell with Wittgenstein, both because the phrasing can be dense and even obfuscatory, and also because he elsewhere seemed to imply a contrary viewpoint. I take this statement, however, to mean that it is possible through a certain mental attitude to shrink the self into the tiny and miniscule entity that it is, and that in so doing, a fuller awareness of reality is available. Interestingly, some proponents of authentic mindfulness make exactly this claim, but their means to the end differs from Wittgenstein's. For advocates of authentic mindfulness, the means involves nonjudgmental attention in moment-to-moment fashion, with everything attended to, whether or not it involves the self. Because most things occurring in a given moment do not involve the self, the counsel is thus largely against self-focus. Wittgenstein's advice is self-focus of such an intensity that the self is obliterated, as if self-focus were a laser than can destroy whatever it is trained upon.

Wittgenstein's perspective on this is dubious, but a potential way to salvage it is to argue that we are inherently selfish creatures, and so to fully accept that reality—to face it and embrace it—may be a step toward moving beyond it. This compromise position is a promising one, because I believe that all except the most excessive faux mindfulness enthusiasts will endorse it; the authentic mindfulness group would, as would I. I thus return to this idea later in the book as a piece of a potential solution to the problem of mindless mindfulness.

I hope that the foregoing represents a fair conceptual treatment of the collection of ideas and interventions that fall under the umbrella of authentic mindfulness, because I think the topic deserves it. I also have in store some criticisms of the concept, but especially of its defilement. Staying for the moment with its merits, however, they are not only conceptual, they are empirical as well. For example, a group of researchers demonstrated that mindfulness training can improve test scores on the Graduate Record Exam (GRE; used as part of admission to graduate school) and reduce mind wandering.[11]

The training program in question lasted 2 weeks, and involved four, 45-minute classes over those 14 days. During class, the participants sat in a circle on cushions on the floor. The authors described the classes as follows:

> Classes focused on (a) sitting in an upright posture with legs crossed and gaze lowered, (b) distinguishing between naturally arising

thoughts and elaborated thinking, (c) minimizing the distracting quality of past and future concerns by reframing them as mental projections occurring in the present, (d) using the breath as an anchor for attention during meditation, (e) repeatedly counting up to 21 consecutive exhalations, and (f) allowing the mind to rest naturally rather than trying to suppress the occurrence of thoughts.[12]

The class required participants to use these strategies frequently in their day-to-day lives, and to complete 10 minutes of daily meditation (in addition to that which occurred in class).

The emphasis on meditation, circle-sitting, upright posture, exhalations, and the like may set eyes rolling among some skeptics, but the data will tell, and the data produced by this study were convincing. As compared to a group who took classes on nutrition, the group who were versed in mindfulness experienced improved cognitive functioning, which showed in multiple ways, including better GRE scores and an improved ability to stop the mind from wandering. One remarkable aspect of these findings is that the mindfulness intervention changed something that is often viewed as immutable, namely, cognitive ability. Also of note, this same group of researchers has shown that even a single, brief bout of mindfulness meditation (8 minutes) can have detectable effects on cognitive performance.[13]

Related to cognitive performance, consider the "sunk-cost bias." As the name implies, the bias kicks in when one has invested resources in an effort, and because of those invested resources, refuses to abandon the effort and cut losses despite clear signs that that is proper (e.g., the selling of a failing stock; the deletion of problematic manuscript text that required hours of effort; the continuation of unfortunate military campaigns). In a package of studies,[14] researchers demonstrated that mindfulness mitigates the sunk-cost bias. Specifically, they showed that (1) people who have high trait mindfulness are better able to resist the bias; and (2) as compared to controls, participants randomized to a mindfulness meditation intervention were better at warding off the bias. In this study, as in some of the work alluded to earlier, a relatively brief bout of mindfulness meditation (15 minutes) was enough for an effect.

A fair amount of the literature on the effects of mindfulness is of this sort, that is, mindfulness has surprising effects on the ability to succeed in various ways. This direction of thought—"be mindful in order to get ahead in life"—is ironic, in that mindful-ness, in its authentic form, is not about success in life; rather, it is about attunement and connection. Among other critics, Ron Purser and David Loy have noticed this irony. Writing in the *Huffington Post*, and using the memorable term "McMindfulness," they write, "Rather than applying mindfulness as a means to awaken individu-als and organizations from the unwholesome roots of greed, ill will and delusion, it is usually being refashioned into a banal, therapeu-tic, self-help technique that can actually reinforce those roots."[15] Researchers, too, have noticed the irony of McMindfulness, and one group conducted an illuminating study to address the issue. Similar to the study on GRE scores, this study put one group of partici-pants through a mindfulness training course and had another group who did something else (in this case, they were told that they had been placed on a waiting list for a future course). After the mindful-ness training course was completed, participants from both groups were invited in one at a time and found themselves in a waiting area with only three chairs. Two of the three were already occupied, and so naturally enough, all participants sat in the remaining chair. Unbeknownst to them, however, the other two people were confed-erates of the experimenter, as was an additional person, who limped into the waiting room after the participant had taken the third seat, on crutches and with the kind of boot on the foot that signifies a broken bone. The "injured" confederate made somewhat of a display of her predicament, by leaning against the wall and audibly sighing in discomfort.

Buddha tended not to focus on GRE scores and the like; as he said, "I teach one thing and one only: that is, suffering and the end of suf-fering." The researchers were interested in a simple question: Would participants voluntarily give up their seat for the aggrieved confeder-ate more readily if they had received the mindfulness intervention? Would they attempt to relieve a fellow human's suffering?

The answer to this question was clear and also can be viewed as encouraging or disheartening, depending on the context. A mere 16% of those in the waiting list condition—that is, only 3 participants of the 19 allocated to the waiting list—gave up their seats, whereas half of those who had received mindfulness training—10 of 20—did so. Mindfulness training made a considerable difference—three times as many people who had received it than had not showed compassion to a stranger. That is encouraging, but what I think is disheartening is that overall, only 13 of 39 participants helped the injured person.

I suppose a "glass half full" interpretation, is that as many as 13 of 39 helped the injured person *despite* the strong social pressure not to help, that is, neither of the other two seated confederates made the slightest move to give up their seats. Helping the injured person thus required the surmounting of at least two barriers: the reluctance to reach out to a stranger and the hesitation in contradicting the social behavior of multiple others. And yet 33% of the participants did it.

Mindfulness training took this percentage up to 50%, and this with regard to a selfless, noncompetitive behavior. In this regard, one of the authors of the study reminded readers that after all, "Gaining competitive advantage on exams and increasing creativity in business weren't of the utmost concern to Buddha and other early meditation teachers."[16]

We have seen that interventions involving mindfulness can focus the mind, improve cognitive functioning (e.g., as reflected by higher GRE scores), and make some people more compassionate to a stranger in need. More compassion toward others reduces their suffering, but might mindfulness reduce one's own suffering? A group of researchers has thoroughly examined this question, answering in the affirmative. Some of the most compelling evidence involves the particular form of suffering that is major depressive disorder. Despite confusion in various quarters of our culture as to the nature and even the very existence of this and other forms of mental illness, this is a grave and debilitating disorder that can prove lethal. This fact makes the success of mindfulness-related interventions in depression all the more impressive.

For example, in the journal *Mindfulness*, one group of researchers studied depression prevention in adolescents.[17] There is little doubt that these researchers were successful in their project, although as discussed throughout this book, I think there should be at least some reticence in teaching mindfulness to youth, and I view it as potentially worrisome that there is an academic journal called *Mindfulness* (susceptible to becoming an echo chamber).

These researchers randomly assigned high school classes to a group mindfulness program (which also involved depression assessments prior to and immediately following the intervention and at 6-month follow-up) versus a condition that only completed the depression measures. Results indicated clinically significant differences between the two groups postintervention and at 6 months, with the mindfulness classes less depressed than the comparison classes.

Mindfulness training has even been studied in incarcerated youth.[18] Plausibly enough, the researchers expected that the experience of incarceration, because of its many inherent stressors, would represent a cognitive burden and thus degrade adolescents' attentional abilities. This expectation was fully borne out, as there were clear decreases in performance in an attentional task from the study's baseline assessment to its 4-month follow-up assessment.

This research team evaluated whether a mindfulness-based intervention might slow the degradation of incarceration-related attentional abilities in the incarcerated youth. Adolescents between the ages of 16 and 18 were housed in dormitories for their incarceration, and some dorms were randomly assigned to receive a mindfulness-based treatment (there were a total of 147 youth in these dorms) and some dorms (with a total of 117 youth) received an active control treatment (which focused on cultivating more healthy and helpful beliefs and attitudes about issues such as substance abuse and violent behavior). Over a period of approximately one month, both groups received a total of about 12 hours of treatment, which amounts to an hour every other day or two, in small-group settings. Adolescents in the mindfulness condition were asked to keep a written record of time spent practicing the techniques outside session.

As the researchers predicted, the control condition did not forestall attentional deficits in the young participants. By contrast, the mindfulness intervention did, but only for those youth whose written logs reflected regular out-of-session practice.

One bottom-line conclusion from this study, then, is that out-of-session practice is key. Out-of-session practice of what though? This research team's answer would be "practice of mindfulness-based techniques," but because the control condition did not contain a rigorous practice element, a plausible alternative answer would be "practice of anything as long as it is reasonably healthy and done routinely." I incline toward this latter answer, as the health-inducing effects of routinizing basic things such as sleep and exercise schedules are quite well documented. This point will be emphasized in this book's final chapter on ways forward that avoid the pitfalls of faux mindfulness. Nevertheless, the study was consistent with the view that mindfulness can be helpful, and an impressive aspect of the work is the extension to a challenging population, a population one would not necessarily associate with mindfulness or its benefits.

At least as impressive, Mark Williams and colleagues have repeatedly shown that interventions related to mindfulness are not only useful in depression prevention in youth, and not only useful in intervening once depression has occurred, but also helpful regarding some of the most difficult-to-treat kinds of depression (e.g., treatment-resistant depression, recurrent depression).[19] This work, combined with other rigorous research demonstrating relevance of mindfulness-based interventions to problematic tobacco use[20] and prehypertension[21] indicates that authentic mindfulness deserves respect as one means to remediate various problems in living.[22]

I met Williams at a small meeting of mental health professionals interested in scientific approaches to suicide prevention. During the course of a dinner and cocktail party, I intimated my doubts about mindfulness to him. His perceptive, thoughtful, and gentle manner subtly aroused my suspicions at first, because when this otherwise enviable constellation of traits is combined with an interest in things like mindfulness, I have found it can lead to muddle-headedness. Williams, however, is far from muddle-headed. At the end of the evening, he turned to me and said something along the lines of "it's just the idea that your thoughts are merely your thoughts," his tone and demeanor expressing his awareness that this was simultaneously a simple, profound, and powerful statement. There is a beauty to this view, and it is partly in the sentiment that one's moment-to-moment thoughts have an inconsequential character, and thus are not worth getting depressed or anxious about, and not worth, in the case of thoughts of violence (including the self-directed type), of hurting or killing anyone.

The various positive effects of mindfulness suggest that its practice may leave detectable neurobiological traces. Indeed, there is a growing literature attesting to this likelihood. For example, researchers administered Kabat-Zinn's mindfulness-based stress reduction program to adults with mild cognitive impairment and compared them to a similar group who received usual care.[23] Both groups underwent resting-state functional magnetic resonance imaging (fMRI) brain scans both before and after the intervention phase. The study was small and preliminary, but nevertheless suggested that those who received the mindfulness-based intervention were more protected than others from processes such as atrophy of the hippocampus (crucial to memory) and loss of connectivity between key brain regions.

A somewhat larger study compared mindfulness meditation to a wait-list comparison group, assessing brain electrical activity just before and immediately after the 8-week intervention, and then again 4 months after the intervention.[24] The meditators experienced significant increases in brain electrical activity in an area known to be associated with positive emotion (i.e., the left anterior region). In addition, very intriguingly, both the meditators and the wait-list controls received the influenza vaccine at the end of the 8-week period, and when assessed later, those in the meditation condition showed a more robust immune response to the vaccine than did those in the control group (reflecting better immune functioning). There was even evidence that the more left-side brain activation (i.e., the pattern associated with positive emotion), the more rigorous the immune function.

Results like these are enticing, and it is easy to see why they excite proponents of mindfulness-related interventions. As the authors of this work noted, however, caution in interpretation is warranted. All that was demonstrated in this research—brain scans and immune assessments notwithstanding—is that doing something (e.g., mindfulness-related activity) was better than doing nothing (e.g., being assigned to a wait list). "Something" can mean mindfulness or meditation, but it could also mean any number of other things, and indeed, there is strong evidence that the repetition of some activities (e.g., physical exercise), even if done quite mindlessly, produces healthful effects. A recent review[25] of mindfulness neuroscience cites mindfulness meditation–induced increases in dendritic branching, synaptogenesis, and myelinogenesis, and refers to the possibility of mindfulness-induced neurogenesis. The same review notes mindfulness meditation-induced anatomical changes in the following areas: anterior cingulate cortex, posterior cingulate cortex, prefrontal cortex, insula, caudate, putamen, and amygdala. The review authors stated: "However, we acknowledge that many other brain areas are also involved in mindfulness practice." The ways in which these areas may interact with each other in response to mindfulness-related interventions and how these may in turn interact with mindfulness-related changes in brain processes such as synaptogenesis, represent a level of complexity with which current neuroscientists struggle. Moreover, much of the neuroscience literature on mindfulness includes comparison conditions (e.g., relaxation training) that could be improved in terms of methodological rigor—a concern that, as we will see, pervades research on mindfulness in general. Mindfulness neuroscience generates considerable enthusiasm, but the state of the science indicates a more tempered outlook. Similar excitement—and similar concerns—attach to a study on pain management.[26] The research focused on chronic pain sufferers who tended to use more pain medicine than prescribed, and it examined a mindfulness intervention including three emphases: mindfulness itself, reappraisal, and savoring. The mindfulness aspect was similar to that contained in other mindfulness-based interventions discussed here already, namely, attention to and awareness of moment-to-moment experience, without judgment. Interestingly, the other two aspects—reappraisal and savoring—in a sense contradict mindfulness, because each requires judgment, at least of a kind. Reappraisal requires that one interpret a difficult experience as growth-promoting, and savoring demands that one preferentially dwell on positive events. Reappraisal's interpreting and savoring's narrowing of attention run counter to mindfulness' guidance to pay attention in the moment to all features of the moment, with no filtering or judgment.

The three-pronged package of mindfulness, reappraisal, and savoring outperformed a nonspecific, traditional support group with regard to the target behavior of opioid misuse and led to reductions in pain-related impairment as well. These improvements persisted throughout a 3-month, posttreatment interval.

Opioid misuse is an enormous public health concern, and chronic pain sufferers clearly would benefit from several rigorously studied treatments from which to choose. These findings may point to one such treatment, but there is reason for caution. One concern is that the mindfulness-related treatment was supported for some outcomes but not for others. Effectiveness seemed indicated for some outcomes, such as overall pain-related impairment, but was not supported regarding desire to misuse opioids. More specifically, the intervention group reported significantly fewer cravings for opioids just after the treatment phase of the study, but this difference had disappeared by 3-month follow-up. A second issue with the work is that, to the degree that the mindfulness-related intervention was effective, it is not apparent which aspect served as its active ingredient. Had participants been advised only to savor or only to reappraise, would results have been similar? And finally, like many studies in this area, the control condition was such that a stringent test of the treatment's effectiveness was not possible. Specifically, in the mindfulness-related condition, participants were instructed to engage in 3 minutes of mindful breathing just before ingestion of pain medicine. The point of this was to allow considered deliberation as to whether the dose was proper, whether the motivation for opioid use was truly pain control, and so forth. This strikes me as sensible and in itself is not a problem; the problem is that nothing similar was done with control participants. If, for example, they had been instructed to toss a tennis ball in one hand for 3 minutes before taking their medicine, would the mindfulness-related treatment still have outperformed the control condition? The design of this study leaves questions like this unanswerable, and this kind of design problem recurs frequently in the mindfulness literature (and, it should be acknowledged, recurs in areas beyond mindfulness too, throughout the literature on psychological treatments for mental disorders).

Understandably, findings such as these on pain management and those noted earlier on brain activation patterns tend to attract the notice of the media. Reporters' readerships want the bottom line and are often uninterested in the details of experimental design, such as the stringency of control groups. Nevertheless, a close reading of these studies reveals enough weaknesses that, to quote from most grant proposal reviews I have ever seen (and not just the reviews of my own grant proposals, though I have certainly received my fair share), "enthusiasm is diminished." What would increase enthusiasm is a sufficiently controlled, large-scale study by a group of researchers who are well-credentialed regarding the design of treatment studies as well as the mindfulness landscape.

Williams' group, mentioned earlier, answered this call in an impressive 2014 study on depression prevention. As the authors noted, a strength of their study "... is that it is the largest trial of mindfulness-based cognitive therapy (MBCT) versus treatment-as-usual to date, and the first with an active control treatment." This latter point is essential: Worryingly few studies of mindfulness interventions contain compelling comparison treatments. Williams and colleagues also note that their sample is large and representative enough that they are likely to generalize to routine mental health practice settings. Their trial had many state-of-the-art features, for example, to decrease the possibility of participant drop-out, which is a well-known problem with studies like these, the researchers conducted a pretreatment interview with participants that focused on shoring up motivation for persistent attendance. They also preregistered their trial, including the public and a priori specification of their hypothesized results.

Perhaps tellingly, the findings were not particularly supportive of a mindfulness-related approach. The participants were 274 people who had experienced three or more episodes of major depressive disorder in their lives, but who were currently depression-free; 255 of these 274 were reassessed at follow-up at some point between 3 and 12 months following termination of treatment—an impressive rate of retention, indicating that the pretreatment motivational interview proved worthwhile. Participants were allocated to one of three groups:

1. Eight sessions of mindfulness-based cognitive therapy (MBCT) were given to the first group.
2. Eight sessions of a treatment that included everything in MBCT except meditation (this was the study's active control) was given to the second group.
3. Treatment as usual was given to the third group.

Neither MBCT nor the active control intervention outperformed the treatment-as-usual group regarding the study's main target, which was the prevention of recurrence of major depressive disorder. More specifically, around half of those in the study experienced a recurrence of depression, regardless of which group they were assigned to.

This illness is notorious for its extremely high relapse rates; without treatment, people who have experienced three or more episodes in the past have as much as a 90% chance of a recurrence of the condition. The good news from the preceding trial is that MBCT cuts that rate approximately in half, and so does MBCT minus the meditation. The bad news, however, is that neither treatment adds significantly to ongoing usual care (e.g., ongoing antidepressant medication). My overall thesis is that the deterioration of mindfulness into solipsism verges on the tragic. I do not mean to suggest, however, that Williams and his group have contributed to this problem. On the contrary, the results can be viewed as an instance in which claims for the power of all forms of mindfulness—problematic or not—tend to outpace their evidence base.

In fact, the article describing the trial went to some lengths to emphasize that there was one subgroup among whom the mindfulness-based intervention appeared to significantly outperform the treatment-as-usual group, which was those who had suffered childhood trauma. As psychologist James Coyne helpfully pointed out on his periodic blog and as noted earlier, the trial in question was officially preregistered, meaning that, in advance of any data collection, the specific predictions, methods, and treatment targets of the study were publically stated. Much as in riflery and archery, it is not very impressive to state one's target after it has been hit; the practice of preregistration of clinical trials is now widespread because it prevents researchers from after-the-fact change of targets. To their credit, Williams and colleagues not only preregistered their mindfulness trial, they also faithfully reported the null effects of the mindfulness intervention.

At the same time, the childhood trauma subgroup was not mentioned in the preregistration materials, and the team emphasized the post hoc childhood maltreatment subgroup result, so much so that many will scan the article's title and abstract and view it as a supportive trial for mindfulness, when it is anything but.

Other researchers reported a highly similar pattern of findings, with null results regarding MBCT in main analyses, and in post hoc analyses, some suggestion that MBCT might outperform controls in those who had experienced abuse in the past.[27] Helpfully, these researchers also focused on cost of treatment. Overall, there was not a significant difference between MBCT and the comparison condition, which was antidepressant medication. With the important caveat that the cost differences were nonsignificant, it is nonetheless interesting to sort through them.

MBCT cost more. Specifically, the price tag for MBCT was 112 British pounds, as compared to approximately 70 British pounds for antidepressant medication (or about US$172 for MBCT vs. US$107 for medications). MBCT was also more costly regarding costs to the healthcare system and overall societal costs. MBCT performed better on out-of-pocket costs to patients and productivity losses. Again, all these differences were nonsignificant. A bottom-line summary of this trial is that it produced another null result for MBCT, and that MBCT saved patients and society no costs.

In similar work, researchers replaced antidepressant medication as the active comparison group with the cognitive behavioral analysis system of psychotherapy (CBASP), a behavior-analytic form of cognitive-behavioral therapy.[28] These researchers also added a third comparison group, treatment-as-usual. Participants were selected for being in the midst of a major depressive episode of a chronic nature; they were recruited at two different treatment sites. In analyses across the two treatment sites, MBCT was no better than treatment as usual, whereas CBASP outperformed treatment as usual. In direct comparison between MBCT and CBASP, CBASP was superior but only to the degree of a nonsignificant trend ($p = .06$). That is, this difference did not clear the bar for statistical significance according to usual scientific convention.

The findings of these three clinical trials derive from very high-quality research designs, and in no case do they support mindfulness-based approaches to depression. A study done by Bowen and colleagues with some similar design features, but with the outcome target of relapse prevention of substance abuse, appeared in 2014 in the august pages of *JAMA: The Journal of the American Medical Association Psychiatry* (formerly—and to my ear always—*Archives of General Psychiatry*). Media coverage of the study implied clear benefit of a mindfulness intervention over standard treatment as usual, and even the title of the article itself conveyed this view ("Relative Efficacy of a Mindfulness . . ."). As we have seen before, packaging and marketing are one thing, and substance may be another. There certainly are areas of science that are "you see what you get," where the packaging and marketing accurately depict the substance of the product.

The case can certainly be made that mindfulness is not one of those areas, and the study on substance abuse is a prime example. The researchers focused on 286 people who had completed an initial hospital-based treatment and had successfully ceased intake of drugs and/or alcohol. Patients were randomly assigned to one of three conditions:

1. A mindfulness-based relapse prevention approach
2. A traditional relapse prevention approach based on cognitive-behavioral principles

3. Aftercare as usual, which emphasized abstinence and involved frequent Alcoholics Anonymous (AA) or Narcotics Anonymous (NA)–style meetings

A positive feature of the research was that both comparison treatments contained active treatment elements (i.e., cognitive-behavioral relapse prevention or AA/NA-type meetings).

As is characteristic of this literature, the actual results are not as impressive as the headlines in newspapers, magazines, and websites would suggest. It is true that the mindfulness-based intervention outperformed the AA/NA-style intervention, but it is also true that the cognitive-behavioral approach did too. It is true that in one analysis, the mindfulness-based approach appeared to perform better than the cognitive-behavioral intervention, but it is also true that it was significantly inferior to the cognitive-behavioral treatment in another analysis. The specific analysis in which the mindfulness-based intervention performed significantly better than the cognitive-behavioral treatment involved days of heavy drinking and drug use in the 90 days preceding the 12-month follow-up assessment. In that analysis, the participants who received the mindfulness-based intervention reported around 3 days of substance use, whereas those in the study's cognitive-behavioral arm reported around 6 days of substance use. However, if substance use days are tallied for the 90-day interval preceding the assessments at 3-, 6-, and 12-month follow-ups, the two groups look nearly identical (and both look superior to the AA/NA-style intervention).

This study relates important truths: Both the mindfulness-based and the cognitive-behavioral approaches performed well and significantly better than an AA/NA-based approach, which itself has proven in past work to be a reasonably effective method. And because the mindfulness-based and the cognitive-behavioral interventions were generally equivalent and also both superior to a standard approach, patients could choose between them based on whatever most suited them, patient self-determination being a good in and of itself. Unless one carefully reads the article describing the study itself, however, these truths are obscured by the misleading slant that this study demonstrated the superiority of mindfulness, when it did not.

In fact, it can be argued that the study demonstrated mindfulness' inferiority. Not only did it lose out to the cognitive-behavioral intervention in a key analysis, but in addition, mindfulness-based approaches tend to contain cognitive-behavioral principles, sometimes explicitly, and often implicitly, while the reverse tends not to hold, at least not as much.[29] Regarding the study on substance abuse, then, this means that the mindfulness-based approach was equivalent to the cognitive-behavioral approach despite adding mindfulness elements to the latter.

Where does this leave us with mindfulness research in general? Mindfulness research on pain management, brain patterns, depression prevention, substance abuse, and so on, has inspired a lot of interest and excitement. This has combined with some of the inherent features of mindfulness (e.g., its cachet because of similarities to Eastern philosophy) to create a major movement within the mental health profession and beyond.

As I have pointed out, the original, authentic version of this movement has admirable qualities. But arguably the best-designed studies to date by highly credentialed teams did not support a mindfulness-based depression prevention program[30] or a mindfulness-based substance abuse relapse prevention approach.[31] If, in the hands of credentialed proponents publishing in the best journals, the depression prevention and substance abuse relapse prevention effects of mindfulness seem to fade under the scrutiny of tightly controlled experiments, one wonders what would happen to the various other positive effects attributed to mindfulness, promulgated by people and in outlets that are not as scientifically rigorous.

If mindfulness-based approaches are more or less similar in outcomes to other approaches, why not let people just vote with their feet and choose whatever suits them? If by "mindfulness" we are talking about what I have termed "authentic mindfulness," I would be comfortable with the idea of people choosing based on whatever factors were important to them personally, as long as the effectiveness of authentic mindfulness is not being overhyped, so that people can make truly informed decisions based on sound information. As we have seen, however, there is evidence that mindfulness may be overhyped, at least implicitly, even by serious and credentialed scholars. Second, the transformation of authentic mindfulness into its impostor version occurs with regularity, and there is every likelihood that faux mindfulness will claim an unfortunate distinction: To be even less effective than authentic mindfulness while being even more loudly and irresponsibly trumpeted as a cure-all. Finally, for authentic mindfulness and certainly for its impostor version, the tone and emphases encourage cultural trends, already well underway, toward self-importance and self-indulgence.

A photo accompanying a January 12, 2014, *SF Gate* article written by D. L. Kirp shows Major League Baseball pitcher Barry Zito, film director David Lynch, and comedian-actor Russell Brand meditating, with dozens of schoolchildren seated behind them doing the same. The article's title is "Meditation Transforms Roughest San Francisco Schools," and documents the sincere belief on the part of school administrators that a meditation-related program called "Quiet Time" is producing many good effects in very challenging school environments. For example, the article claims that a troubled school marked by fighting, the scrawling of graffiti, verbal abuse of teachers by students, poor academic achievement, and high absenteeism among students and teachers alike, has changed into one that is "doing light-years better."

Better as demonstrated by what? The article states that "an impressive array of studies shows that integrating meditation into a school's daily routine can markedly improve the lives of students." The San Francisco superintendent of school agrees: "The research is showing big effects on students' performance." At the particular school in question in San Francisco, suspensions are down 45%, attendance rates are up to 98%, and grade point averages have significantly increased, among other positive developments.

This impressive transformation, the article suggests, was caused by the Quiet Time program, and the article marshals two pieces of evidence for this claim. First, before Quiet Time, dysfunction reigned and after it, the school improved. Second, before Quiet Time, "the school tried everything," listing as examples sports and after-school tutoring, with little improvement.

These facts are indeed consistent with the possibility that the program caused the changes. However, these facts are also consistent with other possibilities, such as economic, policy, and civic changes occurring in the school's area during the same time frame. Like a large proportion of the mindfulness studies reviewed earlier, the claims regarding the Quiet Time program's effects on the San Francisco school are *under-controlled*; other possible explanations are prematurely excluded, mindfulness-related approaches are prematurely construed as particularly effective, and mindfulness is heralded and promoted by memorable devices such as celebrities and athletes meditating along with the schoolchildren. As for having "tried everything," a truism in seasoned clinicians is that this statement almost always refers to having tried a less-than-full dose of whatever intervention is in question, so much so that I advise clinicians in training to use such statements as a signal to encourage patients to try a genuine full dose of whatever intervention they are dismissing.

But what about the research mentioned by the article's author as well as by the school superintendent? I turned to Google Scholar, searched for "Quiet Time," and was puzzled. Many articles came up, and all had "quiet time" in the title, but virtually all were about a phenomenon in astrophysics in which conditions are magnetically or otherwise "quiet." None were about Quiet Time, the meditation-related program for schoolchildren. I then turned to Google Scholar's granddaddy, Google, and within a click or two found myself at the website of the David Lynch Foundation for Consciousness-Based Education and World Peace—the same Lynch who was pictured sitting next to other celebrities meditating in the news article.

The main point of this foundation is the promotion of Transcendental Meditation (TM), and I learned at the website that Quiet Time is simply a name that has been applied to TM. The newspaper article failed to mention this point and also did not mention Lynch's foundation. These omissions are perplexing, especially since Lynch is pictured. One possibility is that the reporter (who seems a supporter of TM) and Lynch's Foundation realize that the term "Transcendental Meditation" will not sit well with all parents. If this was the motivation for the choice of the name Quiet Time over TM—and I do not know that it was—then I view the choice as both a good one (they are right—many parents would react to the TM label as I would, not because I think it would harm my sons, but because I would rather them spend that time either hard at work or at play with their friends) and a mildly deceptive one. I note, incidentally, that the two school-based efforts I have mentioned thus far are in Madison, Wisconsin, and San Francisco, California. There are many U.S. cities where I doubt this would get community support (e.g., my own community of Tallahassee, Florida, a pretty liberal town especially for the region), no matter what it is called.

The term "Quiet Time" has been used by Congressman Tim Ryan, a vocal supporter of mindfulness. His support is ardent enough that a September 2014 *Cleveland Plain Dealer* article described him as "a congressional evangelist," and Ryan himself stated "I am a relentless advocate and proponent." An *Atlantic Monthly* article on Representative Ryan, also from September 2014, labels him "Congressman Moonbeam." Politicians and their staffs are rightly and understandably concerned with branding, and so probably were not fans of the "moonbeam" reference. Ryan's sensitivity to branding may also explain his adoption of the term "quiet time sessions" for his mindfulness meetings on Capitol Hill, as opposed to Transcendental Meditation, the latter being even more certain fodder for his political opponents. Despite his care in branding, the article points out that Ryan has not succeeded in convincing his colleagues; only one is a regular attendee (a Democrat from California).

The website of Lynch's foundation has tabs that correspond to the usefulness of TM to schools, the military, women, American Indians, homeless shelters, prisons, and Africa. The phrasing in the last sentence is the website's, not mine. By "Africa," the Lynch Foundation means African war refugees who are suffering from PTSD; by "homeless shelters" and "prisons," the foundation means the people in those settings (and regarding prisons, the website promises "freedom behind bars" via TM); and by "women," the foundation is referring specifically to female victims of abuse and violence (I could not find reference on the website to whether TM would be helpful to male victims of abuse and violence, but I presume as much, given the website's claims for near-universal applicability and benefit).

To convey a sense of these claims, consider Lynch's own words featured prominently on the site: "I started Transcendental Meditation in 1973 and have not missed a single meditation ever since. Twice a day, every day. It has given me effortless access to unlimited reserves of energy, creativity and happiness deep within. This level of life is sometimes called 'pure consciousness'—it is a treasury. And this level of life is deep within us all."[32] I will just let pass the class issues involved in having the leisure to meditate, even once a day once in a while, much less twice per day every day. Words like "effortless" and "unlimited," however, and reference to a rarified level that, despite being rarified, is universally available, are clues that claims have become unmoored from actual evidence. Claims like this are simply not credible to the seriously minded, and further-more, risk that things of actual measured benefit, such as genuine mindfulness and even TM, are dismissed via their association with trumped-up hokum.

The hype is not limited specifically to TM circles. The first lines of Kabat-Zinn's *Mindfulness for Beginners* are: "You may not know it, but if you are coming to the systematic cultivation of mindful-ness for the first time, you may very well be on the threshold of a momentous shift in your life, something subtle and, at the same time, potentially huge and important, which just may change your life." And later from the same book, regarding mindfulness: ". . . you could think of it as the hardest work in the world, and the most im-portant." These quotes, also from Kabat-Zinn, are from a *Salon* mag-azine article: Mindfulness "has the potential to ignite a universal or global renaissance . . . that would put even the European and Italian Renaissance into the shade," and "may actually be the only promise the species and the planet have for making it through the next couple hundred years."[33]

Regarding the actual evidence, there is research on the effects of TM, and much of it is, at first blush, supportive of its various salutary effects. These effects include stress management, decreased substance abuse, better sleep, better cardiac functioning, lower blood pressure, decreases in plasma cortisol levels (cortisol is "the stress hormone"), reduced anger, and better job performance, among other benefits. If it were really true that TM provided all of these benefits and more, and crucially, provided them incrementally beyond things like a daily 30-minute walk, or working in a garden more days than not, it would be one of the most exciting scientific developments ever, Newtonian or Einsteinian in its scope and profundity.

But it is not true. The TM studies are under-controlled, the same problem we have already encountered regarding some mindfulness research. Yes, TM provides *some* benefits, as compared to weak con-trol activities. But it does not provide *more* benefits than activities with rigorous features. What this means, in my opinion, is good news: If one is inclined to or intrigued by things like TM, then by all means do them, because they do impart some benefits. If, however, one is disinclined to things like TM—and I would add that most of the U.S. population is, which may be why TM for kids became Quiet Time—no problem, engage in a routine healthy behavior that does suit (e.g., walking, other kinds of physical activities, interacting with nature).

Walking is a very interesting comparison activity, for many reasons. First, though not available to everyone, it is an accessible physical activity for a large proportion of the population. Second, whether it is viewed as a hike, a march (in military settings), snow-shoeing, an early evening stroll, a leisurely skate, or getting some fresh air, and whether it involves a dog or not, it is a widely accept-able activity across numerous cultural settings. This is one feature of American neighborhoods that has not changed much over the past few decades (when much else has changed). I sometimes work in a room that looks out over our front yard and on to the sidewalk and street. Numerous walkers of all ages, genders, ethnicities, and cul-tural backgrounds stroll by on a daily basis (this is in Tallahassee, Florida, where the weather is facilitative and we get no ice skaters or snowshoers). Third, there is a compelling empirical base to the posi-tive health benefits of walking, and, in this literature unlike others covered here, the controls are reasonably rigorous. For example, in an article in the *Proceedings of the National Academy of Sciences*,[34] Arthur Kramer and his colleagues studied a year-long walking regi-men for older adults (ages 55–80) that initially involved three 10-minute walks per week and gradually ramped up by the seventh week to three 40-minute walks per week. A comparison condition also involved regular physical activity, but unlike the walking condi-tion, was not aerobically challenging. This control group participated in bouts of stretching, muscle toning, balancing exercises, and also in mindfulness' and meditation's next of kin, yoga. Like the walking regimen, the control regimen built up to three weekly sessions of about 40 minutes.

Exercise can be boring, and so the researchers took steps to keep the regimens interesting, but if anything, they did so in ways that favored the control condition, in which novel kinds of activities were introduced every 3 weeks. And more, the control participants got to do *yoga*, which, to hear my cultured professorly friends tell it, cures all physical, mental, and spiritual ailments (and, I would add, scratches the itch to be—or to appear to be—fashionable, and as a bonus relieves wallets of the onerous burden of money. I don't wish to go too far in the direction of Pat Robertson, who publically stated his belief that there is something literally evil in yoga mats, but one can buy a spray cleaner specifically for one's yoga mat at Whole Foods, at least judging by the single time I was in one in Pasadena, California to attend a highly satisfying college football game of note in early 2014. And to boot, the yoga mat cleaners were on display *in the checkout lines*, much as would be gum or batteries in the grocery stores I frequent. I went there to buy beer, incidentally, naively and wrongly thinking that the Pasadena Whole Foods would carry my usual preferred products). Surely something yoga-related would beat plain old walking, which lacks cache and is free of charge.

But it didn't. Walking increased the volume of participants' hippocampus by 2%. Let's reflect on that statement for a moment: Mere walking—and moreover, just three times a week for 40 or so minutes at a time—affected the size of an area in participants' *brains*. It was only by 2% you might counter, to which I would answer that that is how much is lost in about two years. A gain of 2% thus means a reversal in usual age-related loss by almost two years. You might rebut that a 2% gain probably did not translate into any functional difference. I would first congratulate you on the incisiveness of the point—it is an essential one—but then I would have to add that the gain in hippocampal volume led to notable improvements in spatial memory (the hippocampus is a well-known seat of memory processes). Lastly, you might inquire as to whether the yoga and such at least kept hippocampal volume steady, but I would have to reply that no, it did not—volume shrank in those participants.

Before leaving the topic of Whole Foods, it seems I am not the only one who has noticed some of its quirks and contradictions. Writing in the *Huffington Post*,[35] Kelly Maclean wrote, "Whole Foods' clientele are all about mindfulness and compassion ... until they get to the parking lot. Then it's war ... I see a pregnant lady on the crosswalk holding a baby and groceries. This driver swerves around her and honks. As he speeds off I catch his bumper sticker, which says 'NAMASTE.'"

Returning to the unglamorous but effective, an independent group of researchers has reported a similar finding as the preceding, regarding the effects of aerobic exercise on increasing hippocampal volume in women between the ages of 70 and 80, who were showing signs of mild cognitive impairment (a frequent precursor to dementia).[36] Still another group has documented the same effect, now regarding adults at genetic risk for Alzheimer's disease. Smith, Nielson, and colleagues followed healthy older adults (between the ages of 65 and 89) over the course of 18 months; participants were split into four groups based on whether they were physically active or not and whether they carried a specific genetic marker (the apolipoprotein E epsilon 4 allele) for Alzheimer's risk. Brain imaging showed that only one group lost hippocampal volume, and it was the group who were genetically vulnerable and who engaged in low levels of exercise. These participants lost 3% of hippocampal volume, similar to the 2% figure in the study noted earlier. By contrast, the vulnerable group who engaged in high levels of physical activity was indistinguishable from the genetically protected participants, suggesting that exercise offset genetic risk.

This overall trend of physical activity leading to robust health has been replicated time and again across the world. A study from Australia is an example, and furthermore, situates physical activity among other health-related activities in terms of relative health impact.[37] One might wonder, for example, whether one gains more from smoking cessation than from physical activity or from diet changes as compared to physical activity. Of course, one need not choose between these, and each is supported in numerous studies in its own right as beneficial for health. In the Australian study, which was focused on mortality caused by heart disease, physical activity was compared to the following approaches: blood pressure management, weight management, and smoking cessation. Despite the clear power of these other approaches, physical activity generally outperformed them, a trend that became increasingly clear as older and older cohorts were studied.

It is an interesting truth, and one demonstrated many times, that as pernicious as are the effects of something like smoking, the effects of physical inactivity are even more so. Indeed, there are few things that compare to the negative effects of inactivity, and it is interesting to consider the one factor that regularly rivals it, namely, loneliness. To choose just two of numerous strands of research on loneliness and health, first, it has been shown that not only do lonely women have more difficult pregnancies, they also experience more postpartum depression and even have babies with lower birth weight, all as compared to women who are not lonely. Second, loneliness and insomnia are reciprocally inductive of one another; lonely people tend not to sleep well, and insomnia is lonely because one is up at night whereas everyone else is not.[38]

Physical exercise and social connection are easily among the most powerful health-inducing activities. Not only has it not been demonstrated that mindfulness-based approaches are incrementally helpful beyond these tried-and-true (indeed ancient) approaches, but some forms of mindfulness-related activities involve physical *in*activity in socially isolated settings.

Of note, incidentally, the best characterized walking regimen involves three brisk walks per week, each of approximately 45 minutes. There is a strong likelihood that these effects will occur for other aerobic activities (e.g., stationary biking) and possibly regarding even shorter bouts of exercise. Indeed, in a 2014 presentation to the American Academy of Neurology, Spanish neurologist Manuel Seijo-Martinez reported that a regimen of roughly 18 minutes per day of stationary biking led to improved cognitive functioning in adults who averaged approximately 80 years of age. Those assigned to a control group involving enjoyable, nonphysical activities (e.g., card-playing, reading), by contrast, saw declines in overall cognitive abilities. The average weekly tally of exercise was around 134 minutes, quite similar to the weekly tally of walking regimens of 45-minutes per bout, three times a week. An interesting and open question in this literature involves the minimum amount of physical activity necessary to attain cognitive benefits. There is obviously a lower limit, because the nonexercising card-playing controls in Seijo-Martinez' study experienced decreases in cognitive functioning. But how far above zero does one have to go hold steady? To get actual increases? We have solid evidence that 18 minutes per day of brisk activity (e.g., walking, stationary biking) suffices. It will be interesting to see if future work suggests an even lower limit (e.g., 10 minutes per day).

In my relatively frequent conversations with successful writers, and in my even more frequent reading of writers' biographies, I have discerned a pattern. If writers are able to devote themselves to their writing full time, they often fall into a daily schedule along the following lines: wake up (usually but not always fairly early); accomplish the day's writing (usually in around 3 hours or so of concentrated work, but of course the duration varied); break for brunch or lunch; engage in a bout of fairly lengthy and moderate exercise (usually a long walk, sometimes swimming); sit for an hour or two of reading; eat dinner; and finally, socialize in some form. Ideas for the next day's writing frequently formed during walks or swims, while reading, and while socializing. Should any of those activities be replaced with mindfulness-related activities, it is a fair question as to whether writing quality and productivity would have decreased. After all, in some forms of meditation (but not mindfulness-based meditation, it should be noted), a goal is emptiness of mind, and for those who have experienced writer's block (as most writers have), emptiness of mind does not necessarily sound inviting. It should be emphasized that authentic mindfulness does *not* advocate emptying of the mind. As mindfulness proponents rightly point out, this is a frequent mischaracterization of genuine mindfulness. Instead, what is encouraged is moment-to-moment, dispassionate awareness. It is conceivable that this would help with some aspects of creative writing (e.g., attention to sound, color, ambience, etc.). What I am questioning is whether it would help more than a long walk, swim, or talk with friends. More, what I am especially doubting is the benefit of moment-to-moment nonjudgmental awareness in an endeavor that requires long arcs of intricate and interconcatenated thought.

I am aware of a selfless and well-meaning mindfulness advocate who, when challenged to let his mind wander during mundane tasks so as to spur creative thought, balked, the reason being his understanding that when doing a mundane task, it is the mindful thing to do to keep one's mind fully in the moment and on that task. At risk of hyperbole, I view this as a tragedy. It is tragic because a very fertile mind, who may produce a valuable or even profound insight while, for example, doing the dishes, instead is being led by his understanding of mindfulness to focus on dishes and soap water. I believe that he has misunderstood genuine mindfulness, but given his selfless nature, at least his mistake is not the same as that of the unseemly Narcissi. While the latter dwell on the wonder of their thoughts, feelings, and bodies, the selfless advocate is yeoman-like, and in choosing between the two, it is quite impossible to overstate my preference for the latter. But I would advise the selfless soul of a third way (and so I believe would the few people who understand genuine mindfulness): Mindfulness is moment-to-moment nonjudgmental attention, *on purpose*, to the teemingness of the present moment (with the recognition that one's own subjectivity is but a grain of sand in a beach of infinitude; this latter piece is of course where the Narcissi stumble). Though it is perhaps arguable, I take the "on purpose" part to mean that one can introduce thoughts of one's choosing into the present moment (as long as one remains nonjudgmental about them and open to the rest of the moment too). These introduced thoughts could include where a novel one is writing can or should go, what other books one might write, and so on and so forth.

To a person, successful writers I have queried on this point immediately agree that these kinds of reveries are indispensable to their work. It is why, I believe, the daily long walk or swim, and the nightly conviviality, are so common among writers who can manage to live that schedule. (Not coincidentally, this is the schedule one finds, more or less, at writers' colonies or at the Rockefeller Foundation's Bellagio retreat in Italy. I have instituted a long weekend version of this for my PhD students at St. George Island, Florida, with excellent results.) Writers and other creative professionals, at least those of my acquaintance, would vigorously reject the counsel to keep one's focus on mundane activities; it would cost them too much in the precious specie of *ideas*.

Because of the impressive findings regarding aerobic walking (and there are many others besides those described), and because of the mundane nature of the activity, it strikes me as an excellent candidate for a rigorous, active control condition for any study that strives to claim great power for interventions such as TM, yoga, and mindfulness. If an intervention is so profound and revolutionary (e.g., as Lynch claims for TM and Kabat-Zinn for mindfulness), then it should surely outperform a lowly three-walks-a-week regimen.

I recently received a mass email from the Lynch Foundation, and it read in part, "Can a simple meditation technique that dates back over 5,000 years help people ... overcome toxic stress, boost T-cell count, and improve quality of life?" A 2014 study published in the journal *Cancer* might, at first glance, suggest the answer is yes, but deeper scrutiny of the study reveals its answer is no.[39]

The project included 88 distressed breast cancer survivors who had completed cancer treatment at least 3 months prior. The participants were randomized to one of three conditions:

1. A mindfulness-based condition, using a group therapy format, which included mindfulness meditation as well as "gentle

Hatha yoga," involved eight weekly group meetings, each of which lasted 90 minutes, and also included an additional 6-hour retreat. Moreover, participants were encouraged to practice frequently at home, and were provided with written materials for this purpose, along with compact discs to guide them through meditations and "mindful body movement."

2. A supportive-expressive therapy condition, using a group therapy format, emphasized emotional expression and social support between group members. The therapy involved 12 weekly meetings of 90 minutes duration each.

3. A one-time, 6-hour didactic stress management seminar was offered.

The point of the study was to determine which if any group affected telomere length. Telomeres form the protective ends of chromosomes and help maintain the latter's integrity, somewhat like the plastic sheath at the end of a shoelace, called an "aglet," does for the shoelace. Just as when an aglet weakens or breaks, a shoelace frays, so when a telomere shortens, a chromosome frays. Chromosomal fraying is undesirable. When it happens, duplicating the chromosome and all of its essential information cannot proceed fully because the "frayed" information is lost. Information loss is not a good thing and can eventuate in many problems, including cell death. Shortened telomeres have been implicated in several illnesses, including heart disease and diabetes, and are predictive of earlier death in certain forms of cancer.

Did mindfulness meditation and/or yoga—millennia-old traditions as the Lynch Foundation reminded email recipients—protect telomere length? No, not as compared to the supportive-expressive therapy group. This finding is worth dwelling on. Although the mindfulness-based intervention surely included supportive-expressive elements, and then added on to them a heavy emphasis on meditation and yoga, including among other things a full-day retreat, the mindfulness-based intervention added nothing beyond supportive-expressive therapy, at least regarding telomere length.

Surely, however, the mindfulness-based intervention outperformed a 6-hour didactic lecture. By the severe strictures of science, which requires that findings clear certain hurdles (e.g., $p < .05$), it did not. In no analysis was the criterion of statistical significance met. In fact, the closest was an analysis comparing the control group (who received a long lecture) to the *combined* group of those receiving either the mindfulness-based intervention or the supportive-expressive therapy. This approach obscures the weakness of the mindfulness intervention, because in absolute terms, this group fared worse than the supportive-expressive group (though not worse to a statistically significant degree), and combining the two groups allows the mindfulness group's mean to be "helped" by that of the supportive-expressive group. Even given all this, nonsignificant results were obtained.

Had the researchers compared the mindfulness group directly to the group receiving a lecture, the findings would have been very clearly nonsignificant. The researchers did not report this analysis (why I do not understand), but it is easy to see from the results they do report that this is the case. Meditation and yoga, notwithstanding their 5,000-year-old traditions, performed no better than a lecture. And this was despite participants in the mindfulness-based group spending 18 hours of total time engaged with the intervention, as compared to the 6 hours of lecture in the control group, and despite the mindfulness intervention encouraging additional ongoing practice and providing compact discs and other materials to facilitate it.

Regarding the lecture, incidentally, the researchers explained that they used it to decrease the chances that those randomized to the control condition would feel demoralized. Put yourself in the position of the breast cancer survivors in the study: You have agreed to participate with fully informed consent in a study that you know to involve a fashionable approach that the larger culture views (with very little substantive reason) as verging on the miraculous, and you end up attending a lecture, and a very long one at that. I do not necessarily suggest that the likelihood of demoralization for the lecture attendees was *maximized*, but I do doubt that it was much *minimized*. That a mindfulness-based intervention performed similarly to a long lecture is not encouraging.

But, that is not how the results are described by authors who, to their credit, clearly state their conflicts of interest, including that two of the study's authors "have received royalties from New Harbinger Publications for a book on mindfulness-based cancer recovery." The article's last sentence reads: "Although interpretation remains difficult, the results of the current study nonetheless provide provocative new data that suggest it is possible to influence telomere length in cancer survivors through the use of psychosocial interventions involving group support, emotional expression, stress reduction, and mindfulness meditation."[40] Interpretation of these data is not difficult: This is a null finding, unsupportive of the intervention under study.

In a similar vein, consider a 2014 report that appeared in the *Journal of Alternative and Complementary Medicine*.[41] The researchers compared three groups on their overall well-being. All were Zen trainees from Japanese monasteries: those who had trained in Zen practices for less than a year, those who had trained for between 1 and 3 years, and those who had trained for three years or more. The authors implied that the latter group reported the highest well-being, and attributed these differences to more practice with techniques like meditation.

This implication was largely borne out, but not completely. For example, there were no significant differences between the groups on a measure of social functioning, nor on an index of overall physical well-being, and although the most experienced meditators differed from the least experienced on an overall measure of mental well-being, there was no significant difference on this index between the moderately experienced and the most experienced meditators.

Several differences did nevertheless emerge between the three groups on things such as vitality and bodily pain. I would suggest, however, that this is a foreordained and highly unremarkable result and one that could very well operate via a different mechanism than meditation practice. It is foreordained and unremarkable because any group that persists in training for more than 3 years will be more hardy than novices, and therefore more likely to report high well-being, and this is so pretty much regardless of what the training is (e.g., Zen practice, athletic training, military training). Indeed, one sees a similar pattern in the military: Those who have reenlisted are hardier and healthier as compared to first-time enlistees. This effect, whether in the military or in Zen monasteries, is not wholly attributable to the effects of training; some of it is accounted for by attrition. Those who are less hardy and otherwise less well to begin with, tend to drop out earlier.

But certainly training over time will have some salutary effects, and it is important to understand the various components of training, here in Zen monasteries. The authors of the article focus on the practice of meditation, and while this is certainly an aspect of the regimen, it is very far from the only one. For example, in most such settings, wake time is regimented to be early in the morning, and early waking by itself, if adhered to consistently, tends to confer benefits in health and well-being domains. The lifestyle in Zen monasteries is inherently healthful in many other ways too. There is an element of physical rigor in prostration and manual work; there is a sense of camaraderie; there is a shared purpose; and there tends to be an avoidance of illness-inducing behaviors (e.g., smoking; excessive alcohol intake; overeating). The lifestyle is programmed for health and well-being, and it is thus little surprise that those who have been exposed to it the longest—and who also have the discipline and grit to persevere in it—have high levels of well-being. These factors would encourage health in the absence of meditation, and it is at least questionable whether meditation can incrementally add much beyond them.

In fact, there are numerous examples of people who experienced many physical and behavioral health problems, who were then subjected to a newly routinized lifestyle with no meditation included, and whose health improved dramatically as a consequence. One would not recommend prison as a health intervention; however, it is remarkable how healthful many previously quite unhealthy people find incarceration (and this is despite its many potential terrors, about which we should remain clear-eyed). To take just two of many examples, prison psychiatrist A. M. Daniels (whose writing pseudonym is Theodore Dalrymple) related the following exchange in the book *Second Opinion*:

DALRYMPLE: "Is this going to be your last sentence?"
PRISONER: "I hope not."
"You mean you want to come back here?"
"I've only been outside prison one out of the last ten years, doctor."
"You prefer it here?"
"I do, really."[42]

In a second example from the same book, the psychiatrist described an individual who had spent most but not all of the last 16 years in prison. "Do you prefer life in prison?" he asks the man, who replies, "I feel safer."

The memoir *The Splendid Things We Planned: A Family Portrait* describes the relatively brief life of the author's troubled brother. From very early in life, the signs of dysfunction in the brother were readily apparent and would unfold to include an unfortunate list of miseries and outrages. These included repeated physical assaults against family members, including the man's own mother; several serious car accidents, at least one near-fatal, including the totaling of a sports car given to the man by his rather patient and generous father; peculiar sexual proclivities and interests; the unsolicited and aggressive kissing on the mouth, tongue extended, of both his father's new wife and his own brother (the latter was asleep and was awoken by the incident); and his death by suicide in his early 40s.

His death in this manner was hardly a surprise to his family; indeed, as happens in most but not all suicides, the man had verbalized his desire to die to a friend, and specific to this case, family members had discussed the possibility of the man's eventual suicide with one another. In the aftermath of the man's death, the author reports, the family was left with a grief complicated by the fact that, in candid moments, they felt relief at his passing, both on his behalf and on theirs.

Of his 40-some years, virtually all were marked by some sort of very noticeable behavioral difficulty, true even in the earliest years of his life. Five years, however, were exceptions to this rule, and these were the years he spent serving his country in the Marines. These were easily his healthiest and most functional years, and it is a testament to the lifestyle and the values of the military that they can be salutary even in the face of the grave challenges this man presented. I do not mean to suggest that these years were all idyllic; there can be little doubt that this man plagued and was plagued by his superiors, and one of his peers later remembered him as a problematic drinker during his years in service. Nevertheless, the military's daily routines, sense of togetherness, mission and purpose, and physical rigor significantly improved this man's physical and mental health when nothing else did or even came close.

The same pattern can be detected in the life of a far different and more functional personality, that of the second man on the moon, Buzz Aldrin. During his time first at West Point, then as a fighter pilot in the military, and then as a NASA astronaut, Aldrin excelled and generally thrived (you don't end up on the moon otherwise). However, his post-NASA life was vexed, including serious episodes of depression and severe problems with alcohol. In his memoir *Magnificent Desolation*, Aldrin wrote, "... when I left NASA and the Air Force, I had no more structure in my life. For the first time in more than 40 years, I had no one to tell me what to do, no one sending me on a mission, giving me challenging work assignments to be completed. Ironically, rather than feeling an exuberant sense of freedom, an elation that I was now free to explore on my own, I felt isolated, alone, and uncertain."[43]

Fallen Israeli hero Jonathan Netanyahu (Prime Minister Benjamin Netanyahu's older brother, who was later killed in the raid on Entebbe), in a letter to his family wrote, "Strangely enough, I think the army has improved my health." It is understandable that Aldrin sees this as ironic, and Netanyahu as strange, but it is in reality a fairly common scenario.

As clear an example as these and the previous one were, perhaps even more so was a case study conducted by the intramural research program of the National Institute of Mental Health (NIMH).[44] The case involved a man with bipolar disorder, who was admitted to an NIMH facility in the midst of a florid mania. The term "facility" is misleading in this instance; it evokes images of inpatient psychiatry, when in actuality, the man was installed in a nicely appointed room that would remind one more of a thriving hotel than of a hospital. There were, however, some differences between a usual hotel room and the man's room. The latter was scoured to ensure that there were no dangerous materials that could be used in a suicide attempt. The worry was not that the man was suicidal at admission—he was not, as few in a florid mania are—but rather that he would rapidly become so if he cycled out of mania into a mixed or depressive state. There is, incidentally, a science and an architecture to making a room safe in these scenarios, and a lot of it involves removing not just potential ligature materials (e.g., a belt) but also ligature points (e.g., a coat hook on the back of a door) as well as other dangers, such as potential asphyxiation agents (e.g., plastic trash bags). Also related to safety but pertinent to the research as well was that the man was closely monitored in multiple ways, including actigraphy (which measures the amount of physical activity engaged in over time, with a readout somewhat similar to a seismograph). Finally, unlike the usual hotel room, the man was not free to come and go, and the lighting was controlled such that the lights dimmed to darkness at around 10:30 PM and were turned back on around 8 hours later, at 6:30 AM.

On the first night, still in a severely manic state, the man did not sleep at all, but instead paced, talked, and explored the room in absolute darkness for the entire night. This is actually quite a feat in itself (imagine trying it if you doubt that) and conveys the power of illnesses like bipolar disorder. His actigraphy ratings for this first night, unsurprisingly, were "spiky" in the same way a seismograph is during an earthquake. The second night resembled the first, though there was an activity dip in the middle of the night along with a few minutes sleep. On successive nights, this middle-of-the-night calming followed by sleep continued to expand to the point that, around a week later, it included a full night's sleep. Remarkably, a floridly manic man was restored to a euthymic state with the sole intervention of strict management of the lights out and lights on in his room; he was not medicated during the time he spent in this facility. Of course, the mere passage of time would have assured an eventual return to euthymia, in that almost all manic phenomena are time limited. However, the immediate and accelerating response of this individual to the lights-out-and-lights-on regimen suggests that it specifically was therapeutic.

Not that I recommend the management of bipolar disorder without medication; as I will return to explain shortly, I most certainly do not. The point, rather, is the power of entraining natural biological rhythms (e.g., sleep–wake cycles) through behavioral management of routine and regimen. It is powerful enough that it can deflate a florid mania (albeit, granted, in a highly unusual setting), and as we saw earlier, powerful enough to produce years of adequate functionality in a man whose life was otherwise woefully dysfunctional.

It is worth noting, incidentally, how little emphasis is placed in these settings on the self. In Zen monasteries, in the military, in the man's hotel-hospital room, and yes, in prison, the regulations are one size fits all, and it is inescapable that these encourage health and well-being for a sizable proportion of those who undergo them, whatever their other rigors and challenges may be. Contrary to the current cult of individualized this and individualized that, an unfeeling, highly disciplined, and deindividualized set of routines fosters *individual* health and functionality. That this contradicts certainties in the modern mind is its virtue, not its drawback.

Not only do routines foster health and functionality, there is surprising evidence that they enhance one's sense of meaning in life. Samantha Heintzelman, Laura King, and colleagues have shown that routinization leads to a sense of coherence, and that coherence, in turn, induces a sense of life's meaningfulness.[45] In a representative experiment, these researchers showed participants photographs of trees. The pictures were specifically chosen to show trees that were clearly photographed either in fall, winter, spring, or summer. Half of the participants saw pictures of trees that were in the natural order of the seasons: They first saw a picture of a tree in the fall, then one in the winter, and so on. The other half of participants saw these exact same images, but in random order. Those who saw the trees in seasonal order later rated their sense of meaning in life as higher than those who saw the same trees in random order. Interestingly, seasonal order was not necessary for the effect; it also emerged when there was an arbitrary, non-seasonal, but nonrandom order (e.g., spring, winter, summer, fall; spring, winter, summer, fall; etc.). Furthermore, these researchers demonstrated that the effect is not dependent on stimuli related to nature; it also occurred when reading word triads with a coherent versus incoherent theme. That is, those reading coherent triads, such as "falling, actor, dust" (common associate word is "star"), reported more meaning in life than those reading incoherent word triads (e.g., "belt, deal, nose").

It is intriguing that something as simple as this affects a higher-order state, such as life's meaning, and contradicts the notion, held in many modern contexts, including many related to mindfulness, that attainment of meaning is complex, nuanced, and difficult. Further to this point, the researchers obtained data suggesting that their meaning induction was "mindless," in that when asked, participants did not report that they noticed the patterning. Important in this context, these scholars have shown that the effect size of simple routinizations like these on meaning in life is comparable to that for religiosity—and that for mindfulness too.

In studies of those undergoing training in Zen monasteries, then, a telling control group would be people whose lives are highly regimented by some external authority regarding things like sleep–wake cycles, diet, and activity levels, but who are not engaging in specific things like meditation training. Should interventions, such as meditation and the practice of mindfulness, prove incremental in such actively controlled studies, then enthusiasm is warranted. Until then, however, the chorus of exuberance that surrounds mindfulness-based approaches is premature and has the potential to be deceptive.

This chorus is quite loud, and although it is hard to quantify, it seems to me that it is currently the loudest, which is ironic in light of the problems with the evidence base identified here. Some advocates of mindfulness and fellow-traveling approaches (like acceptance and commitment therapy, or ACT) oversell significant findings. On social media, Coyne has gone to some lengths to show that a well-known study on ACT's effects on rehospitalization of psychotic patients, pitched by the authors as very clear evidence of ACT's effectiveness, is equivocal, perhaps even a null trial. Similarly, a meta-analysis of 13 studies of mindfulness interventions for schizophrenia or psychosis at first glance appears favorable to such interventions, but reports null results when analyses are limited to studies of rigorous design.[46] I have seen instances in which clearly negative findings are heralded. For example, I chanced upon a symposium on ACT in 2014 and heard three PhD students report on outcomes of the treatment in various challenging populations and environments. The students were plainly bright and diligent, but nevertheless, two of the three studies produced results clearly at odds with the effectiveness of ACT. In behavior therapy circles, or in medicine, I believe the atmosphere would be sober in the face of unsupportive results such as these, and I know it would be at NASA and at most elements of the Department of Defense, but in the symposium on ACT I happened upon, the atmosphere was unfazed and upbeat, as if the results were positive. The dissonance between fact and atmosphere was one I found quite jarring, but I seemed to be alone among those in attendance.

Even had the studies returned significant results, they would still be somewhat unconvincing, because control groups were either absent or relatively weak. But as already noted, few such studies include active, rigorous controls, and when they are included (as in the

Williams and colleagues study on mindfulness-based treatment to prevent depression relapse), null results tend to occur. And as at the ACT symposium I chanced upon, when null results are obtained, they frequently are nonetheless celebrated. A 2014 article in the *British Journal of Psychiatry* did exactly this: A mindfulness intervention was compared to treatment as usual in primary care patients, and not only did more patients drop out of mindfulness treatment than they did of usual care, there were no significant differences in clinical outcomes between the two groups.[47] Undeterred, the trial is framed by the authors as a "noninferiority" finding, arguing that it is useful to know that the mindfulness intervention was not inferior to usual care. I would agree that it is useful to know that, but where the authors and I may part ways is over what to make of that knowledge. Their implication is that mindfulness' noninferiority is a basis for its promulgation and regular use. My conclusion is that at least some skepticism is warranted, and that at most, a noninferiority finding suggests that the intervention may be useful for some patients some of the time.

A similar description pertains regarding a meta-analysis of mindfulness-based interventions targeting current depressive and anxiety symptoms (the focus on current symptoms is noteworthy, because it differs from other work, including the impressive Williams and colleagues trial, which focuses on the prevention of future depression). The meta-analysis pooled the results of 12 studies on 578 patients with a diagnosis either of a mood or an anxiety disorder.[48]

At first glance, as is often the case, the bottom-line conclusion from this meta-analysis can be read to support the effectiveness of mindfulness-based interventions, because there was indeed a sizable pre–post effect of the interventions. That is, patients left mindfulness-based interventions substantially less depressed and anxious than when they began.

Upon closer examination, however, there were three notable problems. Granting for the moment the conclusion that there were significant pre–post effects associated with mindfulness-based interventions, the results themselves significantly qualify this conclusion. Yes, there were such effects in some analyses, but not in all: Effects were clear for those with depressive symptoms, but not for those with anxiety problems. Effects were clear for one specific mindfulness-based approach (mindfulness-based cognitive therapy), but not for another specific mindfulness technique (mindfulness-based stress reduction).

This mixed pattern of findings alone is enough to create at least some doubt about the power of these interventions, but there is still more reason for doubt. Specifically, there was an issue with what is called "publication bias." Although one index of bias suggested a low likelihood of a problem, another indicated that among the studies with large mindfulness-based intervention effects, studies with small samples were overrepresented. The least reliable studies (because of their small sample sizes) produced the largest effects, the opposite of what would likely occur if there were a true, underlying large effect to be detected.

The most important of the three problematic issues is, here yet again, the question of inactive versus active control groups. Mindfulness-based interventions easily outperformed inactive controls, but were a tad worse than active controls (but not worse to a statistically significant degree). The overall pattern, again taken from pooled analyses across numerous studies with hundreds of participants, should be of considerable concern to mindfulness enthusiasts. Not only were effects found for one outcome but not another, and for one type of intervention but not another, and not only is there evidence in the publication bias result to undermine the claims, often boastfully made, of extreme effectiveness, but also the results directly contradict the idea that mindfulness-based interventions are at all special or unique. They are not, in the sense that they do not outperform active controls.

Further still, it is essential to understand that for some people, mindfulness-based techniques might be more than just ineffective; they might also be actively harmful. In the January 23, 2016 issue of *The Guardian*,[49] journalist Dawn Foster reported on this very phenomenon, including a woman she called Claire. Claire attended a 3-day mindfulness course, arranged by her place of employment, during which traumatic childhood memories became increasingly salient. Claire said, "I had a breakdown and spent three months in a psychiatric unit. It was a depressive breakdown with psychotic elements related to the trauma, and several dissociative episodes." According to the article, several years later Claire is still affected, in and out of the hospital and waging a fight against alcoholism. The article also refers to another individual who dissociated while meditating, became catatonic the next day, and was treated for bouts of psychotic depression over the course of the next 15 years.

These, of course, are isolated instances, but the negative effects of mindfulness-based techniques are not rare. One study found that 63% of those who attended retreats like the one Claire attended reported at least one negative effect, and, like Claire, 7% reported extremely negative effects (e.g., panic, depression, pain[50]). Regarding such negative experiences, the *Guardian* article quotes a researcher that "... mindfulness researchers have failed to measure them, and may even have discouraged participants from reporting them by attributing blame to [the participants]."

That reports such as these *should* concern mindfulness advocates is unfortunately not the same thing as that it *does* concern them; it plainly does not worry many of them, judging by the ongoing trumpeting of its virtues in magazines, workshops, and alas classrooms. There is potential harm in this, beyond mindfulness activities directly injuring people like Claire. An additional source of harm involves misleading scholars and clinicians who do not have the time to check the facts for themselves (a large group, if my own experiences are any guide). Relatedly, and even worse, another source of potential harm is the distraction of vulnerable people away from actively effective treatments and toward things that may be popular but not as effective. I turn to this and related issues in the next chapter.

The Perils of Distraction
from Evidence and of
Other Flights of Fancy

C ONSIDER THE MISERY AND WOE OF THE PERSON IN THE
midst of a severe episode of major depressive disorder. Consider
further that this person did not respond to a host of aggressive
treatments, but finally was stabilized on a powerful but hard-to-
tolerate antidepressant (a monoamine oxidase inhibitor [MAOI]).
Imagine that the individual was stabilized for years and did a prodigious amount of extremely successful creative work over the course
of more than 2 decades while on the drug. Assume that, for some
reason, the person became persuaded that remaining on the medication long-term was unwise and therefore discontinued it. And finally
imagine a disastrous outcome, such as a vicious recurrence of the illness, no longer responsive to treatment including the very treatment
that had been so successful for so long, ending in the person's death
by suicide.

Unfortunately, this occurred not just in the imagination, but in
real life. This is the true story of the life and death of novelist David
Foster Wallace, whose very severe depression was well controlled by
an MAOI medication that he stayed on throughout his 20s, 30s, and

into his 40s. During this time, he produced fiction that some consider the finest of the last half century or so, and he produced a lot of it—his best known work, *Infinite Jest*, was more than 1,100 pages. In his mid-40s, he stopped taking the medication. The depression roared back, now unresponsive to any treatment, even the one that had kept him alive for approximately 25 years. He was dead by suicide within months.

The reasons Wallace discontinued his medication are hard to discern and were likely multiple. For one thing, this class of medication requires careful dietary restrictions, and there is some indication that in the days and weeks prior to discontinuing his medicine, Wallace unwittingly violated one of these restrictions and was faced with some very unpleasant physical consequences as a result.[1] Whatever the reason, he was diverted from a plainly effective regimen with a catastrophic outcome.

Confusion about the relation of mental disorders and medications is by no means limited to artists such as Wallace. Should one, however, converse casually on these topics with artists, humanities professors, lawyers, businesspeople, military officers, scientists, and physicians, as I myself have done on numerous occasions, it is unmistakable that the artists find the issues the most fraught (with the humanities professors not far behind). Their vexations tend to come in two main forms: (1) an intellectually moribund, paranoid, and misinformed view of "big pharma," which sees large pharmaceutical companies as solely focused on profits and, at best, unconcerned with the effects of their drugs on people, and at worst, determined that their medications will wreak the utmost havoc; and (2) the intertwined opinion that mental illness can spur creativity and that psychiatric medicines usually dull it.

Regarding the so-called evils of big pharma (a phrase that seems to gain traction in some conspiratorial quarters in part because it is resonant with the Orwellian phrase "big brother"), pharmaceutical companies of course are focused and should be focused on profits. That is what companies do, and doing so provides them incentive to excel in competitive markets. That this system and its incentives are imperfect is as obvious and sophomoric an observation as I can imagine and to make it with the knowing air of the seer, as I have seen many professors do, is to commit the grave sin of saying something utterly lacking in profundity with an air of profundity. The very messy and effective free market is at play here (and in this case, not completely free as evidenced by the U.S. Federal Drug Administration) and to imagine that physicians, hospital administrators, and similar others are either co-conspirators or just plain dumb, beggars all imagination. I have seen professors malign "big pharma." These same professors whose voices and very lives, along with those of their loved ones, were saved by "big pharma" products. I reiterate that the messiness and imperfections are very real and just as real as shareholders' profits and life-saving and life-enhancing medications. I am aware that there are book-length arguments to the contrary, most too vapid to counter. Exceptions may include Robert Whitaker's books *Mad in America* and *Anatomy of an Epidemic*. Although the best of the genre, even they are not very convincing because of basic flaws in reasoning, such as misunderstanding the important truth that initial underlying severity of illness is a key reason that people with schizophrenia on antipsychotic medications fare more poorly than do people with schizophrenia never treated on antipsychotics (i.e., those with more severe illnesses to begin with are more likely than others to be medicated).

Side by side with this conspiratorial view of drug companies often exists a similarly confused view of how mental illnesses and psychiatric medications affect creativity. Mental illnesses are powerful forces of nature. They derange and devastate the mind and body and therefore constitute a strong deterrent to any kind of productivity. This is true regarding all forms of productivity, ranging from the relatively simple (e.g., caring for one's own hygiene) to the relatively hard (e.g., writing a novel of quality). Those who hold a romantic notion of the inspiring properties of the mental suffering involved in these illnesses are revealing their lack of experience with or lack of understanding of the actual illnesses.

A useful litmus test for whether what someone is saying about mental illnesses is sensible is to ask, "Would it make sense to say that of cancer?" Ideas such as "it's just in your head" and "she's just trying to get attention" and "if he would just try harder" would be appalling to say of the cancer sufferer. These are equally inappropriate things to say of the sufferer of mental disorders. Thus to say "the suffering of mental disorders is romantic and inspiring" is akin to saying that the ravages of cancer and the world-tilting nausea of chemotherapy are romantic and inspiring.

I am aware from repeated and tedious experience that those who most need to hear these messages won't take them from me. I am too—in their terms—"scientistic" to be trusted with matters of such subtlety and nuance as the human mind, heart, and soul. Then take it from Jeff Tweedy, the leader of the band Wilco, who is as soulful and as artistically credentialed as they come. An interviewer, who himself seems to harbor the view that from mental suffering springs great art, asks Tweedy his view. To which Tweedy replies,

> I've struggled with the idea of the tortured artist a lot in my life and I've been through addiction, I've been through periods of pretty serious depression . . . and I don't personally subscribe to that idea. In fact, I think it's a very, very damaging mythology that has grown up around the idea of art being a product of pain, as opposed to being something that's created in spite of pain . . . the part of me that is able to create managed to create in spite of the problems that I was having . . .[2]

Or take it from the life and death of Wallace: on medication, depression-free and able to produce great art for approximately 25 years; off medication, lacerating depression, and death by suicide.

Or take it from the life and death of a physician who found himself in a peculiar scenario. He was under the care of a psychiatrist (as well he should have been given a very serious form of bipolar disorder), but it was a psychiatrist who did not believe in mental disorders. One would think this a mythical creature, and perhaps it is becoming more and more one (though nature abhors a vacuum, and so I suppose this niche will always be filled, no matter how undesirable a niche it is), but in the cohorts trained between the 1950s and1970s, there were several such psychiatrists. One of them was Thomas Szasz, the title of whose most famous book epitomizes his view, *The Myth of Mental Illness*.

Among many other things, Szasz' work inspired, in my opinion, one of the best closing lines to a scholarly work ever penned. The work was on the genetics of schizophrenia, led by psychiatrist Seymour Kety, and the line is "If schizophrenia is a myth, it is a myth with a high genetic loading."

It was alleged in court that Szasz' views also led to the death of the physician with bipolar disorder mentioned earlier.[3] Initially under the care of another psychiatrist, the man had responded very favorably to lithium, as many did and still do who have bipolar spectrum conditions. For reasons that are not clear, the man decided to seek an additional consultation with Szasz, who mentioned that it made little sense to take a powerful medicine (lithium) for an illness (bipolar disorder) that is a myth, that does not exist. Unfortunately, Szasz' patient was persuaded by this, discontinued lithium, and was dead by his own hand within months, in circumstances very similar to those of the suicide of Wallace. Quite understandably, the man's widow sued Szasz, who settled the case instead of contesting it (or more likely, whose insurance company insisted that he do so). It would seem certain that there are more cases like this in Szasz' files.

Szasz died in 2012. As it happens, I met him when he spoke at a social work colloquium held at Florida State University (FSU), which, to the best of my memory, was in 1999 or 2000. Then as now, I viewed his ideas as preposterous and poisonous, and thus was prepared to dislike him immensely. In fact, candor forces me to rephrase to say, "I hoped to dislike him immensely." My hopes were dashed, because he was modest, humorous, friendly, and erudite. I could not decide whether this made his ideas all the more poisonous, and I remain unsure of the answer to that question.

His charm is perhaps one reason that he still has admirers. Among this group who are at all sympathetic to Szasz and his ideas, it is an interesting exercise to try to find one who is at the center, or even center-left, of the political spectrum. In my experience at least, they are all very far out on the flanks of the left, which is curious, because Szasz himself was not.[4]. Though I have not (yet) tested it out, my strong suspicion is that Szasz' admirers are unaware of this fact, and that awareness of it would immediately cool their admiration toward him. This is notable, because what has *not* cooled them is clear evidence that Szasz' thought and action led to misery and death; what *would* cool them, I expect, is learning that Szasz likely voted for Goldwater and Reagan. The priorities on display here are of course questionable.

In his *Shrinks: The Untold History of Psychiatry*, Jeffery Lieberman profiled a contemporary of Szasz, R. D. Laing. Unlike Szasz, Laing at least believed in the existence of mental illness, but he attributed it 100% to disordered family relationships, especially in the domain of parenting. He assigned blame for mental illness to parents, until later in his life, that is, when it became clear that he himself was the parent of a daughter with schizophrenia. After that point, he was described as "disillusioned with his own ideas" and "a guy asking for money by giving lectures on ideas he no longer believed in." The author Lieberman met Szasz many times, and he wrote, "Same with Szasz ... He made it pretty clear he understood that schizophrenia qualified as a true brain disease, but he was never going to say so publically."[5]

Antipsychiatry stances facilitate atrocity. The deinstitutionalizations it caused did nothing for patients except to remove them from treatment and safety, leading directly to several current problems, including homelessness, an explosive growth of mentally ill people in prisons, and mental health insurance coverage cutbacks. (For why, the insurance companies reasoned, should they pay for mere "lifestyle choices" and "problems in living," which is what antipsychiatry proponents believe mental disorders are?)

The grandfather of cognitive-behavioral therapy, psychiatrist Aaron "Tim" Beck, was interviewed for Lieberman's book *Shrinks*. Beck told Lieberman the following anecdote: "I had been treating a potentially homicidal inpatient who made contact with Thomas Szasz, who then put direct pressure on the hospital to discharge the patient. After he was released, the patient was responsible for several murders, and was only stopped when his wife, whom he threatened to kill, shot him."[6]

Ideas can kill (and it would be fair to raise the point that this truth applies to ideas arising from many quarters). This is well known, or should be, to anyone with passing familiarity of 20th-century history. Ideas like those that held sway in Cambodia, for example, or Nazi Germany as another example, were evil on their face, which may have misled us into thinking that only obviously evil ideas kill. The anecdotes enumerated about Szasz and Wallace illustrate that other ideas can kill too. It is not necessarily evil to question the nature or even the existence of mental illness, as Szasz did (it was naive and unwise and also ruinous for the families involved, who may well think of the ideas as evil). It is not evil that Wallace wondered whether he might discontinue his medication and be stable or even be the better for it (it was unwise and misinformed, and it led to disaster, but it was not evil for him to wonder). These ideas were not (necessarily) evil, but they did kill.

There is a professional mental health conference called "Freud Meets Buddha: Mindfulness, Trauma, and Process Addictions." I have no doubt that many mental health professionals are drawn to such meetings, and I do not begrudge them their enjoyment, any more than I would if they all decided to go to Disney World at their own expense. I do insist, however, that certain treatments work, others make people worse, and others have no effect at all. I insist that when "Freud meets Buddha," there will be plenty of talk—some of it high-minded, some of it coherent—and there will be self-satisfaction among many participants, but that those with grave illnesses, such as schizophrenia, borderline personality disorder, and major depressive disorder, are unlikely to be helped as a result, either directly at the meeting or indirectly as the participants apply what they learned to sufferers in the ensuing weeks. And at least some of this will occur at taxpayers' expense. An individual pays (and may write off) $529 for the full experience, for which, sad and needless to say, psychologists can obtain continuing education credits sanctioned by the American Psychological Association (up to 24 units, to be exact). The mental health profession has always tended to go starry-eyed at any mention of Eastern philosophy, no matter how confused, and was fertile ground for this newest flight of fancy, mindless mindfulness.

Mindfulness is a collection of ideas (a mostly sound and beneficent collection); faux mindfulness is also an idea (or a distortion of one, an impostor for one). Even faux mindfulness is unlikely to be directly harmful. The point of delving into the histories of Wallace and Szasz and of discussion of current views on medications, creativity, and mental illnesses is that distraction from what truly works can *indirectly* cause destruction and death.

We have encountered Representative Tim Ryan before, a self-described "relentless advocate and proponent"[7] of mindfulness, and one who hopes to introduce what he views as its many unique benefits to his colleagues in Congress and to other elements of the U.S. government. One such element is the National Institutes of Health (NIH), and a major institute within the NIH is the National Heart, Lung, and Blood Institute (NHLBI). In this connection, it caught my eye in September of 2014 when Rep. Ryan issued a press release that one of his constituents had won a sizable NHLBI grant. The study is called "Mindfulness-Based Stress Reduction for High Blood Pressure," and a goal of the project is to allow people with hypertension to manage it without medications but with things such as meditation instead.

Let us hope the project succeeds. It is in capable enough hands it appears (part of the research team is at Kent State University in Ryan's home state of Ohio), and the more scientifically supported approaches there are for major public health menaces, the better. The topic and the congressman's announcement of the project, however, lead me to wonder about unintended negative consequences. For example, it is somewhat unusual for an elected federal official to announce the awarding of a federal scientific grant—usually it is the public relations office of the researcher's university or the public relations personnel at the granting agency (here, the NHLBI). For Ryan to issue an announcement unnecessarily raises questions in the public mind about his undue influence. To be clear, I have no doubts that the process was fair; I know from many first-hand experiences that NIH grant proposal reviews are rigorous. The congressman's announcement, however, may undermine that reality in some people's eyes.

The larger problem is the potential implicit message that projects on mindfulness and health may send, which is that one's illness stems from one's mindset. An *Atlantic Monthly* article on Congressman Ryan includes a quote from a former NFL football player whose career was ended by a hit that left him paralyzed for several months. Describing his successful recovery including yoga and meditation, the former Pro Bowler stated, "I was tapping into the modality that we inherited to heal ourselves. We have this within us all."[8] On first blush, this seems uplifting, but I doubt it is much of a lift to those with similar injuries who did not recover well. One thing we most certainly do not have within us all is the world-class physical rigor required to play in the National Football League, at a Pro Bowl level no less. That the player had it is a highly likely factor in his favorable outcome. The same article includes a quote from someone who believes meditation cured his post-traumatic stress disorder (PTSD)—a former marine, who, by virtue of being a former marine was by definition more physically and psychologically hardy to begin with as compared to the norm. I do not begrudge these admirable individuals

the solace they get from meditation and yoga. I do, however, feel
for those who are injured or ill through no fault of their own, who
are led to believe that they would be better if they could just have a
better attitude. The evidence that a positive attitude has something
to do with the course of illness, for example, cancer, is not only thin
and riddled with problems, it sends the message one is to blame for
having cancer. That is, if only one's attitude were slightly rosier, one
would not be so ill, which is a view that Barbara Ehrenreich demol-
ished in her book *Bright-Sided*. The kind of victim-blaming that
Ehrenreich skewers literally adds insult to injury.

Every fall (and then some) from when I was 7 to 17, growing up in
Georgia, I played football, and learned a lot about the endurance of
pain, the limits of stamina, and placing one's team before oneself.
If someone were seriously injured (e.g., to take one true example,
an arm broken so badly that it dangled at a 90-degree angle several
inches below the wrist), the reaction was quick and kind, pretty much
as it would be today. But if the injury were lesser, one was very unlikely to be gently encouraged to be mindful, and very likely to hear
the phrase "tie it on, tape it up, and suck it up." I heard the phrase
dozens if not hundreds of times, as did much of my own and previous generations in settings like the football fields of the American
South, Texas, Oklahoma, and much of the Midwest. That football has
problems—concussions, suicides, domestic violence—is important to
heed, and it is also key to note that these are problems in the wider
society too, civilian and military alike.

Despite forecasts to the contrary, football in America represents
an enduring institution, as can be seen on my younger son's bedrag-
gled countenance after spring football practice in the North Florida
heat. (The season is in the fall and a few weeks of spring practice is
standard. Our family's expression for when things really get intense
is that "the coaches got all coach-ish.") But even enduring institutions are influenced by the broader culture. For example, my son
(and my wife) think the idea behind "tie it on, tape it up, and suck
it up" is "dumb"—mindless, as it were—whereas I am not so sure.
I think there may be situations in football and beyond in which it
remains apt.

The mention of "trigger warnings" is one such situation. The concept will likely be familiar to university-based readers, because as

with many similar things, it has gained traction and spread within the academy, especially and predictably within the humanities. The idea is that the professor should issue a public alert to all students regarding any course material that may trigger a negative emotional reaction (e.g., an exacerbation of PTSD). The concept of triggers is pervasive enough that one sees it regularly mentioned in official university policies and correspondence (e.g., I recently saw a memo using the idea as a rationale to exclude a student from a certain course of study).

There should be a movement of those of us whose only trigger is trigger warnings. The concept is an affront to human resiliency and an insult to those who actually do have triggers, in the sense that they have been severely traumatized and suffer from actual PTSD. Even they, however, should not be coddled (unless they individually ask for consideration as I will discuss later) and should receive scientifically supported treatment for the condition, which tellingly, encourages *confrontation* of the trauma and the *prevention* of avoidance of trauma cues. This irony bears repeating: State-of-the-art science and treatment for genuine PTSD counsel gradually but fully facing one's trauma (as hard as this is), whereas the trigger movement would have people avoid things, even great works of art, that happen to cause some emotional distress.

A reporter for *Al Jazeera America*, having spent some time in war-ravaged Afghanistan, seems to agree. The reporter wrote,

> It's hard to feel any sympathy for a student discreetly taking a professor aside to discuss the content of the assigned reading and its impact on the psyche after you've watched a bunch of Afghans twitch slightly at yet another bomb and keep going because they have very little else available to them: no therapy, no shrink, no Xanax, no vociferous student union caring about their feelings, no professor who might carefully comb a reading list for potential triggers.[9]

I could not agree more, except for one thing: People with genuine and under- or untreated PTSD should be empowered to discreetly take a professor aside and ask a question along the following lines: "Could you please give me a heads up about any reading on the theme of x?" And x, by the way, has been formally defined (in this case by the University of California, Santa Barbara student union) as "rape, sexual assault, abuse, self-injurious behavior, suicide, graphic violence, pornography, kidnapping, and graphic descriptions of gore."

The *Al Jazeera* reporter continues in a vein with which I am in agreement: "It's hard not to think that the desire for trigger warnings isn't simply evidence of a younger generation's need to 'toughen up,' but yet another manifestation of the very American desire to limit one's experience to 'pleasant' things rather than fully understanding the world around us." One can quibble with how American this really is—it strikes me more as modern human— but it is certainty true that it is hard not to view the trigger phenomenon as a sign of the populace's newly delicate constitution, one that smiles upon itself and frowns upon sucking it up, tying it on, and taping it up.

The phenomenon not only coddles that which should usually not be, but undermines the very point of a university. Writing in the *New Yorker*, Rebecca Mead observed, "The hope that safety might be found, as in a therapist's office, in a classroom where literature is being taught is in direct contradiction to one purpose of literature, which is to give expression through art to difficult and discomfiting ideas, and thereby enlarge the reader's experience and comprehension."[10] This is one of the better answers to the question of why we should we bother with art. And I have heard many such answers, including many unpersuasive ones from artists themselves.

If any book should be slathered with trigger warnings, it is probably the Bible. As Todd Gitlin noted in the March 13, 2015 edition of *Tablet*, writing specifically of the Old Testament, "Lot's two daughters slept with him in order to continue his line (Genesis 19). Joshua slaughtered 12,000 Canaanites in one day (Joshua 8) and soon thereafter 'smote all the country of the hills, and of the south, and of the vale, and of the springs, and all their kings: He left none remaining, but utterly destroyed all that breathed, as the Lord God of Israel commanded' (Joshua 10:40)."[11] As it happens, I am an unreligious person, but I have read the entire Bible more than once. Why? Because it is a foundational text, perhaps the most important single one, of Western culture and civilization, slaughterings and crucifixions and all notwithstanding. And because some of the writing is very beautiful. To have not read it is to leave one's schooling incomplete (and is to be hypocritical if one claims Christian piety). To have not read it because of its violence and so forth strikes me as absurd, akin to not having a sound foundation for a house because one is spooked by basements.

Although not referred to specifically as trigger warnings, there is a similar issue within suicide prevention circles. Specifically, there is concern (partly warranted) that inappropriate media coverage of suicidal events may encourage suicidal behavior in susceptible people. Just as triggers are thought to elicit painful emotion from vulnerable individuals, so may sensationalistic, glorifying, or overly detailed reporting of suicidal phenomena lead to increased suicidality in those exposed to the coverage. In fact, there are dozens of correlational studies showing an association between things such as media coverage of a celebrity suicide and suicide rates in the population. A meta-analysis of this literature suggested that population suicide rates increase by 0.26 per 100,000 during the month following a celebrity suicide, and this effect is higher still if the celebrity is especially famous.[12]

Nevertheless, there are reasons to think twice about a puritanical orthodoxy regarding this topic, just as there are reasons for skepticism regarding trigger warnings and regarding a reflexive, self-regarding version of mindfulness. For one thing, there are prominent examples in which the coverage of a celebrity suicide was extensive and yet no increase in suicidality in the population was observed. Perhaps the clearest example of this was the death of Nirvana frontman Kurt Cobain, by self-inflicted gunshot wound in 1994 in his Seattle home. Cobain was extremely famous, and Nirvana's fan base clearly included numerous young and vulnerable people. Yet there was no increase in suicide deaths in Seattle following Cobain's suicide—a fact that may be because of responsible reporting of Cobain's death.[13] However, there is another reason for at least mild skepticism about the notion that exposure to certain imagery and phrasing leads to increased suicidality. To my knowledge, the literature to date includes no study in which exposure to media materials was experimentally manipulated to conclusively show that exposure heightens suicidality or anything related to it. Accordingly, my colleagues and I conducted exactly that sort of study.

In an effort led by psychologist Michael Anestis, we randomly assigned undergraduates to one of three exposure conditions. In the first condition, students read an article that had run in *Newsweek*. The article included a detailed description of the death of a suicide decedent and also included several photographs of celebrities who went on to die by suicide; the photographs were flattering if not glorifying or romanticizing. When this article was published, there was indignation from some quarters of the suicide prevention community that the media reporting guidelines had been neglected. A second group of undergraduates read the same article, but with the supposedly offending material removed. A third group read an article about the experience of cancer, selected to be about as detailed about pain and suffering as the suicide articles were.

Immediately after exposure, and then 1 month later, students were assessed for any changes in mood or suicide risk. The entire sample was examined, as was an important subsample: Those who, at baseline, seemed vulnerable to begin with, and thus could be particularly susceptible to the effects of exposure. And there were effects, only not the ones that the indignant crowd would expect. Rather, one of the only clear differences between the groups was that those who saw the supposedly dangerous version of the suicide-related article fared *better* than others, in the sense that they reported a lower likelihood of future suicide attempt than those in the two control conditions. In the subset of those who had harbored suicidal ideation in the past, the effect was similar but even stronger. In this subgroup, those who read the revised article, meant to "cleanse" it of putatively offending material, reported the highest likelihood of a future suicide attempt of the three groups in the study (no participant attempted suicide during the 1-month study).[14]

Responsible reporting makes good sense, however, hysteria about responsible reporting is counterproductive, in that it can shut down needed public discourse about suicide and its prevention. Trigger warnings carry the same danger in the classroom, where we lose the ability to discuss sensitive topics even in great works of art in exchange for no demonstrable gain. Inauthentic mindfulness poses a similar threat, which is the simultaneous glorification of the self at the expense of virtue.

The eminent clinical psychologist Paul Meehl noticed this same general tendency more than 50 years ago. In his classic article, "Why I Don't Attend Case Conferences," he wrote of the then-current mental health landscape what could easily be written about the now current one:

> One undesirable side effect of the mental hygiene movement and the overall tradition of dynamic psychiatry has been the development among educated persons (and here I do not refer only to professionals

but to many persons who get an undergraduate degree in a variety of majors) of what I call "the spun-glass theory of the mind." This is the doctrine that the human organism, adult or child (particularly the latter), is constituted of such frail material, is of such exquisite psychological delicacy, that rather minor, garden-variety frustrations, deprivations, criticisms, rejections or failure experiences are likely to play the causative role of major traumas.[15]

What I have termed "authentic mindfulness" has admirable qualities: If understood properly, it is conceptually appealing in its dispassionate consideration of each moment's facets, including the mind's own products (but extending far beyond them); it has clinical and other forms of practical utility; and it has garnered a fair amount of empirical support. Unfortunately, on each of these fronts, there are countervailing forces that directly undermine either the conceptual or empirical basis of even authentic mindfulness, including, for example, the tendency to neglect rigorous control conditions such as walking and the routinization of other mundane activities. Moreover, there are consequences to this. I have scratched the surface of this latter aspect in discussing topics like the deaths of Wallace and those linked to the thinking of Szasz, as well as trigger warning phenomena. In upcoming chapters, I will delve further into the various other nefarious consequences, especially those produced by the noxious combination of mindfulness with a culture of narcissism.

Earlier in this chapter, I questioned the truth of the assertion that things such as Transcendental Meditation (TM) and mindfulness meditation outpace mundane activities like walking regimens. Judging from an evolutionary standpoint, why would they? Daily walking is easy to understand as beneficial, given that our bodies have been sculpted over eons to do just that. Indeed, there are accounts that attribute to our ability to walk and run very long distances (and to thereby outlast hunted animals), an essential role in our evolutionary development. It is similar for frequent gardening, as we co-evolved with plant life and have cultivated crops for millennia. Similar things are true for nonhuman species as well (e.g., ants cultivate fungus farms). I would contend that for most things good and true, one can find a reason why their variant might have been adaptive in ancestral settings (taking care to avoid the "just-so" fallacy), and parallels can often be found in other animals. Even thoroughly modern things, such as reading or writing a book on a computer or some kindred device, have resonance with the ancient development of language, interpersonal communication, and storytelling, and it is far from challenging to find nonhuman examples of social communication (e.g., rats "chat" constantly, but out of the narrow range of our meager hearing).

To what in ancestral conditions does TM trace back? Where are the nonhuman meditators? Tellingly, the only possible candidates are sleep and its extreme version, hibernation. In the case of sleep, it is one of nature's virtual invariants, applying in some fashion to the daily lives even of bacteria and plants. To paraphrase Keats, sleeplessness breeds many woes, the obverse of which of course is that sleep cures many, which incidentally, makes sleep improvement another candidate (along with walking) for an active, rigorous control intervention. To imagine something like TM being incremental beyond it, or even related to it, requires exactly that tendency toward fantasy encouraged by the strands of our culture that this book decries.

Consider David Lynch's starry-eyed description of the benefits to TM mentioned in Chapter 1, but substitute terms related to "sleep" for TM: I started [sleeping well] in 1973 and have not missed a single [night] ever since ... It has given me effortless access to unlimited reserves of energy, creativity and happiness deep within ... And this level of life is deep within us all." With this substitution of the products of eons of evolution for the implausible meditation-related claims, the words gain at least some level of credibility.

I am thus proposing evolutionary and cross-species yardsticks that can be used, together with rigorous outcome data, to gauge the credibility and plausibility of techniques of behavior change. Walking regimens fare well on this criterion, as do sleep improvement strategies. TM, yoga, and faux mindfulness, less so (e.g., in the study mentioned in Chapter 1 on hippocampal volume gain, walking beat out yoga). Interestingly, however, authentic mindfulness is credible and plausible as judged by evolutionary and cross-species metrics: Moment-to-moment awareness of the details of one's environment has obvious adaptive benefits, and it is not especially difficult to witness forms of this occurring in nonhuman animals (the deer in my neighborhood are hyperaware and, I must assume, are often more "mindful" than I, in that they see me more than I them).

Authentic mindfulness loses some points, however, given its non-judgmental emphasis. As emphasized throughout this book, life itself is by definition judgmental. One common criterion to differentiate between animate and inanimate things is responsiveness to stimuli, and this responsiveness tends toward decisive judgment. Matthew McConaughey's *True Detective* character, pressed about being judg-mental, replies, "Everyone judges, all the time." Indeed, plants orient toward the sun, decisively (for a plant), consistently, and without mindful deliberation; sea slugs withdraw their gills and siphons in response to disturbance with very little reflection and in a decisive, judgmental manner; ants who are infected and thus sick leave the nest to die with as much resolve and intent as a human who has decided to end his or her life; cows range through pastures in such a way as to avoid the larvae of intestinal worms in their waste, and they do this reliably, decisively; a baby who sees a box suddenly and inexplicably move startles and does so with immediacy and clarity. Life judges—we judge—and to counsel us to do otherwise is to mis-understand the natural world. Ecclesiastes, full of searing wisdom, reads, "You who do not know how the mind is joined to the body know nothing of the works of God."[16]

As long as I am subjecting authentic mindfulness, daily walk-ing, faux mindfulness, TM, and yoga to evolutionary and cross-species tests, how do other approaches to behavior change per-form? Psychoanalysis—or rather the diverse collection of ideas and methods, often at cross-purposes with one another, that is called *psychoanalysis*—fails dramatically, doomed from the outset by self-contradiction as well as by first premises that fundamentally mis-understand human nature and nature itself. For example, Freud not only believed, but recorded in print, his belief that humans developed the capacity for self-control because had they not, then men would have given in to the irresistible urge to urinate on campfires, ex-tinguishing the fires and with them all that they allowed (e.g., the cooking of game, shared culture around meals, ritual, and culture in general).

I encourage you to try this material out on a true believer. I recently took the opportunity to do so with a colleague after he informed me that he was an expert on psychoanalysis. Informed readers may have already deduced that this was a humanities professor, as these days the claim for psychoanalytic expertise is becoming nearly pathognomonic for such employment. Even the glare of this colleague's especially prominent earring could not distract me from noticing his angry perception of my psychoanalytic ignorance. I was loudly challenged to cite chapter and verse regarding the "urinating on campfires" statement, and when I attempted to politely demur, was alerted to the facts that my conversation partner had read everything Freud had ever written, "at least twice" and that his certainty that I was mistaken was total. A small crowd of other humanities professors had gathered by then, and I resisted the impulse to murmur "Eppur si muove" and instead responded, "I seem to remember it being in a footnote, maybe in *The Future of an Illusion* or *Totem and Taboo*, but it's certainly possible I'm mistaken, and anyway, how about them Noles?" (we had just been at an FSU Seminoles football game).

Indeed, the Noles were great that weekend, and indeed the material is contained in a footnote, but it is in *Civilization and Its Discontents*. It appears on p. 41 of the paperback Norton standard edition. Freud characterized the idea, quite accurately, as a "fantastic-sounding one," and it reads in part as follows: ". . . primal man had the habit, when he came in contact with fire, of satisfying an infantile desire connected with it, by putting it out with the stream of his urine." This is fantastic-sounding for sure, but Freud is ready with more, claiming that urinating on fires ". . . was a kind of sexual act with a male, an enjoyment of sexual potency in a homosexual competition. The first person to renounce this desire and spare the fire was able to carry it off with him and subdue it to his own use." For Freud, primitive man was naturally homosexual, and the one individual who heroically controlled his own homosexual impulses thereby was Adam to us all, culturally speaking. This is incredible material—just to pick out two implications of it, it means that the natural state for all men is homosexuality, and that the development of high culture necessitated the suppression of homosexuality. These claims are so discordant with truth and with the modern ear (which do not always correspond), that I even feel a pang of sympathy for my well-dressed humanities colleague. If I were a fan of psychoanalysis or of Freud, I too would want to forget or deny that such passages are there in black-and-white in one of the most seminal books of the entire psychoanalytic canon.

I shared the citation with my professorly acquaintance via email. I got no reply. I have had much more fruitful exchanges with the remaining few academic clinical psychologists who say things like, "I know there are major problems with it but there seems to be something there, something valuable" (indeed, a patron saint of the profession, Meehl, tended to say just that, although he also allowed that for every decade he aged, he believed considerably less and less of it). When I share the urinating on campfires story with this latter group, they tend not to get inappropriately angry but rather to mournfully shake their heads and say "I know, I know . . . but still, I occasionally find it useful."

I trust that the layer upon layer of misunderstanding reflected in some of Freud's writing—and the extinguishing fire story is quite far from the only one—underscores my assertion that psychoanalysis fails as a technique of behavior change on multiple criteria, including plausibility and coherence, never mind the evolutionary and cross-species gauges. What of other approaches?

Cognitive-behavioral therapy (CBT), although not prone to flights of fancy like the campfire story, is not above reproach on the evolutionary and cross-species counts. On the one hand, its original and basic emphases pass the test. That is, the recurring fundamental questions of the cognitive-behavioral therapist (e.g., According to logic and evidence, how likely is that *really*? According to logic and evidence, what *really* would be the consequences of that?) are of obvious benefit both now and ancestrally, and versions of them clearly occur in creatures of all sorts. On the other hand, CBT practitioners tend to frequently depart from the basic script, and when they do, their drift can be away from basic behaviorism and straightforward cognitive restructuring toward more complex constructs (e.g., early maladaptive schemas) and faddish topics, such as mindfulness. This is not necessarily a problem in itself, assuming the practitioner in question knows rigorous schema-focused therapy and practices authentic mindfulness instead of its impostor version.

In remarks to an American Psychiatric Association meeting in 1949, D. L. Thompson said, "Everything spiritual and valuable has a gross and undesirable malady very similar to it." This was a point of my 2014 book on murder–suicide, called *The Perversion of Virtue*, which contended that perpetrators of murder–suicide, as they are enacting atrocity, are under the sincere impression that they are behaving in accord with one of four essential virtues: justice, mercy, duty, and glory. Of course they are disastrously mistaken, but they are unaware of the fact, and more, it is possible to detect elements of actual virtue in the woeful logic operating in the minds of murder–suicide perpetrators. Regarding authentic mindfulness, I am not certain it is accurate to characterize it as "spiritual," but it is valuable, and it has a gross, undesirable, and perverted version that has similarities to it. Buddhists are aware of this same distinction and have terms for " right mindfulness" (samma sati) and " wrong mindfulness" (miccha sati). In a *Huffington Post* blog referred to in Chapter 1, Ron Purser and David Loy wrote, ". . . decontextualizing mindfulness from its original liberative and transformative purpose, as well as its foundation in social ethics, amounts to a Faustian bargain. Rather than applying mindfulness as a means to awaken individuals and organizations from the unwholesome roots of greed, ill will and delusion, it is usually being refashioned into a banal, therapeutic, self-help technique that can actually reinforce those roots."[17] An essential engine for this refashioning is our culture of narcissism, which is the focus of the next chapter.

Our Culture of Self-Regard
The Stare of Narcissus

T HE MYTHICAL NARCISSUS WAS TAKEN BY THE BEAUTY of his own reflection in the water of a spring. At least he had to exert himself enough to walk to the spring and lean over it to look. The 21st-century versions—plural, for they are legion—need not be put out to that extent. They carry their reflecting pools in their pockets and use them frequently to snap self-portraits and then to gaze at their likenesses—plural, for each individual youth does this ad infinitum. There is even a no longer very new (but definitely tiresome) word for this development, if it can be called a development, and unlike many neologisms, this one is very apt: "selfie."

Even more apt is my wife's occasional mispronunciation of the term. English is her second language, leading to humorous and otherwise charming phrasings, such as "taking a selfish" in place of "taking a selfie." This particular instance occurred, incidentally, in response to a person taking a "selfish" with a "selfish stick" at the site reputed to be where Jesus was crucified, anointed with oils, interred, and resurrected—Christendom's most holy site—the Church of the Holy Sepulchre in Jerusalem.

Comedian Doug Stanhope said "any time you complain about the kids today you know you're walking on dangerous ground of being a pathetic old [expletive deleted] . . ." Perhaps so, and maybe my attitude on "selfies" and the like is just my own "kids these days" attitude, a tired refrain of each generation about the next. In context of this possibility, consider the following words, also uttered by a middle-aged man: "The children now love luxury; they have bad manners, contempt for authority; they show disrespect for elders and love chatter in place of exercise. . . . They contradict their parents, chatter before company, gobble up dainties at the table . . . and tyrannize their teachers." Or how about these, also written by an older man: "I see no hope for the future of our people if they are dependent on the frivolous youth of today, for certainly all youth are reckless beyond words. . . . When I was young, we were taught to be discreet and respectful of elders, but the present youth are exceedingly impatient of restraint."

You may detect in the phrasing that neither quote is from the 21st century, but what century then? Maybe the 20th or, at the earliest, the 19th century? Wrong, by well over 2,000 years. The first quote is from Socrates, written in the fifth century BCE, and the second is even older, from Hesiod, in the eighth century BCE.

We could go century by century and find similar quotes. It would be tedious to do so, but here is one last example. Writing in the 1800s, Ralph Waldo Emerson termed his time "the age of the first person singular." Emerson himself did not hesitate to give voice to the age in some of his thinking and writing (e.g., "Here's for the plain old Adam, the simple genuine self against the whole world," from his *Journals*), and his younger colleague Henry Thoreau tended to wax even more self-referentially. The fact that century after century one can find "kids these days" kinds of sentiments suggests that it is in fact an illusion. While it certainly appears to each successive generation that their juniors are feckless, perhaps their juniors are actually not any more so than they.

In this context, I have decried—and will decry again—the phenomenon of the "selfie", but it is worth remembering that this is not a uniquely 21st-century activity. "Dandyism" was fashionable, and within this trend, having a self-portrait made (the "selfie" of the time) was not uncommon.[1] Honoré Daumier's 1871 painting *Dandy* satirizes this activity. In the painting, a self-satisfied individual is depicted, dressed as one might expect a 19th-century dandy to dress, nose upturned, chin jutted out. The subject is depicted not once, not twice, but three times. The first depiction is the painting itself; the second, in the mirror in which the subject is smugly gazing; and the third, in a previous self-portrait that is depicted hung on the wall. As an aside, a prominent scoring system for the Rorschach inkblot test counts seeing things in the blots as reflecting one another as an indicator of narcissism.

So there were "selfies" of a kind back then (I've tried several times to type "selfies" without the quotation marks and cannot bring myself to do so, the imprimatur of the *Oxford English Dictionary* notwithstanding). But was there a queen of the "butt selfie?" Did these depictions involve the painter's very prominent and grinning self-portrait using a funeral as backdrop? How about a clearly despondent homeless person as a backdrop? How about a desperate person about to jump to his death from a highway overpass, again as setting for a leering "selfie?"

I can find no examples of such in the 19th century, few if any in the 20th, and cannot help but see them in the 21st. I suppose it is true that people have scratched their names, initials, and so forth, into humanity's great architectural treasures for centuries, but it was only in the 21st century that two Americans (ages 21 and 25) were arrested as they took a "selfie" of themselves and what they had just carved into the Roman Colosseum.[2] One shudders to think what they would carve in the moon if they had the chance. All that Neil Armstrong and Buzz Aldrin left was a stainless steel plaque embedded in the moon's Sea of Tranquility: "HERE MEN FROM THE PLANET EARTH FIRST SET FOOT UPON THE MOON, JULY 1969, A.D. WE CAME IN PEACE FOR ALL MANKIND." No one's initials emphasized, no one's name blaring, not even much mention of the particular country responsible, the citizens of which paid for, designed, built, planned, risked, and manned the trip. No one has carved into it (yet).

The young American carvers' antics are actually quite tame, relatively speaking. " 'Selfies' at funerals" is alas a real thing, as is " 'selfies' with the homeless," and should you doubt this, there are Tumblr sites of those exact titles showing many such images. (Tumblr is a little hard to describe for the nonuser, but it's a combination of microblogging and social media. In other words, it lets the user share quick items of interest, such as an appalling "selfie" with a sleeping home-less person, often organized by topic, such as the appalling "selfie with the homeless" category. Tumblr's self-description is "Tumblr lets you effortlessly share anything," which is accurate enough, but also neglectful of the adage that often a trouble shared is a trouble doubled. Speaking of which, let's just avoid the topic of "butt self-ies," except to say that not only are there "selfie sticks," which are extensions so that "selfies" can be taken at more of a distance, but also apparently "belfie sticks," extensions for taking "selfies" from the back. I say "apparently" because I hope that the belfie stick is an *Onion*-esque spoof, fear that it is not, and am disinclined to research the matter further.)

Notice, incidentally, the fully self-focused nature of the selfie stick. Not only does it facilitate the taking of one's own picture, but it discourages interpersonal involvement. That is, whereas before one needed to greet and ask the favor of taking one's picture of an actual human passing by, now, thanks to the selfie stick, the self is fully in recursive relation to the self. I struggled to think of what the next innovation would be, but quickly was confronted with a contender: the wireless "selfie" remote. When I first chanced upon it at the Tallahassee airport, I could not conceive of its point, but have since learned that such devices serve the same function as the selfie stick , but do so remotely, thus extending navel-gazing's range. Before I could form the thought, " 'Selfie' drones are next I'm sure," I was alerted to the existence of "selfie" drones. In trying to imagine what is next, I am at a loss.

In April 2014, a man in the throes of misery scaled the railing along a southern California interstate with the intention of jumping to his death below. One might imagine that this was newsworthy in itself, but that is unlikely. There are more than 100 U.S. suicides per day, and virtually all receive no media coverage whatsoever (and the few that do are covered with varying degrees of propriety). Or perhaps the event was newsworthy because of the effect on interstate traffic. Indeed, the incident led to closure of the interstate and thus to a massive traffic jam. However, only the lack of traffic in southern California would be news. No, what caused media attention to the sad affair were the numerous "selfies" with the distraught man in the distant background. The celebratory expressions and gestures in many of these photographs are jarring, even as compared to those in the neighboring "funeral" and "homelessness" genres. "The genus *Selfie* of the family Narcissus contains many species," as the now-defunct news website Gawker pointed out.

"Selfies" have not only been taken with scenes of death as backdrop, but have also been linked to numerous deaths. In the presence of their two young children, a couple became focused enough on taking their own photograph that they stepped backward over a cliff and fell hundreds of feet to their deaths. In a separate incident in 2014, a couple died in a private plane accident when their plane went into an aerodynamic stall, and it is possible (though not entirely clear) that the stall occurred because of the distraction of taking a "selfie." In a June 2015 incident, an individual (later characterized as "some moron" by an Air Force general) posted a "selfie" he took standing in front of an Islamic State (ISIS) headquarters building. Air Force intelligence saw the "selfie," located the building, and 22 hours after the picture was posted, destroyed the facility, presumably killing everyone inside. In September 2015, a young man intended to take a "selfie" with his gun; the gun discharged accidentally, instantly killing the man. In July 2015, Russian law enforcement authorities released a brochure on the dangers of driving while taking a "selfie," after at least ten deaths of exactly this sort occurred over the span of several months. A January 2016 report in *Priceonomics* tallied 49 "selfie" deaths since 2014, and the average age of the decedents was 21 years. The report notes that a rash of such deaths led one national government to issue what I consider a blessed law: There are 16 " 'selfie'-free" zones in India.

A commentator writing in the *Irish Times* stated of the "selfie;" "It's hard to think of a more appropriate—or more depressing—symbol of the kind of society we have become. We are living in an age of narcissism, an age in which only our best, most attractive, most carefully constructed selves are presented to the world."[3] True enough, as far as it goes, but the "funeral," "homelessness," and "suicide crisis" examples show it does not go far enough. If there remain any doubts at all on this point, "Auschwitz selfies"—with the Narcissi smiling—should allay them once and for all (yes, that really exists). It is depressing indeed to observe that we are living in an age in which others' suffering and tragedy serve as fashion accessories.

In my polemics against "selfies" and their dismal accoutrements, I am bemoaning the deterioration of *individualism* (everyone has inherent dignity and rights and also responsibilities and self-reliance) into *individuality* (everyone is unique, like a snowflake—and as resilient and thoughtful as one I would add). This crucial distinction animates my current argument, but also was noticed by early 20th-century social theorists among others. For example, Georg Simmel argued that, although individuality may have derived from individualism, it became so distorted in the process that it turned on its predecessor. Simmel wrote, "First, there had been the thorough liberation of the individual from the rusty chains of guild, birthright and church. Now the individual that had thus become independent also wished to distinguish himself *from other individuals.*" Simmel continued, "The important point no longer was the fact that he was a free individual as such, but that he was this specific, irreplaceable given individual."[4] Simmel attributed responsibility for this turn to Romanticism, calling it "the channel through which [the idea of individuality] reached the consciousness of the nineteenth century."

In the late 19th century, the great sociologist Émile Durkheim made compatible observations. Of the growth in the cult of individuality, he wrote that it has become a "cult of personality on which all our morality rests," and that the individual has become sacred, "even most sacred ... something which no one is to offend ... [The individual] has become tinged with religious value; man has become a god for men."[5] Durkheim was interested in this process because he viewed it, alas mistakenly, as something that would lower population suicide rates.

In fact, this process can be viewed as one full swing (back and forth) among a series of pendulum swings in selfhood over centuries. In the 15th and 16th centuries, church authorities assured us of our centrality in the universe. A given human may not be that unique or significant, but humanity certainly was the center of the cosmos, placed there by an attentive God. Galileo and colleagues refuted this view, and thereafter the Enlightenment prospered. One bounty of this was a flowering of political thought, including among provincial farmers in Virginia with education, time on their hands (because, it should be noted, of slavery), and a bone to pick. These Virginian individuals and their fellow travelers in Massachusetts and the 11 other colonies articulated a view of *individualism*, unrivaled before or since. (Although they could not really understand how to widen that view to all people. They saw the potential of it, writing, "We

hold these truths to be self-evident, that all men are created equal."
But they left the *doing* of it to an American war on American soil,
devastating a country, and killing hundreds of thousands of its citizens. And even that was not enough.) But the self will out, and did
so, as Simmel noted, partly on the waves of Romanticism. (Simmel
viewed this trend much more positively than I do. One wonders what
he would think in the 21st century.) Romanticism was no match for
the horrors of the American Civil War and World War I, not to
mention atrocities yet to come. The view of the self thereafter settled
about where it was in the Enlightenment, and perhaps not coincidentally, another scientific day dawned, crowned by achievements such
as Apollo 11 (and fueled, to be sure, largely by Cold War national-
ism). This brings us to the last few decades, which in my reckoning
is a Romantic revival.

I am not the only one to think so. Writing in *The New Criterion*
in 2013, Bruce Bawer opined of the 1950s and some of its artists,

> ... with their glib contempt for capitalism and mainstream society,
> their romanticization of criminality, drug abuse, and the tragedy of
> mental illness, and their narcissistic rebranding as virtues of their
> own shiftlessness and dissolution—they would turn out to be, to an
> amazing extent, the seed of pretty much everything that was rotten
> about the American 1960s and their aftermath. Echoing Burroughs's
> dictum that "the only possible ethic is to do what one *wants* to do,"
> Kerouac—who viewed himself as one of history's "great ravaged
> spirits," along with Dostoevsky, Nietzsche, and Hitler (yes, Hitler)—
> justified his colossal selfishness by pretending it was a philosophy
> of life, which he called "self-ultimacy." It's hard to decide which is
> more of a miracle—that all these self-regarding pseudo-intellectuals
> managed to find one another, or that they then managed to spark a
> cultural revolution that transformed the Western world.[6]

These last several passages represent an admittedly highly selective and American-centric view of history, but its main point is
the swings of a pendulum of selfhood. In this process, a backlash
against the cult of the self occasionally emerges and recurs. In recent
times, however, it is but an infrequent murmur among the constant
and deafening roar of the Narcissi. One form of the backlash occurs
every spring now at high school and college graduation ceremonies,
in which the speaker's main point to the new graduates is "you are

not special." Genuinely noxious trends tend to end sooner or later (even if less than gracefully), and often relatedly, tend to catch the attention of regulators. One possible beam of sunshine in this regard is concern about "ballot box 'selfies.'" For example, skewering the Narcissi who dabble in "funeral 'selfies'" is hamstrung by First Amendment issues, as are other deplorable activities like the Westboro Baptist Church picket activities or Ku Klux Klan rallies. The ballot box, however, may be different. The relevant law in New York State admonishes anyone who "keeps any memorandum of anything occurring within the booth; or directly or indirectly, reveals to another the name of any candidate voted for by such voter; or shows his ballot after it is prepared for voting, to any person so as to reveal the contents" has committed a misdemeanor. In Wisconsin, anyone who "shows his or her marked ballot to any person or places a mark upon the ballot so it is identifiable as his or her ballot" has committed election fraud, which is a felony. Bans on "ballot box 'selfies'" attempt to keep at least one place sacred and "selfie"-free, but, predictably, in accord with the cultural trends examined here, there are ongoing legal efforts to undo these bans on First Amendment grounds.

Cultural trends tend to be apparent in advertising; so much is riding for Madison Avenue on getting these trends right (especially regarding their usual marketing target, young people) that advertising is arguably the best single barometer of cultural trends. One massive advertising campaign involving millions of dollars takes as its entire premise the importance of the self. Taco Bell commercials deride sharing, encouraging viewers to take all for themselves. In one glaring example, it occurs to a TV ad character that a silver dollar of extreme sentimental value and family history is, among other things, a dollar, and thus can be used to buy a 99 cent taco. This he contentedly does. I nominate this image as our time's emblem: A keepsake heirloom passed down over generations tossed across a greasy fast-food restaurant counter in exchange for an even greasier amalgam of meat and flour, which is a dismal meal, one of three in a dismal day, one of thousands in a dismal life, all the while turning away from or never knowing about the honor, diligence, and sacrifice over generations required for the liberty and luxury of a 99 cent taco.

My cell phone camera's default is for taking "selfies," as opposed to taking photos outward, you know of, say, other people or things. My worry is that society's default is becoming similarly set. I recently attended a somewhat edifying lecture on a specific swami's views of Hinduism, for which brochures had been preprinted. Which phrase do you suppose was highlighted on the front of the brochure—"Each soul is potentially divine" or "Give up this little life of yours?" The latter was viewed as the epitome of the particular swami's teaching, but did not appear on the brochure; the former did, in large and ornate print.

It would be reassuring to those currently worried about our future to imagine that there is nothing new under the sun, that what is has ever been, including the older generations' distaste of the younger generation's self-love. Reassuring, that is, if it were true. However, there is growing and convincing evidence that it is not true, that despite the fact that many generations in the past have seen the sky falling in the faces of their irresponsible youth, only to find the sky very much intact a generation later, the sky may actually be falling now. If not falling outright, many strands of evidence suggest that it is at least chafing.

As part of my work I train psychologists, and a common activity of psychologists is psychological testing, including intelligence quotient (IQ) and other cognitive assessments. A standard aspect of the assessment process, naturally enough, is clear and usable feedback to the testee about test performance. In a recent training meeting, a younger colleague of mine asked the still younger PhD students to raise their hands if they found it difficult to convey to people that their IQ and other results were normal (i.e., average). I was surprised, because I expected the question to be about results that are well below average, including down into the range which meets formal criteria for a diagnosis of mental retardation. I expected the PhD students to share my surprise, and to stare back at my colleague with puzzled expressions. But, as is often enough the case when the instincts of the senior person misalign with those of a more junior, more plugged-in colleague, virtually all the students raised their hands. That is, they expressed discomfort with the idea of accurately informing people of their IQ level, unless that level happened to be above average.

The headline of a May 2014 *National Journal* article read "Average Americans Think They're Smarter Than the Average American." Given the current cultural zeitgeist, this hardly comes as a surprise, but what was somewhat surprising was that only around 60% of people thought they were intellectually above average (and above average in other ways too).[7] No wonder the TV game show *Are You Smarter Than a Fifth Grader?* was popular; everyone thinks they're smarter not just than a fifth-grader but smarter too than pretty much everyone else. If younger and younger cohorts are more and more impressed with themselves, this percentage may rise, and the implications of a population of which 75% or so think they are a smarter than everyone else are disquieting.

Self-regard and self-reference are all around us, so pervasive that they go unnoticed even when obviously absurd. As I have mentioned, the first time I tried to use the camera on my new phone, I was befuddled, because regardless of where I aimed the camera, the image was of me. It dawned on me that the camera was to take a picture of *oneself*. The well-known pop singer Taylor Swift counsels her fans "Just be yourself"—sound enough advice—but then adds "there is no one better." In one night of recent TV viewing, I saw a billboard at an English Premier League soccer match that read "Make the next 12 months count, the year of you," a commercial that asserted that "every woman deserves to be a star," another equating extremely dangerous life-threatening behavior with one's own sense of power and agency, still another commercial involving a boy practicing swinging at a baseball, and a reality TV show set in a pawn shop.

The ad with life-threatening imagery features an individual making a big landing, the idea being that if one subscribes to the satellite television company DirecTV, one will have made an impressive landing, complete with control and connectedness. So far, so good I suppose, but the problem is that these "landings" are powerful and destructive toward innocent bystanders. In perhaps the most egregious example, an individual makes his "landing" on a frozen lake. His impact destroys the very thick ice, and while he himself makes a nifty escape, there is a couple ice skating on the lake. The commercial leaves the specific fate of this couple unclear, but things do not look good for them: They are some distance from shore on the now-broken ice, and our last glimpse of them indicates concerned expressions on their faces and suggests that they are starting to fall. Even allowing for the fact that such imagery is not meant to be interpreted literally, the undercurrent is nonetheless disquieting.

I imagine that the special effects imagery is designed to appeal to the senses, as well as to viewers' desire to feel powerful. A moment's reflection, however, reveals the appalling implication, even if fictional, that a modest increase in one's own sense of agency is worth the terror, agony, and deaths of others.

The commercial about the boy practicing baseball began with the boy tossing the ball into the air, swinging, and missing badly ... strike one. With a determined expression, he tries again, and misses just as badly ... strike two. Now with an uncertain expression—and accompanied by dramatic background music—he tries a third time.

Given the self-aggrandizing cultural tendencies this book decries, I expected a "Rocky"-esque triumph for this youngster—perhaps a home run—but my expectations were disconfirmed ... temporarily. The boy misses badly ... strike three. A momentary ripple of disappointment passes over his face, followed by an expression of growing revelation and his exclamation, "I was meant to be a pitcher."

This commercial was of the public service variety, sponsored by a state or regional educational council, and meant to encourage optimism in youth. There is certainly a place for optimism in many life contexts, but—and this is where I found the commercial aggravating—there is also a place for learning from one's mistakes, facing failure and disappointment, and moving on to other pastures that might be greener or otherwise more suitable.

Almost as if planned (or perhaps it was planned), this hyperoptimistic commercial was embedded within the show about the pawn shop, in which a woman expressed the desire to buy a ring. She was asked if the occasion were perhaps an engagement, to which she replied, with a self-satisfied smile, that she wanted to commemorate her commitment to herself.

This is not an isolated example. There is a movement afoot called self-marriage (with news articles on the phenomenon using phrases like "with this ring I me wed"). For the self-marriage ceremony, invitations are issued, a wedding ceremony is held, and often there is a reception afterwards as well, all as with a traditional marriage. A cultural development of this sort tends to come with neologisms, and this one is no exception: Self-marriage is also known as "sologamy." It should be noted that the idea is not entirely about self-centeredness; instead, it is motivated, at least in part, by a desire to buck societal pressure to get married. Nevertheless, the self-focus of the movement is undeniable; one of its tenets is "Becoming your own lover, best friend, and parent/child." To view one's self as one's own lover is a questionable start, and then to add that one should *also* relate to one's self as one's own child can be viewed as creepy.

Needless to say, the idea is being marketed online, with people offering self-marriage courses for a fee. A typical one costs $200, which buys weekly group "telecalls" on self-marriage topics as well as a one-on-one 20-minute coaching session. A slogan of one of these programs is "You are invited to walk down the aisle of your own heart and meet yourself unveiled."[8]

My wife is Mexican and thus Roman Catholic in culture if not in faith; she therefore wanted us to be wed in a Catholic church in Mexico City, and as often happens, she got what she wanted. The priests viewed me warily for a few reasons I imagine, one of them certainly being that I am not Catholic. My wife and I needed to be quite diligent and persistent to finally persuade them, and even then, I doubt we spent 10 total hours in marriage training, even though we did participate in Pre-Cana (a required course of premarital consultation; the name is from the biblical wedding feast at Cana, which is where Jesus turned water into wine, alas a service that was not offered to us).

Pre-Cana was enjoyable for my wife and me, and through it we did more formal premarital consultation than most everyone we know. But we did not do as much as what is contained in the self-marriage courses, and this strikes me as discordant. If you are marrying yourself, shouldn't you do less not more premarital counseling, because you already understand how the person you're marrying (you) runs a household or handles finances?

This is certainly no rant in favor of "one man, one woman" marriage, with its cringe-inducing slogan of "it's Adam and Eve, not Adam and Steve" (for me one source of cringing is that I cannot hear this in my head in other than the voice of a loud and large American white male, rather lacking in mental acuity, and with a Southern accent. It doesn't help my cringing that all but two of the last sentence's descriptors apply to me [I am neither especially loud nor lacking in mental acuity]). Rather the argument is against the extreme solipsism of self-marriage. If one wanted to marry a virtue or a profession, as some functionally do, I would respect the sense of devotion to principle and service. It is noteworthy that in professions in which honor and service are particularly salient themes (e.g., the military, law enforcement), there are ceremonies formally marking an individual's sustained commitment, not unlike marital vows. These events are often moving because of their emphasis on serving others and sacrifice; I have looked, but cannot find the sacrifice and service in self-marriage.

There is a recursive aspect to an idea like self-marriage, with the self being reflected back onto the self. I do not intend to be too hard on advocates of self-marriage—there are aspects of it that people find both freeing and centering, and if one has felt burned or excluded by the institution of marriage, one might be compelled to spurn it in turn—but, depending on the context, recursion can feel creepy. One possible example of creepy recursion is described in Michael Bailey's book *The Man Who Would Be Queen*. I say "possible" example, because the book's main claim is very controversial and hotly debated (the extreme and drawn-out nature of this controversy is described in Alice Dreger's 2015 book *Galileo's Middle Finger*).

Bailey believes that all transgender men who, through surgical procedures, become women, fall into one of two non-overlapping groups. The first, mostly uncontroversial group includes those who easily "pass" as women. According to Bailey, these women really *are* women in identity, in their own minds, in the minds of others, and postoperatively in their bodies (interestingly, to my knowledge, among the very few people who in any way contest the womanhood of this group are certain feminists, who contend that because these women had been men, and therefore enjoyed all the favors society unfairly bestows on men, they can never truly understand full womanhood, and thus can never embody it; feminist Germaine Greer endorsed this view in late 2015).

The other, highly controversial group according to Bailey is made up of those who do not easily pass as women, certainly preoperatively, but also postoperatively. In Bailey's view, members of this group are men in their basic identity, but desire the body of a woman for fetishistic reasons. Bailey's term for this group, following that of sexuality researcher Ray Blanchard, is *autogynephilia*.

Many individuals whom Bailey would view in this way heatedly dispute the perspective, insisting that they are women trapped in men's bodies (or were preoperatively). Perhaps they also resent the characterization of a fetish so pronounced that one undergoes sex reassignment surgery to satisfy it. They would of course rightly resent the characterization if it were false, but might also if it were true and they wanted to conceal the fact. I am unsure as to whether Bailey's claims are overstated or not, but given the reasoning and evidence he marshals, it strikes me as more likely than not that autogynephilia exists, at least in a few individuals. If so, it's a free country, and I have no interest in judging people's interests, values, and identities (as long as they do not unduly infringe on those of others, e.g., as self-indulgence often does). There is little doubt, however, that many will find this condition (if valid) as unsettlingly recursive, the self surgically altered not to enhance appearance in the eyes of others (as with many procedures in plastic surgery), but primarily to enhance its relationship with itself, and a sexualized relationship at that.

In this time of ineffectual and hysterical North Carolina bathroom laws, I rush to reiterate that none of the foregoing is intended or should be used to detract from LGBT (i.e., lesbian, gay, bisexual, and transgender) rights. Indeed, an impetus for the movement for equal rights is the individual's freedom, equality, and access to justice *in relation to* the rest of society. Animating this view is the construal of the self as at once autonomous and as a small, single member among many of a larger polity, implying both individual rights as well as responsibility and duty to others. This view, as we will see, not only occasioned the stunning David-and-Goliath-type victory on the North American continent of isolated colonial settlers' children and grandchildren over a world superpower, but is also one that held sway over stoic philosophers at about the time of Jesus' birth. I have nothing but reverence for this set of values and ideas, as well as for the women and men who serve, protect, fight, and die for them on all of our behalf. In these pages I protest recursive egoism, as well as its manifestation in movements like corrupted mindfulness (but not authentic mindfulness). If Bailey's presentation of autogynephilia is correct, it would be a sign of the times *not* because of connection to LGBT rights—the latter not so much a sign of the times as a sign of progress toward full human rights—but rather, a sign of the times because it epitomizes the self in recursive relation to the self, just as does self-marriage, "selfie" obsessions, and narcissistic personality disorder.

Barbara Ehrenreich has noticed, in my view quite accurately, the self-contained and recursive aspects of a fellow traveler to the mindfulness movement, gratitude. In a *New York Times* editorial, she points out the highly ironic truth that an activity that should be by definition interpersonal and humble is often reduced to a self-focused and inane recursion. She wrote, "... it's possible to achieve the recommended levels of gratitude without ... uttering a word. All you have to do is to generate, within yourself, the good feelings associated with gratitude, and then bask in its warm, comforting glow. If there is any loving involved in this, it is self-love, and the current hoopla about gratitude is a celebration of onanism." She concludes that authentic gratitude "may require getting up from the yoga mat."[9]

The dissertation of my former student, Jen Hames, PhD, was motivated in part by the suspicion that the benefits of gratitude have been exaggerated, and that there may be some people for whom gratitude exercises carry no benefits and maybe even some costs. She recruited undergraduates who, according to their scores on various measures, were vulnerable to depression and suicidal thinking, and randomly assigned them to one of three conditions: (1) daily listing of five things for which one was grateful, for 2 weeks; (2) daily listing of five priorities, for 2 weeks; and (3) daily typing of five random words, sent to participants by the researcher, for 2 weeks. Two months after the interventions had ended, participants were assessed for things like depression levels and suicidal ideation. Those randomly assigned to the gratitude condition had the worst profile of the three groups, which is a worrisome finding in light of the fact that gratitude, like mindfulness, has become pervasive. In my travels in the first half of 2016, I stayed in perhaps a dozen hotels, almost all of which had a placard on the bed promoting Arianna Huffington's book on sleeping better; the final tip read "Before you turn off the lights, write a list of what you are grateful for." Another of the tips, inevitably, includes reference to meditation and yoga.

I have always been impressed with the rather ingenious study design used by anxiety researchers to show that facing one's fears is stronger medicine than medicine. The idea is to randomize anxiety sufferers to one of two groups. One group is treated with medicine, but specifically advised to not face their fears; the other group is treated with placebo and is encouraged to get out and about and face up to feared situations. A difference in anxiety levels would point clearly to the active ingredient in anxiety reduction. Results indicated that medicine absent facing fears did not work, whereas facing fears absent medication did. One wonders what similar designs testing the effects of gratitude and mindfulness regimes would produce. If a group is told to practice gratitude and/or mindfulness but is advised to be physically sedentary, and another group was told to be physically active but encouraged to be mindless and/or ungrateful, I would bet on the latter doing better than the former. I would bet on this in general, but, in light of the findings from the dissertation just described, I would particularly bet on this pattern of findings for the depression-prone.

One possible reason for the potential backfiring effect of gratitude is that depression-prone people may find generating gratitude levels challenging and thus dispiriting. Another possibility relates to Ehrenreich's observation: Perhaps it is not best for vulnerable people to be in mental conversation with themselves about how positive they should be feeling. Indeed, recursive thought in the form of rumination about one's flaws and emotions is highly characteristic of major depressive disorder.

The occasional recursive process can be charming, for example, a cat's chasing its tail. It is charming because it is not self-conscious, and indeed, that is what also makes it mildly humorous. In addition, it is a useful training exercise for hunting, allowing practice for tracking and occasionally catching something that is behind the cat and moving from the cat's peripheral vision into its blind spot behind it. Navel-gazing in humans lacks all of these properties and thus lacks charm.

Indeed, nature tends to frown upon most recursions. It offends the mind when in the illogical form of a tautology; it offends nature when in the form, for example, of inbreeding; and it offends our bodies when in the form of virulent biological recursion machines like various viruses and cancers. The writer of Ecclesiastes (1:5) frowned upon recursion in the following lines of lament:

> The sun rises, and the sun goes down,
> and hastens to the place where it rises.
> The wind blows to the south
> and goes around to the north;
> around and around goes the wind,
> and on its circuits the wind returns.

It is no coincidence that these same verses contain the phrases "all things are full of weariness" and "all is vanity."

The current mindfulness scene is steeped in recursion, and this can apply even to the more credible aspects of it. For example, acceptance and commitment therapy (ACT) is a collection of clinical strategies, with empirical support,[10] emphasizing experiential nonavoidance and behaving in ways consistent with a commitment to one's values. One of the slogans for an ACT meeting called the "Founders BootCamp" in 2014 was "values feeding values"—a frank recursion. Furthermore, I cannot let the topic pass without noting the irritation and even offense caused to my perhaps over-serious mentality by the title Founders BootCamp. First, though I realize it may be unfashionable and I am more aware than most of their shortcomings, I revere the actual Founding Fathers of the United States (especially but not only Jefferson, Madison, Monroe, and Washington, in that order) and resent any hint of the comparison of the living to them . . . and that is anyone living, and certainly the originators of ACT. Second, I have never heard the self-reference "founder," not once in my more than 50 years of listening, to be anything other than an exaggeration of the importance of the individual in question, and I have never heard the actual founders of important intellectual movements to self-refer as "founders." Third, it is my impression that those involved in ACT tend not to have served in the military, and even tend to hold at least mild antimilitary sentiments. The use of the term "BootCamp" may thus not sit well with some of our men and women in uniform and our veterans who are familiar with actual boot camps. My guess is that they would have a similar reaction, incidentally, to a company called "Warrior One." Despite the name, the company has little to do with active duty service members or with veterans. As documented in the June 18, 2015, *Wall Street Journal*, "Warrior One" is a mindfulness coaching firm, founded in the San Francisco Bay area. The reference in the company's name is intended as an homage to the mystical warrior-kings of Tibet.[11]

Recursion and superficiality tend to encourage one another. In describing one of his prodigiously self-regarding psychopathic patients, psychiatrist Hervey Cleckely in *The Mask of Sanity* quotes the patient thusly: "I am in love with love."[12] The reference of the quote were his many sexual relationships in which he took advantage of women. The shallowness and superficiality of the patient's words and attitude are plain to see. In his book *Farewell Fear*, Theodore Dalrymple commented on the current "systematic over-estimation of the importance not so much of emotion, as of the expression of emotion—one's own emotion, that is. . ... Saying nothing, but with sufficient emotional vehemence or appearance of sincerity, has become the mark of the serious man."[13] (Woman too, if professors I know are representative).

Recursion is not randomly distributed across society, and this certainly includes the academy. Rather, it clusters in a clump of disciplines, fields, and intellectual movements—psychoanalysis, much of the modern humanities, faux mindfulness. To choose but one of many examples, I served on the committee of a humanities dissertation and heard a committee faculty member pose to the young aspirant the question "What is a postcolonial writer?" I was not certain of the answer myself, and so was mildly eager to hear it and learn. The answer, however, was "a postcolonial writer is one who engages with postcolonial themes." It was said with gravity and a certain amount of emotion and flourish, and no one except me batted an eye. As everyone in the room blankly stared at me in my lack of attunement, I stared back and noticed that I was alone in yet another regard: Everyone else's hair, male and female alike, was teased up with product. The experience left me unable to discern whether that meant anything other than I was the only member present of the "bald community" (to use Larry David's memorable *Curb Your Enthusiasm* term). Regarding the sketch of the posturing professor near the beginning of this book (which I have already characterized as a "lampoon" and was tempted to describe as a "caricature," but resisted because the type is so common on campuses), if you do not recognize the type on your campus, I can infer two probable things about you: (1) You are in a science department; and (2) you have not looked hard enough, especially at departments in the humanities and allied fields.

That these quarters of the campus tend to tease up flourishes, if not always in their hair, then in their ideas, is unmistakable. The flourishes are often trivial or obtuse, can be byzantine in their ornate detail, are improvised from basic and sound principles, and in the process sully those very ideas, and then are treated as if they were not totally derivative, but have meanings on their own, sometimes profound ones. I have the impression that this tendency has been encouraged as an unfortunate byproduct of an otherwise legitimate intellectual effort, namely chaos theory, with its emphasis on emergent properties of complex systems.

I have nothing against genuine complex systems, those the complexity of which has an actual point. For example, the vehicle that will take astronauts to Mars will be a stunningly complex work. In the building of this marvel, the National Aeronautics and Space Administration (NASA) and perhaps others will add complexity essentially only for two interrelated reasons: (1) to add layers of redundancy, so that if one system fails, another is ready to back it up; and (2) when a complex solution is demonstrably the best one for mission success and survival. Nature evolved complexity in life for similar reasons. This is complexity as a means to a clear end. The modern versions of complexity one struggles to bear in some areas of the campus have no end, no point, other than complexity itself—a full recursion.

I have encountered several times a version of this trend that I have come to think of as "the novelist's fallacy" (it could also be called "the poet's fallacy," or perhaps more inclusively, "the artist's fallacy"). The notion is that fiction is or can be truer than truth; the wiser the holder of such attitudes is, the more likely that he or she will qualify the statement along the lines of "great fiction can be *almost* truer than truth, giving us an enriched and deeper perspective to understand reality itself." I can more or less accept this latter, wiser version, though it seems to me that there are many ways to refine one's perspective other than reading fiction (e.g., reading non-fiction). One of my most recent encounters with the fallacy, however, was not of the qualified sort: An individual, in all seriousness and with no sarcasm, stated in an National Public Radio (NPR) interview that in his medium he produced "the *true* true."[14] His medium is not fiction, or actually, in a way, it is: He scripts what will occur in bouts of professional wrestling. The fallacy can occur even to artists of genius. Of his sculpture *She-goat*, Picasso remarked that it "seems more real than a real goat." I had the privilege to see the Picasso sculpture exhibit at New York City's Museum of Modern Art in October 2015, including the sculpture in question. The collection represents a colossal achievement on Picasso's part, but not one of the sculptures struck me at least as "more real than real," and reading that quote in the museum's notes detracted (albeit in a very minor way) from an otherwise stunning exhibit. The artist's fallacy, at least in its unleavened and rather dull version, enshrines flourishes on truth as truth itself. This recursive instinct is a sign of our times; ideas bend back on themselves and people take "selfies" of, well, themselves.

The mindfulness literature is replete with recursive elements. In Kabat-Zinn's *Mindfulness for Beginners*, he encourages readers to ponder questions like "Is my awareness of my fear, my trepidation, my worry, my anxiety frightened?" "Is my awareness of the pain in pain?" and "Is my awareness of my sadness sad, my depression depressed, or my feeling worthless worthless?" These questions are intended to be helpful, even profound, and to give perspective—and in certain contexts if explained well they can—but I think it is just as viable to view them as confusing. Moreover, they are vulnerable to the charge on logical grounds that they produce an infinite loop (as recursions not seldom do), in that the pondering of awareness of awareness invites awareness of that, and then awareness of that new awareness, and so on, without end. Perhaps the pondering of this infinity strikes some as philosophically exciting, but it is just as defensible to view it as futile. Notice, too, the self-directed nature of the questions: They are about *my* suffering, not the substantially more important question, in the scheme of things, of others' suffering.

In this age of self-administered feces checkers (yes, that exists, and not to monitor illness along with a physician, mind you, but rather to gaze inward at one's own gut environment) and turning one's own DNA into art (also true), creepy forms of recursion are unsurprising. And we will encounter them again later—they will recur in these pages just as they do elsewhere.

In the 2012 book *Farewell Fear*, Theodore Dalrymple described an incident in which people unbeknownst to them had been poisoned at their work place by a serial poisoner: ". . . despite being hardly able to walk or to hold anything down, they insisted that they would soon be all right, and continued to try to work. Above all, they did not want to make a fuss, until some of them were admitted as emergencies to hospital." Dalrymple characterized this, admiringly, as "deeply old-fashioned stoicism and devotion to duty." The incident occurred in the 1970s.

On a wall at NASA's Launch Control Center in Cape Canaveral hang mission patches corresponding to every crewed spaceflight launched there. Each patch, with two exceptions, has a corresponding small plaque noting the launch and landing dates. The two exceptions are *Challenger* and *Columbia*; both launched, neither landed. There are thus blank spots on the wall where the two landing dates should have been. Both spots are discolored, the source of which is the touch of thousands and thousands of hands. As Margaret Dean observes in her absorbing 2015 book *Leaving Orbit*, these were not the hands of tourists, because tourists are very rarely permitted in the Launch Control building. No, these were the hands of "controllers, managers, and engineers who have been touching these empty spaces with their hands, on their way to and from doing their jobs."[15] There are similar phenomena at Clemson and Notre Dame, for example, as their football players touch a sacred spot on the way out to defend home field; as much as I love college football, the NASA example is the most moving.

Compare the reaction of the poisoned staff described by Dalrymple, or of NASA staff, to the modern professoriate, among many others, for whom the slightest physical discomfort often seems not only an excuse for inactivity but an opportunity for self-focused celebration. The woman mentioned earlier who wanted self-focused celebration in the form of a self-marriage ring was not interviewed about her past accomplishments, but whatever they may be, I expect that they will not compare well to those of Russian cosmonaut Alexei Leonov. He was the first human spacewalker, and when interviewed about the experience, he did not refer to things like self-commitment, but rather stated, "I was just a little speck of sand compared to that infinity."[16] Aldrin, the second man on the moon, wrote of the Apollo 11 effort, "Personally, in reflecting on the past several days, a verse from Psalms comes to mind: 'When I considered the heavens, the work of Thy fingers, the moon and the stars which Thou hast ordained, what is man that Thou art mindful of him.' "[17]

Armstrong, similarly accomplished as Aldrin and Leonov and the first human to set foot on any other heavenly orb besides earth, said of the first lunar landing, "It was special and memorable, but it was only instantaneous because there was work to do ... That's why we were there, we weren't there to meditate, we were there to get things done and so we got on with it."[18] Aldrin said in a 2014 *GQ Magazine* interview, "People want to put down in writing something about how [we] were feeling. Look, we didn't know what we were feeling. We weren't feeling." He added, "It's something we did. Now we should do something else," referring to a trip to Mars.

Months before the Apollo 11 triumph, Armstrong was training for the mission in a vehicle that simulated the lunar module he and Aldrin would later fly to the moon. The vehicle badly malfunctioned; within a few seconds it careened back to earth in a fiery explosion that lit up the Texas morning sky. An instant before impact, Armstrong ejected, saving his life. Later that same morning, Armstrong was back at his desk, just like he was routinely whenever not training, calmly at work, as if he had not almost died a couple of hours before. His astronaut colleagues love to tell that story about Armstrong, and they told it to an interviewer, who asked him about the incident. Armstrong answered, ". . . well, yeah, there was work to be done back at the office and so I thought I better go get on with it."

Armstrong and Aldrin have consistently sounded this refrain in the decades since the magisterial journey of Apollo 11 (Armstrong died in 2013). An exchange observed between Aldrin and a production crew by the 2014 *GQ* article author went like this:

> "What were your emotions as you walked on the surface of the moon?"
> "Fighter pilots don't have emotions."
> "But you're a human!"
> "We had ice in our veins."
> "Was there a feeling of awe and majesty?"
> "There wasn't any time to do that, really."

Some may dismiss this as astronaut bravado and posturing, and indeed both Armstrong and Aldrin have stated that they experienced profound if brief moments of exhilaration in the seconds after landing the lunar module on the moon. I am not one of those who would dismiss the genuine brevity of these moments and the prevailing ethic of "we have work to do," and would add that you dismiss people like this at your peril.

People like Armstrong, Aldrin, and Leonov were clear-eyed about their place in relation to things like the infinitude of the cosmos, or the epic accomplishment of Apollo 11, and yet they actually *were* unique in their accomplishments. (And, in a perfect touch, the Apollo 11 astronauts departed from tradition and refused to have their names on the mission patch. Aldrin said, "We felt the mission had a bigger meaning than that of the individuals involved."[19]) A similarly heroic sentiment appears in these words, from a Jewish man born into Nazi Germany in the 1930s: "I have come to a conclusion about myself. In 1938, I escaped the deportation of Poland, I got out of Germany in the Kindertransport, I was sent to Australia on a ship and the ship was torpedoed and nothing happened, I got back to England and was in the army, why all these coincidences, and I've come to one conclusion, I was meant to survive, not because myself, but so that Jews would survive, and I would bring up another generation, and they would live, and I look at my children and my grandchildren and I know there was a purpose to my life." These words from the 2000 film *Into the Arms of Strangers* were said with genuine emotion rising exactly in proportion to the selflessness of the sentiment.

People like this man and like the astronauts and cosmonauts would likely have trouble understanding the concept of a self-commitment ring or of Swift's views about everyone's uniqueness. They might also have trouble understanding the view that the self-esteem of children has to be protected at all costs, as if each child's self-view were as delicate and significant as the Ark of the Covenant itself (notice I did not say "each child" but rather "each child's self-view," for if it were the former, I would argue for significance but not delicacy). In 2013 on social media, a "news" story circulated that a community in Ontario, Canada, decided that youth soccer should be played with no ball so that the children's self-esteem would be spared the negative effects of competition. The story was a satire, but it was not viewed as such by wide swaths of social media, who took it as a true news report. The fact that the report seemed believable to so many reveals the extent to which the culture of the self is ascendant.

There are a few strands of evidence that support that trends in self-view are generational, even if Socrates voiced his "kids these days" complaints more than 2,400 years ago. One strand is local and anecdotal, and thus would not be persuasive except that it converges well with very rigorous research. My professional life is structured such that I have contact mostly with two age groups—PhD students in their 20s, and professors and other professionals who average approximately age 45. In social settings, I have asked members of each group a version of the following question: "Imagine that tomorrow NASA calls you and needs you to volunteer to go on a mission to Mars; imagine further that it all starts soon, like tomorrow. Would you agree to go?"

Human nature being what it is, there are of course a variety of responses, but they tend to fall into one of three categories: (1) an instant and enthusiastic agreement; (2) an even quicker and more visceral refusal; or (3) a tentative agreement, usually contingent on assurances that one's children would be provided for.

The first category of immediate agreement tends to occur in the group that is old enough to remember NASA's heyday, including Apollo 11's grand achievement. The question makes them become nostalgic, even a little misty eyed; the thought of being "Mars' Neil Armstrong" elicits feelings of honor and glory but also of selflessness and service. In my informal polling, around 7 of 10 in this age cohort have this reaction and are agreeable. This 70% figure squares well with that referred to in an April 22, 2013, *New Yorker* article. The author, who had worked at NASA's Jet Propulsion Laboratory (J.P.L.), wrote, "While I was at J.P.L., I heard talk of a survey, perhaps apocryphal, which asked astronauts if they'd go to Mars on a one-way trip. Three-quarters supposedly said yes." Unlike my informal poll, this survey (if it occurred) was specific to astronauts, and so high percentages of agreement are not surprising. However, unlike my little poll, this supposed survey is explicitly about a one-way trip, yet agreement remained high. Reflecting on this, the second person to set foot on the moon, Aldrin, said, "The pilgrims on the Mayflower didn't hang around Plymouth Rock waiting for a ship to take them back."

The 45 and older crowd tends to be agreeable in response to my little thought experiment. In contrast, the second category of response is instantaneous disagreement, and it is almost unique to the 20-somethings. They find the notion not just disagreeable but unimaginable and even revolting. Facial expressions of disgust at the idea are not uncommon in this age bracket. When queried, the dialog tends not to progress, because they cannot get past sentiments like "But why in the world *would* I go?" If presented with Aldrin's words about the pilgrims not waiting around for a ship to take them back, responses would include blinking incomprehension, or else comments like "Why'd they go in the first place?" The contrast between this reaction and the "one small step" feeling of the older crowd is stark indeed.

I do not wish to be excessively harsh in views of the younger generation. Perhaps it is simply smart to wish to avoid a trip to Mars. The novel *The Martian* (later made into a movie) describes an astronaut whose team had successfully ventured to Mars and established a small base, but who was left for dead in a frantic, storm-forced evacuation procedure. Against all odds, according to the story, he survives, and when NASA realizes the fact, his astronaut colleagues unequivocally want to rescue him, despite a likelihood that he and they will die as a result. They want to go nevertheless. "Naturally," says a NASA administrator, "astronauts are inherently insane. And really noble."

Maybe it is better—smarter—to be "sane" than noble. Facebook CEO Mark Zuckerberg told an audience in 2007, "Young people are just smarter."[20] (Many parents wish it were so [including me], but, to use 2007 lingo, LOL).

Moreover, in my Mars mini-survey, there certainly are several of the 20-somethings who volunteer eagerly. And, there are those who are 45 and older who are plainly mystified by anyone volunteering for a Mars trip. For example, in September 2013 on the ESPN radio show *Mike and Mike*, the hosts Mike Greenberg and Mike Golic—both older than 45—discussed the news item, current at the time, that more than 200,000 people applied to be considered for a one-way trip to Mars (a hoped-for—and, it should be noted, problem-ridden—venture of the non-profit Mars One Foundation). The reaction of the radio hosts was along the lines of "it's amazing what people will do for fame" (apparently a reality TV show is part of the planned venture), and also "how bad does your life have to be to want to be sent off to Mars?" Of course it is true that any number of motives is at play in why these 200,000 souls are willing to live and die on Mars, but among them are duty, honor, mission, and the good of humankind, things that in this instance escaped the usually clear-eyed Mike and Mike.

Similarly, after noting that the more than 200,000 willing space travelers came from 140 countries (with the United States, India, and China leading), NPR's Barbara King asked, "Still my question is this: Are people eager to leave behind everyone they love—for the rest of their lives—good candidates to succeed at forging a tight-knit colony on Mars? A colony that surely will require great sociability, shared good feelings, and cooperation to succeed?"[21] For this question to be at the forefront of one's mind requires forgetting or never knowing about the self-sacrifice, gregariousness, and bonhomie of the Apollo astronauts. One might counter, "yes, but NASA selected them," to which I reply "in a pool of 200,000, there will exist some of the 'right stuff.'" One might also counter, "yes, but the Apollo astronauts weren't leaving for the rest of their lives," to which I would reply, "tell that to the families of the Apollo I astronauts" (all were killed in a fire inside the rocket).

Regarding differences in attitudes on travel to Mars, we are talking trends here, generational rules-of-thumb. As a general rule, at least according to my amateurish research project on willingness to go to Mars, enthusiastic agreement tends to characterize the older crowd, while instantaneous rejection usually issues forth from the younger cohort.

There is a third category of "Yes but wait, what about my children?" and it occurs in parents of course, but more specifically, in parents of preteen children, the parents of teens and young adults having already adjusted, at least partially, to their children's "flying the nest." For the parents of preteen kids, once the fantasy is detailed such that the kids are well taken care of, this group comes to resemble the first, in that they mostly agree with the fantasized mission.

There is a clear generational trend to the results of my Mars survey, but of course, this little exercise is open to many criticisms and alternative explanations. Given its anecdotal and otherwise uncontrolled nature, perhaps it is so error-filled as to be meaningless. What would be a lot more convincing is a national poll, not necessarily on willingness to go to Mars specifically, but on things in general like patriotism and trust in others.

Happily, the Pew Research Center provided exactly that in a poll reported on in March 2014. Among the more striking results were historically low levels of social trust and of patriotism. In fact, more than 4 of 5 of those born between 1980 and 1995 (they were between 18 and 33 years old at the time of the survey) responded that, generally speaking, people cannot be trusted, and fewer than half believed the phrase "a patriotic person" applied to them. Perhaps their concerns are not with other people or their flag or country, but rather with something that supersedes all of them, like religion or the environment? Evidently not—only about a third are religious, and fewer than one in three endorse environmentalism as important.

Using the nationally representative General Social Survey of adults from the independent research organization NORC at the University of Chicago (1972–2012; N = 37,493) and the nationally representative Monitoring the Future survey of 12th-graders (1976–2012; N = 101,633), Jean Twenge and colleagues reported something similar in *Psychological Science* in 2014. They wrote, "Between 1972 and 2012 ... Americans became significantly less trusting of each other and less confident in large institutions, such as the news media, business, religious organizations, the medical establishment, Congress, and the presidency." In fact, levels of trust reached historic lows in 2012, lower even than during Watergate, during the Iran hostage crisis, and during the economic downturn of the late 2000s. While these researchers found that trust was declining in all age groups, they also noted that high school seniors in 2012 expressed notably lower trust than did their elders when they were at the same age of around 18. I confess that it is hard for me to argue with one of this team's dispiriting concluding sentiments: "The decline of social capital is a profoundly negative trend for a democracy, a system of government predicated on the few representing the interests of the many."

These trends are not only worrying for our polity, but they produce scenarios that are strange if not perverse. For example, if there were ever a time that one should have trust in medicine, ours is it. The advances have been staggering across numerous fields and almost all illnesses; however, never has trust in medicine been lower.[22] This paradox produces fertile ground for the undoing of decades of astounding progress (e.g., anti-vaccination views). This rather dismal trend may stem from people's increasing confidence that they are smarter than average; if they believe they are smarter than the average person, perhaps they think they are smarter than the average physician. That this is vanishingly unlikely appears to exceed their reasoning abilities, a profound irony.

Most everyone these days seems to feel special, and yet, relatively few believe that others are particularly special. What this adds up to is a lot of people whose self-perceived uniqueness goes unrecognized by others, a recipe for increasing levels of disappointment and anger. A recent study has shown increasing levels of disappointment and anger ... on the faces of Lego minifigures. Researchers found increasing negativity on the faces of more recent versions of the figurines.[23] Interestingly, the authors worried what effect this may have on children going forward (a reasonable question), but it is also worth focusing on where the trend came from, and a plausible explanation involves increasing levels of entitlement and distrust in the adults designing the toys.

Younger cohorts appear not to care much, then, about things like patriotism and trust in each other. What *do* they care about then? Their own economic future, for one thing. For another, gay rights. These two things may seem irrelevant to one another, but they do have one commonality: Both are about *self*-determination (one's own economic freedom in one case, the inherent rights of individuals regardless of sexual orientation in the other). If a focus on the self is driving the overall response patterns of this age group, one might expect very high rates of self-focus. Using "selfies" as an index of self-focus, this expectation is borne out, as well over half in the younger age cohort had not only *taken* such a photograph but had also *posted* at least one online. Compare this to the situation in those 50 and older: Large percentages had not only never taken a "selfie," much less posted it online, but do not know what the term itself even means (despite the fact that it has gotten plenty of attention, including being named "word of the year" by Oxford Dictionaries in 2013, another sign of the times).

If this younger age group views themselves as special and unique individuals, then not only will they post "selfies" and other personal information freely, but they will simultaneously be of the view that people generally share too much information online, that is, they are the special, individual exception to a general rule that applies (to everyone else). In fact, 90% of people in this age group endorse the view that people share too much personal information online, even as they themselves regularly post just such information.

This last poll item—the one on whether people post too much online—is one of the very few that meets both of the following criteria: Quite substantial majorities endorse it (more than 90% in the case of "too much online"), and no generational differences—people in their 20s and those 50 and older and everyone in between agree on "too much online personal information." What this means is that for the older groups, sentiments and behaviors are aligned; they endorse "too much private information online" *and* are sparing in what they actually post online. By contrast, the younger group (called "Millennials," wryly referred to on the website Jezebel as "history's most pesky generation") endorses the "too much online" view and frequently violates it.

Of course this kind of "everyone has to follow the rules except me" attitude is not limited to younger people. A glaring example occurred in Florida in 2014, when 71-year-old Curtis Reeves shot and killed a man inside a movie theater, because the latter refused to stop texting. The man's wife was also shot but survived. Reeves' egregious deed was made all the more so by the fact he himself had been texting in the theater just minutes before. In fact Reeves had been texting his adult son his seat location in the theater, so that the son could find him. The son found the father only in the flash of the gunshot (and tried to save the wounded man but was unable to). The victim, too, was texting with his child at the time of the incident.

Returning to the findings and implications of the Pew survey, the older age groups' behavior is of course key for comparison, to make better sense of the younger generation's reported attitudes and values. In the foregoing, it is implied that younger people are substantially less patriotic, less trusting, and so on, as compared to older cohorts, and that is often true (e.g., regarding social trust, the Millennials are at 19%, whereas no other group is below 30%). What is also frequently the case in this Pew survey is that the 18- to 33-year-olds are being compared to older groups *when the latter were 18 to 33 themselves*. The pattern is thus not easily attributable to youth or aging; rather, it seems *generational*—when one generation was young, they mostly responded differently as compared to how to the Millennial generation is responding in their relative youth.

A similar issue arises regarding my little Mars survey. Perhaps the pattern of the older respondents' eagerness to go really is not about generational differences, but rather about age differences. That is, had the 40-somethings been interviewed 20 years ago, when they were in their 20s, their reactions might have been like those of modern-day 20-somethings; and had those currently in their 20s been interviewed 20 years hence, when they will be in their 40s, their reactions might have involved the nostalgia, pride, and selflessness of the current 40-somethings.

The Pew results, however, do not support this possibility, and neither does an unsettling note from the "Findings" section of the November 2013 issue of *Harper's Magazine*: "Young white Americans feel more empathy for beaten puppies than for identically beaten adults." This latter phenomenon is robust and can be seen in numerous contexts, including people's reactions to movies: If a human is killed, not much of a reaction; if a pet is killed, reactions of horror (if you doubt this, see www.doesthedogdie.com). I will resist moral commentary and just state a related fact: There are studies in which, in hypothetical scenarios, people choose to save their dogs over a human stranger. In one such study,[24] 40% of participants reported that they would save their own dog over a foreign tourist; the percentage dropped, but only slightly, to 37% if, instead of a foreign tourist, the human in question is a hometown stranger. A further percentage drop occurred if the human in question is now a distant cousin—now 23% would save the dog instead of the cousin. Relatively few would save their dog over their best friend, their grandmother, or their brother, but the figures are all above zero: 6%, 3%, and 2%, respectively. When asked if they would save a *strange* dog over their grandmother, more than 2% indicated they would.

The authors of a 2015 *New York Times* opinion piece[25] helpfully noted some limits to this lamentable truth. This authorship team accepted that "... [w]hile a single crying child or injured puppy tugs at our heartstrings, large numbers of suffering people, as in epidemics, earthquakes and genocides, do not inspire a comparable reaction." However, the team described a study identifying conditions under which the reactions are reversed.[26] Participants in the study read excerpts about children who were refugees from Darfur, Sudan. Half of the participants read about eight such children, whereas half read about only one such child. Within these two groups, participants were further subdivided into those who were given the impression that they would be asked to make a financial donation to aid the refugee(s) and those who did not have that expectation. The subgroup who read about eight children with no expectations of financial obligation felt more empathy toward them than did the other three subgroups.

It would appear, therefore, that empathic reactions and related states such as selflessness can be nudged into salience. This in turn has practical implications of how to rein in selfishness, mindless mindfulness, and their ilk.

Scholarship conducted by psychologists Twenge, Keith Campbell, and others has established that, indeed, characteristics like narcissism and low empathy are more prevalent in today's youth as compared to the youth of yesteryear. In a representative study, these researchers pooled data from 85 different samples of young American adults, all of whom had completed a measure of narcissism when they were in college between 1979 and 2006. In a combined sample of well over 16,000 respondents, there was a very clear association between year of data collection and narcissism levels, such that those who completed the measure in the late 1970s and early 1980s had substantially lower narcissism levels than those who were assessed in more recent cohorts. In fact, approximately two-thirds of recent participants scored above the 1979–1985 mean narcissism scale, reflecting an overall increase in narcissism of around 30%.[27]

It is intriguing to view these results in light of the Pew survey mentioned earlier. Over the same time frame examined by the narcissism researchers, the Pew team found compatible results, despite being a fully independent group, with different conceptual frameworks and using different assessments and different samples. The convergence of findings adds confidence to the bottom-line conclusion of a recent surge in indices related to self-interest.

Still, there have been critics of this work. At websites like Gawker (now shuttered, as noted) and Jezebel, one can regularly read articles and commentary ridiculing the "Millennials are selfish" line—these editorials do not offer much analysis beyond outright dismissal, and nearly all are written and read, it should be remembered, by a virtually 100% Millennial group. Psychologist Chris Ferguson, writing in a 2015 issue of *American Psychologist*, referenced the term "juvenoia," a neologism coined by sociologist David Finkelhor. As neologisms go, this one is not bad; it is meant to denote the sin of blaming or demeaning today's youth (a sin—if it is one—of which I am and will be again guilty). Perhaps more substantively, some have raised such questions as whether the measure often used in this research (the Narcissistic Personality Inventory) is valid, and whether one can generalize from college students to other young adults. In reply, the measure is imperfect, but usable, as dozens of studies have shown, and similar results have been produced with other measures (e.g., see the Pew findings). Regarding the focus on college students, entry to college has become more inclusive over the years, and one would think that this would produce less and less narcissistic cohorts, and yet the opposite is true. It is certainly the case that college students are not perfectly representative of young adults in general, but it is also the case that college campuses represent an increasingly diverse cross section of the young adult population.

Other criticisms are more conceptually interesting, but here again, they seem to mostly miss the mark. For example, one scholar has pointed out that as narcissism levels rose, levels of impulsivity did not, reasoning that this pattern undermines the narcissism findings because narcissism levels and impulsivity levels should rise and fall in lockstep.[28] This argument is based on the assumption of a close connection between narcissism and impulsivity (the tendency to act rashly without much forethought), an assumption that is dubious in its own right. There are many individuals who are entitled and grandiose but who have reasonably good impulse control, just as there are many who, in part because of their poor impulse control, do not feel very good about themselves (much less entitled and grandiose). Adding stable impulsivity into the overall picture of a rise in narcissism does not change or undermine the story; rather, if anything, it makes it more ominous. One interpretation of the overall pattern of results is that more recent cohorts have become more narcissistic while retaining reasonable impulse control and can thus be unwavering in their selfishness.

Thus, although there have been some doubts raised about it, the preponderance of the evidence does seem to indicate a cultural swing toward self-regard, and this conclusion has emerged across a variety of methods and samples. A cultural shift toward narcissism would have numerous consequences, for example a turn toward the narcissistic can make mindfulness more mindless.

An important aspect of narcissism is *entitlement*, and one wonders whether more recent cohorts' rise in narcissism and entitlement may stem in part from growing up in times of relative bounty. In such circumstances, things may come more easily, leading to the attitude that it is in the nature of things that everyone deserves or is entitled to easy bounty. In fact, there is evidence to this effect.

Researchers reported that materialism has substantially increased over the last few generations.[29] This, in itself, is not necessarily a bad thing, because interest in nice things, money, and the like may serve as incentive to work harder. Alas, these researchers found that the rise in materialism was accompanied by an increasing distaste for work, a noxious combination.

There are rays of light peeking through the clouds, however. Starting from the premise that economic downturns will be especially hard on newcomers to the job market, a 2014 study reported that those who were in their early 20s at the time of an economic recession were significantly less narcissistic than their counterparts who came of age during better times. This finding was detected in a sample of more than 1,500 respondents, and then replicated in a sample of approximately 30,000 others.[30]

The effect even applied to CEOs. The latter study included more than 2,000 CEOs and focused on the discrepancy between the CEO's salary and that of a company's next highest paid employee. The discrepancy was significantly smaller for CEOs who came of age during challenging economic times.

Taken together, these findings suggest a braking mechanism on increases in narcissism. The rise in narcissism appears to be a real phenomenon, as it has been repeatedly demonstrated in an array of contexts. However, the serious economic recession starting in 2008 may restrain narcissism, such that those born around 1990 may prove to be *less* narcissistic than the cohorts that preceded them. However, there is recent evidence of parents' roles in fostering their children's narcissism: Parents who excessively coddle their children tend to have children who are narcissistic.[31] Those born around 1990 may not be less narcissistic if their parents' overvaluing them offsets any limits on narcissism created by coming of age during an economic downturn.

Several distinct lines of evidence are compatible with the view that attitudes toward the self have shifted in the last several decades. Twenge and colleagues' results on narcissism and materialism and the Pew results on several attitudinal trends paint a similar picture. If it is the case that features like entitlement have increased, this should be apparent in the grades that college students feel entitled to receive. As with these other generational trends, a change in grade distributions would be amenable to a number of explanations—for example, perhaps students and their parents have come to view themselves as consumers and universities as businesses that sell a product (part of that product presumably being A's as grades). Whether this latter outlook is itself a manifestation of a rise in narcissism is interesting to ponder, but in any event, it should be acknowledged that processes like rising grades are likely multidetermined. The convergence of trends across disparate domains like narcissism and the Pew societal findings, however, suggests that entitlement could be one driver of ever-increasing grades.

And make no mistake, grades are on the rise. It is rather astounding to report that in 1960, the most commonly assigned grade was not an A, not even a B, but rather, a C (in passing, it is interesting to note that President George W. Bush, a famous earner of C's in college, attended in the 1960s, the heyday of the C). Approximately 35% of all grades were Cs, followed by Bs (around 30%), and As and Ds were assigned at about the same 15% rate. By the time my generation matriculated, in the 1980s, inflation had begun: B had dethroned C as the most commonly assigned grade. By the 2000s A had not merely attained the throne, but stormed it: At Princeton, 47% of grades were A's, enough of a problem that the university instituted policies to try and rein in the rate to 35%. The effort worked, sort of: The rate went from around 47% to around 42%.[32] At Yale in 2012, 62% of grades were A's. This discrepancy between rates of earning A's of course dissatisfies Princeton undergraduates (who by policy will have lower grade point averages than their Yale counterparts), a fact that has undermined Princeton's efforts to drive the rate to about half that level—in fact, largely for this reason, the Princeton faculty voted to abandon the policy in late 2014. Mention of Princeton and Yale may suggest that this is a problem only among elite institutions, but that is not so. The problem is rampant across the American university landscape, as, to take examples of deep personal familiarity, professors at Tallahassee Community College and Florida State University regularly bemoan.

In a soliloquy decrying modern self-importance on the HBO show *True Detective*, Matthew McConaughey's character states, "In fact, everybody's nobody." Woody Harrelson's character retorts with a sentiment along the lines of "folks around here don't think like that," and his is the more likable and humorous view. But I think it may be a flawed one. I think Seamus Heaney got closer to the truth in the poem *Personal Helicon*:

> To stare, big-eyed Narcissus, into some spring
> Is beneath all adult dignity.

And so did Tony Judt, who had the excuse to be self-focused because he was dying from amyotrophic lateral sclerosis, but nevertheless wrote, "Why should everything be about 'me'? Are my fixations of significance to the Republic? Do my particular needs by definition speak to broader concerns? What on earth does it mean that 'the personal is political'?"[33]

Maya Angelou's last tweet, sent 5 days before her death on May 28, 2014, was "Listen to yourself and in that quietude you might hear the voice of God." What intrigues and vexes about such sentiments is that they can be and are interpreted in diametrically opposed ways. These statements can be seen to mean "you are inherently unique and important" or they can mean "you're an inconceivably small—indeed beyond trivial—bit of the universe, but, being a part, you therefore are literally of the stuff of the cosmos, just like everyone and everything." Angelou's poetry, other work, and previous statements can be viewed as supportive of either sentiment, and so can at least some of the current mindfulness scene—an ambiguity that the culture of the self has rushed in to resoundingly resolve in favor of self-importance and self-indulgence.

My dad's suicide was on a Wednesday, his body was discovered on a Friday, and we buried him on a Monday. On the intervening Saturday, I sobbed my life's hardest tears, in front of my mom, my uncle, and the undertaker, in the latter's office, as we were choosing my dad's headstone. I did not cry again for 10 months, until the morning of my next birthday.

When I woke on my birthday, my sequence of thought was something like "it's my birthday, my dad is dead, and this is the first birthday he's not around for," and I burst into tears. I am ashamed of this.

I am not ashamed of my dad or his death, any more than I would be if he died from a heart attack or cancer. He was a good man killed by a grave illness. I am not ashamed that I cried for him; in fact, I am rather glad I did. I am not ashamed that I sobbed in the presence of my mom and uncle, nor of the fact that a stranger was there too.

I am ashamed of the self-regard inherent in the "this is about me" line of thought and the consequent birthday tears. I am ashamed that I thought more about myself that birthday morning than I did about my dad and the misery he experienced before his death and the physical anguish he experienced during his death; thought about myself more than about my mother, whose husband just killed himself as her father had 20 years before; thought more about myself than about my sisters, the younger of whom was 11 years old at the time, and both of whom still lived, along with my mom, in the house from which my dad left in the middle of the night to kill himself. During those 10 months between my dad's death and my first subsequent birthday, the birthdays of my dad, mom, and both sisters passed, and I did not cry. I cried for mine, and I am ashamed of it.

And I learned from it. Around 25 years later, some of my friends and I were talking over drinks, and one of my friends told a tale about some guy's dad. The gist was that the dad was particularly fearsome and had even killed someone in a knife fight. My friend concluded, "Wouldn't we all like to have a dad who killed someone with a knife?" This struck me on many levels. First, I did have a dad like that; that is how my dad died. Second, no, I would not necessarily like to have had a dad who killed someone with a knife, suicide aside. Third, I had many doubts about the original story's veracity in the first place. In the modern culture of the self, this would have justified a long, histrionic harangue on my part, focused on my own aggrievement, pain, and so forth. In the event, I said not one word, and felt the better for it.

We humans are prone to fits of self-pity, some more so than others, and we can all get better at warding them off. Specific ways to do so are covered in a later chapter, but for now in the next chapter, I turn to more consequences of the toxic decline into self-centeredness.

The Adam of Your Labors
Further Societal Consequences of Solipsism

J UST AS THE MONSTER IN CONVERSATION WITH VICTOR
  Frankenstein refers to himself as "the Adam of your labors," so
has the cult of self-regard gone badly awry, running amok and tram-
pling on our culture. It is important to emphasize that this is a general trend, one which would have occurred even if faux mindfulness
did not exist. My argument is thus not that mindfulness is necessary
for proliferating self-obsession; rather, faux mindfulness has been
the key conduit, the Trojan horse, through which the larger culture's
turn toward the self has infected the mental health field and profession. As that infestation has progressed, mindfulness has departed
more and more from its original, sensible version.

Mindfulness can directly encourage solipsism and, especially recently, it does. An example has the sound of satire a la *The Onion*
and will remind readers of a certain age of a *Saturday Night Live*
sketch done by a now-senator, but it is from the *Wall Street Journal*:[1]
The article reports that at a college of law, under the umbrella of a
mindfulness program, "... students have bonded over an assignment

requiring them to stare at themselves in the mirror for five minutes and say loudly, 'I love me.'" The same article has a balanced approach and quotes mindfulness skeptics who are also lawyers. The article states that the skeptics "... say they have nothing against stress relief but doubt that a regimen of meditation, daily affirmations, and Qigong training will cure the ills of the profession." One specific lawyer, a criminal defense attorney, said that he thinks mindfulness "feeds the narcissism that being a lawyer should be fun, happy, and pleasant."

Just as I gave a genuine effort at the full-day mindfulness retreat I described already, I tried—at least for the first 90 seconds or so—to do this self-love exercise too. I couldn't stand it any longer, the combination of a literal physical nausea and a plummeting sense of self-respect making continuation impossible. Being familiar with the principles of habituation and of exposure therapies for various anxiety conditions, I am aware that I could, with sustained practice, work through my negative reactions and accomplish the full exercise with relative ease. Unlike those with severe phobias that plague their lives and of which they badly wish to be rid, I have no interest in losing my negative reaction to this self-love exercise. I would be overcome with shame.

In this context of a culture that accepts self-love as important, consider these words from Herbert Hendin's book *Seduced by Death*: "In a culture that fosters narcissism, aging and death are harder to bear." On this view, a swing toward narcissism may affect people's attitudes toward natural and inevitable things. Has it?

There is evidence to suggest so. For example, nowadays people wish to be younger, so much so that census takers know that people underreport their true age and adjust figures to account for it. In the 20th and 21st centuries that is. Before then, census takers also had to adjust, but in the opposite direction—people used to overreport their true age, in an effort to be considered older and thus more respected. As Atul Gawande writes in his book *Being Mortal*, "... studies of past censuses have revealed that [people] used to overstate [their age]. The dignity of old age was something to which everyone aspired."[2]

Moreover, in an ongoing effort led by Florida State University (FSU) psychologist Pam Keel, she and her colleagues (full disclosure: including me) collected information on attitudes, values, and the like, from college students enrolled in 1982, 1992, 2002, and 2012.

Additionally, each cohort was followed over time. This means, for example, that the 1982 cohort was first assessed as college students in 1982, but then assessed again in their late 20s in 1992, their late 30s in 2002, and their late 40s in 2012. At the 2012 assessment, the 2012 cohort was assessed for the first time as college students; also during 2012, the 1992 cohort was assessed in their late 30s, and the 2002 cohort, in their late 20s. This design, similar to the Pew survey, allows glimpses of trends related to aging (e.g., How does a group look in their late 30s, as compared to how its members looked when they were in college?), and it also allows examination of generational differences (e.g., Do college students in 1982 display different attitudes than college students in 2012?).

A focus of the ongoing project was eating disorders, and serendipitously for the present purposes, we used an abbreviated form of a mainstay of eating disorder questionnaires, which contains, in addition to predictable things like bingeing, purging, and body dissatisfaction, a subscale measuring "maturity fears." (The story of why an eating disorder measure would include items on maturity fears is an interesting one in itself, the short version of which is that some strands of mid-20th-century thought, now largely discredited, attributed disorders of eating to arrested development.) If it is true that a culture of narcissism encourages maturity fears, and if indeed an age of narcissism has dawned, then it follows that maturity fears should be on the increase from 1982 to the present.

That is precisely the result.[3] More specifically, every 10-year interval witnessed a significant increase in maturity fears: Those tested in 1992 were significantly more fearful than those tested in 1982; those in 2002, more than those in 1992; and those in 2012, more than those in 2002.

Perhaps, one might counter, these trends were not specific to maturity fears but applied, as well, to other things measured in the surveys. This, however, was ruled out: There were no clear generational trends with regard to things like dissatisfaction with one's body or motivation to be thinner. Maturity fears stood out as a characteristic that steadily rose, decade by decade, from 1982 to 2012.

As we have noted in our publications from this project, all participants hailed from a "selective northeastern university." We usually leave it at that, but the university in question was selective indeed—it was Harvard—naturally leading to questions about whether results would generalize beyond the ivy-covered walls of our country's oldest university (this latter fact is occasionally disputed, not very persuasively).

From 2001 to 2012, we collected similar data from undergraduates from FSU, and unlike in the Harvard sample, we used the full, unabbreviated measure from which the Maturity Fears subscale is derived. We thus had the Harvard sample, collected geographically in the northeast on students who came from all 50 states and from around the world, and we had the FSU sample, who mostly came from the state of Florida. In both samples, the last assessment occurred in 2012, but in the Harvard sample, the interval leading up to 2012 was 30 years whereas in the FSU sample, the corresponding interval was closer to 10 years. Despite these several differences between the two samples, the results from them converged on the same story: Maturity fears are on the rise, whereas comparison variables, such as body dissatisfaction, are not.

If one fears maturity, it stands to reason that one may embrace immaturity (e.g., calling one's home a "crib"). Legion are the hallmarks of immaturity. One is certainly self-centeredness—a central concern of this book—which is a natural state for the toddler, an unbecoming one for the 30-year-old. Another can be extreme pickiness about food.

The eating disorder project just described, from which I focused on maturity fears, showed that, unlike maturity fears, some eating-related things like bulimia nervosa have not changed much over time, but we did not measure "orthorexia." This term, not an official part of the diagnostic nomenclature, refers to obsession with eating only that which is pure or healthy. This is not mere preference or pickiness, which have little to do with self-view and much to do with biologically based aversions to spinach, Brussels sprouts, or what have you. Nor does it have to do with things like veganism or vegetarianism, which can be motivated by any number of things, including morality and philosophy, though here, depending on the attitude of the particular vegan or vegetarian, the distinctions can blur. Rather, orthorexia has to do with psychological obsession and little else, the obsession being ostensibly about healthy and pure eating, but really with how special and even sacred one's own body is. Life is sacred; lives somewhat less so; and selves far less so. It is a failure to appreciate the difference that marks self-obsession and orthorexia (or perhaps it is not the failure to appreciate the difference as much as it is an eagerness to ignore it and thereby glorify the self).

I certainly have nothing against the picky, nor against the genuinely vegan or vegetarian. A childhood friend of mine was picky to the point that he only ate peanut butter on white bread and fried chicken (this was the American South after all; to be picky was one thing, but to be picky against fried chicken, quite another). My dad was an avid outdoorsman and an ingenious cook. He took my friend and me camping on an undeveloped barrier island off the coast of Georgia, where my friend and I caught around 15 live conchs and informed my dad of the fact. He thought a moment and told us to bring them to him. We did, thought little of it, and went on our way, to return a couple of hours later to a delicious aroma and an extremely appetizing-looking stew, which tasted even better than it smelled and looked. My friend was delighted, having found something else he could eat, namely "chicken stew." The dilemma occurred immediately to my father, and noticing his slightly pained expression, then to me. As I was about to blurt out the truth, my dad looked at me in a way that tied my tongue. Ever true to his honest nature, however, my dad's eventual reply was, "Um, I've got to tell you, that was conch stew," and it elicited an immediate vomiting spell in my poor friend, an early lesson to me of the potential power of the mind over the body.

Regarding vegetarianism, I myself adhered for around five years, the reason being the moral arguments of the philosopher Peter Singer. I eventually reverted to omnivore status for the simple reason that it was much more convenient for my wife and (at the time) small sons for me to do so, and that, as I learned more and more evolutionary biology, vegetarianism seemed more and more contrary to my own understanding of human nature. I respect genuine vegetarians and allied others, especially those who are barely noticeable as such; these latter have no pretense and are disinterested in conversion of heathen omnivores and the tedious lectures aimed at this purpose. For them, it is not about self-presentation.

By contrast, there is a contingent whose choice of what to eat has become a mode of expression for their excessive self-importance. I have the suspicion that some among this crowd are ersatz vegetarians, the point for them being not what they eat but rather what they say they eat in order to impress on others their moral valor, compassion, and sanctity.

The kinds of people who speak at length about the special nuances in all sorts of foods and drink—and in so doing, imply their uniqueness—are, satisfyingly, often the worst performers in rigorous taste tests. A corollary of the "body is a sacred temple" notion seems to be an idea along the lines of "pure of body, pure of taste." That is, these types tend to believe that they have superior discernment, their care of what they put into their bodies supposedly producing a particularly refined palate. For many things, maybe even most things, virtually no one has a particularly refined palate despite claims to the contrary. In the many versions of taste tests that my friends, acquaintances, and I have participated in, a regular occurrence is that the most confident and pretentious of the group performs below average. It hardly needs saying, but these experiences of failure have no lasting effect on the confidence and pretensions of the individuals in question, who hurriedly attribute their poor performance to "a bad year for that kind of wine" (to take but one of many examples from my own experience).

In taste tests in which the goal is to discern white from red wine, and under conditions in which there are no visual or temperature-related cues about which is which, a high number of people fail, despite their initial certainty that they will easily succeed. I have conducted some cocktail-party type polling, along the lines of my Mars questioning described earlier, and have yet to encounter someone who allows that he or she may be unable to tell white from red wine. However, when the test is actually run, around a third of people cannot reliably make the distinction. Of course, when the task is to discern kinds of white wine from each other, or kinds of red from each other, performance is worse still, typically hovering around chance levels.

Perhaps my favorite of the various taste tests is one in which the goal is to discern foods like the following from one another: pâté, Spam, liverwurst, and dog food. In one specific example,[4] there were four different kinds of human food and two different kinds of dog food. All were made to look similar (e.g., with garnish and served with crackers). There was some discrimination, for example, the tasters generally preferred the expensive duck liver over dog food. However, almost half of the subjects misidentified the liverwurst as the dog food. In a similar vein from a different area, tasters rank the exact same yogurt as superior if it is eaten from a silver versus some other kind of spoon.

I am pretty certain that I never heard the phrase "my body is a temple" growing up in Georgia, though I am absolutely certain I heard or at least read the following one: ". . . do you not know that your body is a temple of the Holy Spirit within you, which you have from God?"[5] The difference between the two phrases is considerable and significant; it inheres in the distinction between the solipsism of "my body is a temple" and the lack of it in Paul's question to the Corinthians. Had one of us said "my body is a temple" in the Georgia of my youth, the reaction would not have been hostile so much as it would have been perplexed. I readily agree that we may have been behind the cultural times—indeed, many were children, grandchildren, or great-grandchildren of rural Southern farmers. But that is the point: Few people know more about bodies in nature than farmers (and ranchers). They would endorse sentiments like "there is inherent dignity in each and every creature's life" and "life is precious," and many would look favorably on Paul's question and much else from the same book, but every single human body a temple, not because it is a vessel of the Lord, but just because it's a body? They would not know how to respond other than with the kinds of platitudes used by my maternal great-grandmother and both grandmothers, platitudes I came to admire for their tact, and which I learned to read as "let's change the subject," but which were stated along the lines of "well isn't that something?"

These women understood as did their farmer ancestors before them that all bodies, including ours, have a deep and ancient creatureliness, which, while perhaps not pretty, is essential to the clear-eyed understanding of biological life. No amount of denying this fact will change it, though the orthorexia crowd have tried, as have another group who are disgusted by their own creatureliness—patients, overwhelmingly female, with eating disorders. This is a prominent enough feature of the presentation of eating disorders that I have developed the opinion that it needs to be directly targeted in the psychotherapy, actually the behavior therapy, of these conditions. One of the most effective ways to do this is to eat together in session—this is a standard approach—but an element that I have emphasized more in recent clinical work is the creatureliness of eating. What sounds are produced? What is the purpose of saliva? How do humans and other creatures understand that it is time to stop eating? How specifically do different elements of food nourish our bodies, and what is treated as waste and how? Especially at first, these are uncomfortable conversations, the disgust at my forcing these discussions being quite plainly evident in the faces of my patients.

We also weigh ourselves together—creatures have mass—and this happens to work strategically very well for me, because I regularly weigh far more than twice my patients. They are horrified for me, on my behalf, and when they look to me for my own expression of horror, they see instead one of indifference, at which point I shrug and say something like "some creatures weigh more than others." They then weigh themselves as I observe, and it is remarkable how instantaneously they forget the horror of my weight and focus on the horror they perceive in theirs (and it really does not matter what that weight is; in a recent example in an adult female of average height, the reading was 104 lb). They look to me for affirmation of the horror, to which I respond with more indifference and say something like "all creatures weigh something."

Ten or so sessions like this are not necessarily deeply transformative. These patients remain disgust-prone and concerned about topics related to weight and shape. But coming to better terms with their creaturely natures helps considerably, lets them eat multiple meals per day without purging, and changes their view of attractiveness from "thin" to "healthy glow." A recognition of one's creatureliness, it should be reiterated, tends to shield one from an overemphasis on the uniqueness of the self.

Hendin's statement, noted earlier and quoted from his book *Seduced by Death*, was "In a culture that fosters narcissism, aging and death are harder to bear." Our work on maturity fears bears out that aging indeed has become harder to bear for more recent cohorts. But what of death?

In this context, life insurance is interesting to consider. Not only does it necessitate confrontation of one's own mortality (at least to a degree), but it also involves the expenditure of one's own money, in the here-and-now, for the financial benefit of others in the future. In this latter sense, it is an exemplar of a selfless act. If more recent cohorts are in fact more self-centered as well as scared of aging and death, these trends may be detectable in people's life insurance buying behavior. There does indeed appear to be fairly clear evidence of a recent downturn in life insurance sales. A report from the American Council of Life Insurers shows that the number of individual policies sold has decreased every year without exception since 2002, and the 2010 total is about half of the high points hit in the 1950s and 1960s. A May 29, 2014, report from *Bloomberg* quotes a man born in 1984 as saying "I'm not planning on dying any time soon so it's a waste of money." He may be right about this, but the difference in numbers between those who thought life insurance was worth it 50 years ago and those who think so today is striking, and is moreover consistent, at least to a degree, with the possibility that more recent generations' fear of mortality and maturity have increased.

It should be noted that some have interpreted trends like those apparent in the life insurance data not as evidence of increasing self-obsession but instead as indicative of more positive traits. About the life insurance data, the coauthor of the book *Millennials Rising: The Next Great Generation* explained these days young people's lives "are just a bit more on hold which means they're not in an insurance mindset. On the other hand, they are long-term planners." Of course, it is possible not to be in an insurance mindset, to be a careful and long-term planner, *and* to be very selfish, as for example serial killers amply and monstrously show.

In *Being Mortal*, Gawande writes of these generational changes, "The veneration of elders may be gone, but not because it has been replaced by veneration of youth. It's been replaced by veneration of the independent self."[6] My read is a little different. The veneration of elders has been attacked on two flanks: the veneration of youth and a corresponding veneration of the self.

My same-aged friends and I have noticed another generational change from us to our children: Whereas when we turned 16 around 1980, we got our driver's license the instant we could and to do otherwise seemed unimaginable, our children seem in no hurry at all. As I write, for example, the younger of my two sons has been 16 for many months but is not scheduled to get his full license until many weeks after he has turned 17 and is completely unperturbed at the fact (by contrast, my wife and I are regularly perturbed at our side jobs as chauffeur for a very sociable child, though this latter trait has led to him also having many friends with driver's licenses and cars). This generational trend appears not to be specific to my friends and our children; data from the Centers for Disease Control and Prevention indicate that the percentage of high school seniors with a driver's license was 85% in 1996, down to 73% in 2010. Of course, this may have to do with the recession that started in 2008, but I am skeptical, because all of the examples in my experience were relatively unaffected by it. Or, it may have to do with the Internet, for example, one no longer needs a car to shop or to socialize. Consistent with the work on maturity fears, however, it also could have to do with a reluctance to face independence, maturity, and the things that lie beyond like financial responsibility and mortality.

The reticence to fully face aging and its sequelae may have a role in the emergence of "death with dignity" movements. I must rush to add here that the vast majority of proponents of such programs support them because, as the name implies, they respect dignity, self-determination, and the option to end needless suffering. They are quite sincere in these values and they certainly have a point, as reflected, for example, in the growing number of jurisdictions enacting death with dignity legislation. There is, however, genuine debate about the merits of such legislation.

One strand of this debate has to do with a central theme of this book, namely, that it can be illuminating, indeed edifying, to consider things from the perspective of life rather than from the perspective of individual lives. For ardent opponents of death with dignity movements, the dignity of life is paramount and exceeds the significance of individual lives. Their perspective is that life does not care about lives, and they might suggest to skeptics to ask the bones deep in the mud of Flanders about the matter. Comedian Louis C.K. may agree, judging at least from an exchange in his eponymous show on the TV network FX. In the relevant scene, he pleads with a fellow comic who plans to kill himself, saying "It's not your life. It's *life* ... Life isn't something you *possess*. It's something you *take part in*, and you *witness*."

Of course the case for life and against suicide has been made similarly in various forms over centuries. A recent and eloquent one appears in the 2013 book *Stay* by Jennifer Hecht; my colleagues and I make similar arguments in a 2016 *Psychological Review* article. In both Hecht's and our cases, the intellectual debt to the work of

Thomas Aquinas and St. Augustine is considerable. My colleagues and I made our case as follows:

> ... suicide involves the unsanctioned and frequently brutal killing of an innocent; the state of mind that one's own death has inviting properties; the potential deaths of others via suicide contagion (Hecht, 2013), not to mention the occasional actual deaths of bystanders (e.g., those landed upon by suicidal people jumping from a height in an urban setting; those killed by chemical exposure; Joiner, 2014); the deprivation of choice and life to one's future self (Hecht, 2013); the deprivation of choice and future care and comfort to loved ones; and the willingness to devastate dozens of people into a shocked state of bereavement (Cerel, 2015) not infrequently without warning and certainly without their consent.[7]

We might have added to our list that a suicide can affect families for generations, and that it might seem a questionable choice to those who struggle for life and yet soon lose (e.g. those with aggressive childhood cancers) and a questionable choice to their loved ones (e.g., the parents of children with aggressive childhood cancers). Our conclusion was that any one of these rationales, even taken singly, constitutes a sufficient argument against suicide, and that the conjunction of these rationales forms an overwhelming case against it. In this article and in our work more generally, it should be noted, we go to some lengths not to blame suicide attempts and suicide deaths on individuals so much as on individuals' illnesses.

It is plausible to view suicide and death with dignity as completely distinct, the one having to do with serious mental disorders, the other with the desire for a dignified death free of needless suffering. Plausible, but debatable. The main bases on which to debate this distinction are threefold.

First, there is a worrying trend to expand availability of physician-assisted suicide to more and more groups, often very vulnerable groups.[8] For example, in jurisdictions like Belgium and the Netherlands, one basis for physician-assisted suicide is psychiatric illness itself. In the study from the Netherlands by Kim and coworkers, the authors reported on 66 physician-assisted deaths, all of which were conducted because of severe and chronic mental disorders. A quarter of these patients were in their 30s or 40s, and though most had mood disorders, other conditions were represented as well, such as eating disorders and prolonged grief. This not only strikes many as appalling on its face, but it directly contradicts the idea noted above that suicide related to mental disorders and death with dignity policies are completely distinct.

Second, there is evidence to suggest that of those who request physician-assisted suicide and who are deemed to be free of clinical depression, a significant portion nonetheless harbors subclinical manifestations of mood disorders. Stated differently, at the subclinical level, those requesting physician-assisted suicide look more depressed than those who do not, even though all are dying and all are facing similar levels of impairment and pain.[9] In this light, here too, the distinction between suicide related to mental disorders and physician-assisted suicide blurs.

Third, though anecdotal, there are reports of individuals fervently wishing to die in the midst of an exacerbation of a chronic physical illness, and then changing their minds at a later date. The astrophysicist Stephen Hawking is one such individual. In the 1980s during a very punishing downturn in his ALS-caused physical status, he asked his wife at the time to turn off his respirator, which would have killed him. She refused to do so, a decision leaving Hawking decades more of quite productive life. In the 1980s and also much more recently,[10] Hawking voiced clear support for physician-assisted suicide, but in the process tends to leave out mention of this episode.

For these three reasons, then, the assertion that physician-assisted suicide and suicide related to mental disorders are different phenomena is a questionable one. I am not convinced it is a fully false one—it seems plausible that there are examples in which there is no mental disorder, only profound and needless physical suffering. Even here, the examples of people in this same state who choose *not* to die by other than natural means gives one pause.

Yet another mortality-related lens through which to observe the processes in question is memorial services. I have attended them for decades, trying to heed my own advice to my sons and students that showing up to any and all funerals which are at all appropriate for one to attend is a balm for everyone's soul, one's own and those of the bereaved, among others (the same counsel holds for weddings). In my first three or so decades (which spanned 1965–1995), I recall no memorial services, not one, from which I came away with any reactions other than fond memories of the deceased and a sense of renewed connection and community—and this despite the fact that some of the deaths in question were deeply sad and troubling, not least of which was my dad's suicide.

Since around 1995, I have noticed two sets of shifts, which I believe are closely intertwined. First, before 1995, few if any of the services I happened to attend were secular; since then, about half are. Being irreligious, I have no particular qualm about this ... except that it has led to a second phenomenon, namely, the secular services tend to be much longer (e.g., more than 2 hours vs. just under 1 hour) and more disorganized than their nonsecular versions. Here too, on one level, I have no qualm; people are grieving so what is the difference if the service goes long or is disorganized? There would be none, except that disorganization can take many forms. What has rushed in to fill the abhorred vacuum of this disorganization? To my misery and to all of our detriment, the answer seems to be self-focus.

Here, I acknowledge I have only anecdotal evidence, but it happens time and again: Because an experienced religious figure is not involved in planning the service, it goes off its rails and once it does, the speakers begin to talk not about the deceased and the bereaved, but rather, first about themselves-in-relation-to-the-deceased, progressing, if it can be called that, to then talking mostly about themselves. This is a pervasive enough thing that I have even seen it affect an extremely conservative Southern Baptist preacher of many decades' experience, though to his credit he seemed to catch himself about one sentence in and then quickly corrected course, whereas in the versions of which I complain, there is no self-catching and no course correction. I have left these latter services more dispirited than when they started, an experience with which I was happily unfamiliar pre-1995.

As noted earlier, one initial inspiration for this book was the anecdotal impression in my little Facebook world that among the most fervent admirers of mindfulness were also to be found the most self-absorbed. Authentic mindfulness counsels selflessness far more than it does self-regard—mindfulness, in other words, should be *negatively* associated with self-absorption—and yet, the supposedly mindful seemed to me to be squarely among the Narcissi. Something felt askew.

Other independent observations served to corroborate and consolidate my sense that something was amiss. To take an example from the home front, my wife's parting words to me and to my sons, when my sons leave for school or I for work, virtually always contain the advice to "eat well." This had become a reflexive and affectionate inanity, along the lines of "have a good day honey," and for several years, it barely caught my attention.

But it did catch my attention, and as I pondered why, it slowly dawned on me that there was a risible discordance between the sweet and rather high-minded underlying sentiment—"we and others depend on you and love you so while you're away from us care for yourself in our stead"—and the literal words "eat well," that is, engage in a mundane and not so high-minded biological function. The words have now become an ongoing source of humor in our family, only encouraged by our discovery that there is a magazine entitled *Eating Well*.

I began to collect other examples of affectionate, parting inanities, starting with ones from my own childhood and that of my wife. My wife grew up in Mexico, and the usual parting advice of her much beloved grandfather was "vas pero te peinas," a literal translation of which is "go but comb your hair," a better translation of which is "go but get yourself together first." My mother's routine parting counsel was "be sweet," which she used long after it was apt (e.g., when my friends and I were in our late teens, going off into the night to participate in moderate forms of mayhem).

Each of these platitudes has a certain charm, at least to me, but I could not shake the view that my mother's was the best of the three. This is not necessarily my usual bias, which led me to consider the three inanities a little further, and soon enough, the essential issue became clear. My wife's "eat well" and her grandfather's "vas pero te peinas" were about tending to self; my mother's "be sweet" was more about tending to others.

Consider in this context the topic of self-care or self-compassion, seemingly a favorite preoccupation among mindfulness fans, and a revealing example of the movement's tendency toward an inward gaze. The essential idea seems to be that it is not selfish to tend to and even to prioritize one's own needs for care and understanding. After all, this line of thought goes, how can one be available for others unless one is fully present, and how can one be fully present unless one's own needs are met? The reasoning here contains a kind of "trickle down" logic. (The reference is to Reaganomics, rich admirers of which asked questions like "How can we all prosper unless the rich do first?") Of course, self-care in the sense of adequate sleep and nutrition is eminently sensible and compatible with my earlier statements on the benefits of activities like walking. Self-care in this sense seems worth prioritizing in contexts like law enforcement and firefighting, in which healthy sleep and eating can be challenging, and in which the stresses of the job need offsetting by sustenance and rest.

Thus, an emphasis on self-care and self-compassion has merit in some contexts but not in others. For example, frequent airline travelers will have heard that should oxygen masks drop from the compartment above, "secure your own oxygen mask before assisting others." This is a sensible policy, geared toward avoiding a domino effect of people blacking out while they are trying to assist others, who, because now unassisted, in turn may also black out. The policy is also aimed at fairly clear emergency contexts and involves an essential element of survival, namely oxygen.

Self-compassion enthusiasts are drawn to this example as rationale for their perspective, failing to appreciate the difference between actual emergency versus a mildly stressful day, and between an absolute necessity like oxygen versus a luxury that can tend toward the self-indulgent. Of course there are times when one has to tend to oneself first, but these are rare, often life-threatening crises that most people mercifully never experience. In this context, it is ironic and no coincidence that self-compassion and self-forgiveness are alien to cultures such as that at the National Aeronautics and Space Administration (NASA) and at virtually all elements of the Department of Defense, no coincidence that they fail to appear in our founding documents, and no coincidence that they are demeaned in one way or another in American works of genius like Hawthorne's *The Scarlet Letter*, Twain's *The Adventures of Huckleberry Finn*, and Faulkner's *As I Lay Dying*. But you will find them at "Freud Meets Buddha" meetings.

In day-to-day life, self-compassion advocates ask, isn't self-care a prerequisite to caring for others? Let's put aside for the moment fairly obvious answers to this question: that one can be available to others regardless of one's own state through virtues like sacrifice, endurance, honor, and duty; and that one can forget about the self, "be sweet" to others, and trust that in the natural course of things one's needs will get met, more or less, in one way or another, sooner or later. And let's put aside the fact that the most persuasive helpers across human history tended not to emphasize self-care (e.g., Jesus). And furthermore, let's put aside the fact that, again in my little social media microcosm, it seems to me that the most ardent fans of self-compassion are easily the most self-indulgent, focusing not on forms of sensible self-care like sustenance, exercise, and physical affection, never mind virtues like honor and duty, but rather harping on things like lotions, creams, and pedicures (and here I do not mean to pick on the fairer sex—quite the contrary actually, more on which momentarily). The preoccupation with these latter kinds of things left me with the impression that "self-compassion" was code and rationalization for indulging in various things that some people find pleasant. There is nothing at all wrong with pleasant activities in my view, but those already have a name. It's "pleasant activities," and calling them "self-compassion" adds little meaning and unhelpfully obscures the fact that such activities are not essential to survival or health and that they can be foregone in the service of sacrifice and honor. Our men and women in uniform do it every day. Self-compassion enthusiasts seem often to be reflexively drawn to Eastern religions, which is an irony in that many of those same systems preach self-abnegation, *especially* with regard to sensual pleasures.

To a certain and admittedly peculiar cast of mind, things like lotions, creams, manicures, pedicures, and even massage—and also self-compassion—are creepy, in part because of their recursive, self-focused nature. A few sentences back, when I wrote the phrase "harping on things like lotions, creams, and pedicures," I literally shuddered, experiencing what is colloquially known as "the willies." This reaction will be familiar and plain on its face to the minority of readers who happen to share this same disposition with me, but for everyone else, a visual image may assist in your understanding our creeped-out reaction.

Recall Alfred Hitchcock's movie *Psycho*, in which Norman Bates (played by Anthony Perkins) has murdered his mother and her lover, keeps his mother's corpse where he lives in the Bates Hotel, and gives literal voice to his mother by assuming her identity. When Perkins is in the character of Norman Bates, his voice (and general demeanor) are disquieting, but when he is in the character of Norma Bates (the deceased mother), his voice is chillingly creepy. In the movie, the voice is used to hector Norman, but imagine for a moment the voice turning compassionate: "You're a good boy Norman, you deserve some self-care, why don't I give you a massage?" Cut to Norman, in his mother's clothes, massaging his own shoulders.

If your skin is crawling a little bit, or you feel a sense of unease in the pit of your stomach, that is the feeling I and others have about things like pedicure and self-compassion. Why do we feel this way?

As a matter of purely personal choice, there is no issue (as long as it is legal, but the *Sunday Times* reported in August 2013 that many U.K. nail bars are fronts for human traffickers). However, when personal choice gets retooled in to professional practices like self-compassion, recommended by mindfulness experts and others as principle and policy and as on a par with needs like nutrition and hydration, that is different.

As to why we feel this way, when Norman Bates is speaking in his mother's voice, in one sense, there is nothing inherently wrong with what he is doing. He is just a person talking. On the other hand, at least part of what triggers our creep-sensors, and gives us an eerie feeling of uncanniness, is that what he is doing is in a sense almost but not quite normal. If he were doing something alien to most of us, like perpetrating a murder, we would feel revulsion but not necessarily a feeling of eeriness. If he were talking normally to his mother while she were still alive, the scene would trigger neither revulsion nor uncanniness. But when Norman Bates speaks in the voice of Norma Bates, it is eerie and creepy in part because it is in a way almost but not quite normal.

Research psychologists have amply characterized this effect, called the "uncanny valley." The term refers to the dip—the valley—in comfort level as, for example, the image of a nonhuman robot becomes increasingly human-looking. People tend to be perfectly comfortable with a nonhuman robot—think R2-D2 from *Star Wars*—and also perfectly comfortable with humans and even with robots that are fairly human-like—think C-3PO, also from *Star Wars*. However, there is a zone in which a robot is almost but not quite human, and when a person has perceived that zone, he or she has entered the uncanny valley, and will feel a sense of eeriness. Perhaps I am not alone in thinking that a pretty good name for a wax museum—where this phenomenon is more or less the whole point—would be the "The Uncanny Valley." If for some reason you doubt that wax museums trigger our "uncanny valley" reactions, Google "wax museum" and then click "images." Just as Charles Darwin tried in the London Zoological Gardens not to flinch and failed as puff adders struck at him, with a thick pane of glass between him and the snakes, so will most who Google "wax museum images" fail if they try to suppress a sense of unease in the pit of the stomach.

The phenomenon can also be readily observed in any setting in which there is a clown. Fear of clowns is a quite common phobia. In fact in some surveys, it is the most common childhood phobia of all, even outpacing fear of the dark, of needles, and of various animals, and it is common largely because clowns throw us into the "uncanny valley."

Just as clowns and wax museum sculptures elicit in many feeling of eeriness, "the willies," or outright phobic reactions, so does the concept of self-compassion make those of a certain cast of mind shiver with a mild sense of disquiet and distaste. It is probably not a coincidence that the only ones who can get away with extreme and literal forms of self-compassion—hugging oneself or patting one's own arm—are clowns. Anything for which that is true—a clown could do it but probably not anyone else—is an unlikely candidate for a general policy, principle, or prescription.

Further still, self-care (and this is true too of its more extreme cousin self-compassion) will kick in naturally, instinctively, one might say mindlessly. Hungry? You will have the natural instinct to eat, without much thought required, much like famished penguins. Tired? You will be drawn to sleep, with little moment-to-moment subjective awareness needed. Just as we need not encourage adolescents to play video games, they will do so naturally enough, and just as we need not encourage self-regarding creatures to gaze inward, they already do and trends suggest they will do so even more over time, we need not encourage self-care and self-compassion in a gregarious species hardwired to heed instinct. To reiterate, for those who have lost touch with natural signals to sleep or eat, especially for those in stressful professions like first responders and some mental health professions, attention to those signals—self-care in other words—is of course indicated. But this sounds a different note than a constant and self-regarding self-compassion on the part of everyone.

There is an element of self-care and self-compassion which stands in contradiction to authentic mindfulness. The latter advises a dispassionate, nonjudgmental stance about *everything*, certainly to include oneself. Indeed, the most compelling versions of authentic mindfulness are those that encourage a dispassionate nonjudgmentalism *especially* about the self. It is a challenge to be both *dis*passionate and *com*passionate at the same time, and this is particularly true regarding emotionally valenced things like one's own self. I do not argue that it is impossible. I argue that it is unlikely for all but the most self-controlled (who of course already think and act in ways that I doubt would be improved by their immersion in current mindfulness literature), and I argue that the Narcissi and their ilk are far from self-controlled.

Although I am loath to bring it up, in part because it is a favorite topic (tellingly and predictably) of the Narcissi (I suppose as an attempt to show their open-mindedness), the topic of masturbation deserves some consideration in a discussion of self-directed attention, including self-care and self-compassion. The activity is self-focused, in a self-evident way, and it is the prototypical activity that many refer to when impugning something as overly self-focused, for example by calling the activity "masturbatory." However, the activity very often involves a focus on another person (in fantasy). Say what you will about this focus—that it is highly sexualized, that it shows little care for the fantasized other—it nevertheless has an interpersonal aspect, and for it not to is creepy indeed. Moreover, the activity discharges an ancient and powerful instinct, thus its ubiquity.

By contrast, self-compassion is not only not ubiquitous (and my hope is that it stays that way), but it is less interpersonal even than masturbation—a damning indictment and thus deserving of the label "masturbatory." Any behavior that one can even suggest is more self-absorbed than masturbation is suspect on its face. In self-compassion, where is the fantasized other? Where is the interpersonal connection? Is it to the pedicurist? And what ancient and powerful instinct is being satisfied?

To repeat, I have nothing against pedicures and the like as recreation and relaxation. Indeed, much the same could be said for a whole range of behaviors, some of them somewhat unsavory and in some cases technically illegal, but what in the world does it matter what I think, as long as the behavior does not hurt anyone? The Narcissi, however, often promote various self-compassionate activities, not as recreation or relaxation, but as something high-minded, even spiritual, and also as a professional activity that is one facet of a more general professional mindset. Mind you, there are professions for whom I would enthusiastically endorse manicures—surgeons spring to mind—because there is a functional and obvious reason for them. The motivation is not high-minded and certainly not spiritual, but rather is concrete and instrumental.

Some within the Narcissi would attempt to have us believe similarly with regard to mental health professionals. Their argument would be along the lines of, "Just as a surgeon's hands are intricate instruments that must be treated with care, so the soul and psyche of the therapist are sensitive and delicate curative instruments and must be regularly tended to and re-energized." Is there any doubt that surgeons' hands are curative? The merest sliver of contact with reality puts any such doubts at rest. Are the psyche and soul of the mental health professional similarly curative? An affirmative answer is at best arguable and at worst very offensive to surgeons.

Hang around mental health professionals (I certainly have) and surgeons enough (as it happens I have done this too), and some observations and suspicions emerge. The surgeons are at least as essential to the general good as the mental health professionals, and thus at least as much in need of self-care and the like as the mental health professionals, and yet the latter harp on it, the former rarely if ever mention it. When surgeons do mention something like manicure (and of course, it almost always is manicure given the importance of their hands to their work), it is usually something specific and pointed, like "this one area of the nail and cuticle on my left pointer finger was irritating and distracting me, so I had the manicurist clean it up and while I was there had the rest done too." In saying something like this, it is the very rare surgeon who does so with a languid and self-satisfied smile. (Not that surgeons do not have their self-satisfactions; they most certainly do. It is just that they do not tend to cloak them in rationalizations involving self-care and self-compassion.) In stark contrast, mental health professionals—at least those squarely within the Narcissi but also those at their flanks—are pillars upon which various aspects of the self-care industry rest, like farmers for the tractor industry, or a more apt comparison, youth for the gaming industry.

They are certainly not the only pillars of industries like manicure and pedicure. Another pillar of those industries are people, often but not always female, who like to enhance their own physical attractiveness, and if asked, they will tell you as much. It is ironic, because as they are being preened, there is nothing preening in their attitude: They are authentic and honest. They are engaging in millennia-old traditions of beauty—usually but not always of female beauty—that, tellingly, can be seen in analog forms across nature. Thus, mindless mindfulness' emphasis on self-compassion is not problematic because of the specific activities it can entail or because of a focus on attractiveness or enjoyment, but rather, for its lack of honesty, authenticity, and even provenance. That is, it is not hard to find examples of and reasons for enhancing one's physical attractiveness in, for example, the writings of Darwin, in nature itself, and in the ancient world. I have yet to find a reference to self-compassion in the *Origin of Species*.

Perhaps you believe I have exaggerated the place of things like self-compassion in modern mindfulness movements and indeed in modern professional psychology. Indeed I fervently hope you are right; the world would be better for it. But consider the following anecdote, taken from a real and reputable professional psychology doctoral program. Pictures of each doctoral student were posted on a bulletin board, along with three pieces of information about them. One information point was the student's name; a second was the student's area of research interest. So far, so good: These pieces of information are sensible and functional, much like manicures for surgeons (or, incidentally, for manicurists themselves, as well as for pedicurists and masseuses).

What of the third piece of information? Several reasonable candidates come to mind: What about, for example, the person who has had the most influence on you? The book that has made the biggest impact? The world problem you would most like to contribute to reducing (e.g., poverty, hunger, suicide, lack of access to high-quality education)? The phrase in our country's founding documents or in the works they inspired that most moved you (e.g., "We hold these truths to be self-evident"; ". . . that government of the people, by the people, for the people, shall not perish from this earth"; ". . . content of their character . . .")? If those are too high-minded, how about a favorite hobby, sports team, or food?

But alas, after name and research area came "favorite self-care." I looked through the students' responses, holding out hope for at least one rebel to write something like "I'd rather help others" or at least "I'd rather go to a [fill-in-your-favorite sports teams' name] game," but my hope was in vain. As to what was written, the uniformity was as remarkable as it was dispiriting; in fact, among the 50 or so students, there were only three categories of response: yoga, meditation, and exercise.

In defense of the students, they were only responding in the way expected of them. Indeed, it has been shown empirically that if students are trained in approaches that think like this (e.g., acceptance and commitment therapy, or ACT), they not only report that self-care is important,[11] but they are also informed of the "self-as-laboratory" perspective, an inevitable if suspect view in a culture of narcissism, a revival of an approach the rigorous and increasingly slender portion of our field rejected a century ago. It is far from a shocking finding that clinical psychology PhD students, who, given recent selection pressures, are easily among the world's most elite trainees across fields, are able to learn what is taught to them. But all this is exactly my point: Aspects of the mental health landscape are such that trainees not only receive the message that "self-care" is an essential enough aspect of one's identity that it ranks up there besides one's name, but further, that "self-care" reduces to things like meditation and yoga—things alien, it should be emphasized, to vast swaths of the American public.

Vast swaths of the American public are exposed to signage, cover stories, and the like about such things but that is not the same as saying they endorse them. Relatedly, on a recent visit to a U.S. military installation, I looked for but did not find signage on mindfulness, yoga, and meditation, but in the process I noticed other street signs. Stand-alone and understated, they simply read "Integrity," "Honor," "Selfless Service," and so on. These were not the names of streets, but were positioned more like speed limit signs, but smaller and subtler. Truly, which of the two sets of signage is the more admirable, and which would our Founding Fathers have immediately recognized?

That things like meditation and yoga are alien to huge segments of our population can easily be lost on those living in literati or Narcissi bubbles, where such things seem as natural as breathing or walking and from which professors like myself escape only with focused effort. Our federal research granting agencies, like the National Institutes of Health and the Department of Defense, regularly receive proposals to combat things like depression and post-traumatic stress disorder using interventions related to yoga and meditation. And indeed, as we have seen, authentic mindfulness—not too distant a cousin to meditation—certainly can assist people in various problems in living. I have been on grant proposal review panels when these kinds of projects are reviewed and have noticed a pattern.

It is important to appreciate that these panels are made up almost entirely of professors, and so naturally enough, a majority is in principle in favor of yoga, meditation, and the like as a solution for numerous problems. In response, a thin minority bloc (of which I am a member) points out that on an army base, for example, an advertisement or flyer offering yoga as a treatment for something may not have the same effect that it does on say a university campus. The majority, mildly surprised and momentarily puzzled, ponders the minority view, and allows that some wordsmithing of advertisements and flyers may be wise. The word "yoga" is replaced with something like "stretching and breathing exercises," and all reviewers are more or less satisfied and can turn to the merits of the project's science (which, it should be said, in some cases have been considerable).

Speaking of such review panels, I was initially distressed and surprised to learn in participating in one that, in a survey of NASA astronauts on important factors for mission readiness, "self-care" was ranked at the top. However, it only took a second or two for my distress and surprise to lessen, as I intuited that what the astronauts took "self-care" to mean is "mission ready." Of course they value that, and self-care enthusiasts may well benefit from pondering this specific version of self-care. It is not so much the "mission" part that I urge them to ponder, because military-sounding phrasing is not necessarily for everyone. For the present purposes, "mission" could be replaced with "goal," "purpose," "value," and so forth. Rather, the part I think deserves emphasis is "ready." "Readiness" seems to me to be inclusive of most people (i.e., most will resonate with it and few will feel left out by it), and it is also inclusive of the basic and sensible emphases of self-care, in that one cannot be ready, at least not optimally ready, to accomplish a purpose or serve a value unless one is reasonably well rested, fed, and so on. For the astronauts as for everyone, "readiness" subsumes self-care, and in so doing in a sense leaves the self out of it. In fact, it literally leaves the word "self" out of it, and it conceptually shifts the emphasis from the self to the goal, purpose, or value. A disadvantage of the term "self-care" is that no matter what is meant by it, it will discourage some because some will associate it with self-indulgence. "Readiness" as a term does not suffer from this particular drawback.

The astronauts rated self-care as a priority because they took it in the sense of "so that I will not burden or impede the mission and my fellow astronauts." Had they taken it to mean "self-love," I suspect they would have ranked it last and done so with some disgust at the question.

Self-care has reached a level of cultural cachet similar to that of mindfulness (indeed, self-care includes mindfulness, as we will see), no clearer reflection of which is that a car commercial featuring a white-tuxedoed and coiffed Matthew McConaughey references it as he listens to jazz on his way, in the car being advertised, to a luxuriant social occasion. This level of cultural interest tends to come along with a host of how-to recommendations; for example, I am aware of a "self-care" exercise in which one mentally pictures the person one loves most and then mentally pictures oneself. Just as I showed up at and took seriously a full-day mindfulness retreat, so did I attempt this exercise, which, depending on how I did it, caused either a positive feeling or a mild but nonetheless unmistakable nausea. The positive feeling was caused by the image of me as one who tries to be a good father to my sons, a good husband to my wife, a good professor to my students, and a good servant to my department, campus, community, and country. By contrast, I found the notion that I should love myself as I do my sons to be nauseating. I had had my fill of trying these kinds of things out for myself, incidentally, so skipped over soothing self-touch and the writing of a self-compassionate letter to myself.

On the point of self-touch, FSU social psychologists conducted a study in which they induced participants to feel socially excluded; they did this by having them play *Cyberball*, a computerized ball-tossing game between three or more players rigged so that the participant is left out midway through the game. After the social exclusion experience, participants were randomized to different conditions, two of which are particularly relevant to self-touch. In one condition, participants engaged in self-hugging while imagining a loved one, and in the other condition, they self-hugged while imagining a forest. It is important to emphasize that both groups engaged in self-compassion in the form of self-hugging. Nevertheless, self-hugging was not particularly effective at warding off the effects of social exclusion *unless* it was accompanied by focus on a loved one. An outward direction of attention was salutary, whereas an inward one was not, very consistent with this book's skepticism about concepts like self-compassion.

I am not filled with self-loathing, but neither can I claim to love myself, or really even like myself, though neither do I dislike myself. I love and like other people; I know people who I believe love and like me. I suppose I respect myself most of the time, but to reflect overly on even this has too much an air of onanism for my disposition. The self-like–self-dislike continuum does not apply to my own self-view. I am, I exist, with no particular need to judge my likability. The gulf between this legitimately nonjudgmental stance and the supposedly nonjudgmental versions of mindfulness I decry here is an irony.

The question of self-love and self-like strike me as beside the point, or maybe worse, as a recursion without end and without meaning. I do care about myself much as I would care about my spacecraft if I were in space—indeed that is exactly what it is—but loving me or a spacecraft like I do my sons? The idea is alien.

The feeling this inspires in me is similar to that in reaction to a documentary filmmaker's question. He stared at me intently for a few seconds, and then asked, with a flourish and with a sheen of profundity, whether I was happy. In thought I looked back at him for a couple of seconds, and then responded that I neither knew nor cared about the answer to his question; it struck me as beside the point and irrelevant to my daily concerns. He was puzzled, and so I continued that if I were full of negative emotions and at the same time aware that I was making an above-zero contribution to a cause to which I have devoted my professional life (i.e., suicide prevention), I would be in a state that I think he might mean by the term "happy." I do not pretend to be a Neil Armstrong or a Navy SEAL, but did Armstrong bother over whether he was happy as he piloted the lunar module to the moon on fuel fumes? Did the SEALs worry over whether they were happy as they executed the operation that killed Osama bin Laden?

I would be remiss if I did not point out that it can be somewhat inaccurate to think of self-compassion as one general thing, because it has three separate facets.[12] All of my preceding points hold for two of the three components, namely self-kindness and mindfulness. The third, interestingly enough, has the least to do with the self and a focus on the self; this aspect has to do instead with seeing oneself as a part of a common humanity. Why might it be salutary to see oneself as part of a common humanity? As seen throughout this book, one reason is that the selflessness of seeing oneself as both connected to something larger and as individually trivial tends to defang one's own negative thoughts and feelings. I fear, however, that another very common use of "common humanity" is blame externalization, as in "of course I was self-indulgent, I'm only flesh and blood, just like the rest of humanity."

Indeed, self-compassion has a bedfellow, called self-forgiveness. Just as some may skip compassion and go straight to self-compassion, some may skip asking actual forgiveness and go straight to self-forgiveness. A pitfall of the latter is, again, blame externalization, that is, if a transgression has occurred and one forgives oneself, the blame might attach elsewhere. Mild forms of blame externalization are common, perhaps even an aspect of human nature. In fact, John Milton in *Paradise Lost* voices blame externalization in Adam himself with the words,

Did I request thee, Maker, from my clay
to mould me man
did I solicit thee from darkness to promote me?

However, as with other self-involved processes examined in this book, mild blame externalization can transform into a habitual irresponsibility, and this form of it is one of the truest markers of all of many of the most pernicious forms of mental disorder (e.g., antisocial personality disorder). In the November 2013 issue of *Atlantic Monthly*, Robert Wright wrote, "This is the way the brain works: you forget your sins and remember your grievances."[13] This is particularly so for brains afflicted by certain forms of psychopathology.

In February 2013, Florida Governor Rick Scott changed course and decided that he and the more than 19 million Floridians should, after all, follow the law of the country—a country with problems (that is the nature of countries, as commentators regularly overlook), but with a combination of freedoms, wealth, and potential that is unrivaled on the face of the earth. That country is the United States of America—the one First Lady Michelle Obama movingly characterized as "the greatest country on earth" at the Democratic National Convention in Philadelphia in 2016—and the law in question is the Affordable Care Act (i.e., "Obamacare"). Governor Scott decided not because it was an agreed-on law from a process established by people like Jefferson, Madison, and Lincoln, and not because it was virtuous or generous to extend care to people in need, and not because it would cost the state of Florida absolutely nothing for 3 years and then after that would cost it only 10% of the total cost (the rest covered by federal money). No, he changed course because of a *personal experience* (a difficult- and expensive-to-treat illness in a family member). I expect politicians to come to principled policy positions with which I and others may or may not agree, and I do not begrudge personal misery influencing personal outlook. But is this what we have come to: self-reference as a rationale not just for public policy, but for an official elected to high office of, by, and for the people, to follow the very law of the United States of America?

Argus was a hundred-eyed giant of Greek mythology, and James Madison wanted "every citizen an Argus," meaning that all eyes should turn to protect the things he and others wrote about in the Constitution, like the general welfare. Mindless mindfulness, in contrast, turns all eyes inward. The myth goes that when Argus was killed, his hundred eyes were transferred to the peacock's tail—the journey from Madison's Argus to the strutting peacock is an apt metaphor summarizing mindless narcissism-related cultural decline.

Carthage Must Be Destroyed
Potential Solutions

J UST AS THE OCEAN'S TIDES WILL EBB AND THEY WILL
flow, with human influence having little to no effect, so may the
current cultural ebb of mindless mindfulness and towering levels of
self-focus be immune to solutions other than a hoped-for cultural
flow of grounded, clear-eyed realism. There thus may be no real solutions for this chapter to offer, but if there are, many will likely
require a steely resolve, in equal measure to and to offset the current climate of soft-headed self-indulgence. No matter the topic of
the day—water management, tax law, defense, immigration, foreign
policy—Cato closed his political speeches with the phrase "Carthage
must be destroyed," exhorting his fellow Romans to remain single-
minded about combating an existential threat to their very culture.
Destruction is too extreme a remedy for mindless mindfulness, but
it needs curbing. I wish I knew how to put (some) things back into
Pandora's box, but Cato's outlook—a single-minded stoicism—is at
least a starting point. Single-minded about what? Again as a starting point, how about virtue, as defined, for example, in Faulkner's
matchless Nobel Prize acceptance speech? Speaking of the duty of
the writer, he said "[The writer] must teach himself that the basest of
all things is to be afraid; and, teaching himself that, forget it forever,

leaving no room in his workshop for anything but the old verities and truths of the heart, the old universal truths lacking which any story is ephemeral and doomed—love and honor and pity and pride and compassion and sacrifice . . ." Notice he said "compassion," not "self-compassion"; "love," not "self-love"; and "pity," not "self-pity." Faulkner's list of virtues is compatible with two more recent frameworks: Jonathan Haidt's work on moral systems[1] and the one I developed in the book *The Perversion of Virtue: Understanding Murder-Suicide.* Cato's is an example of relentless single-mindedness, and this book endorses the power of single-mindedness. The backdrop for this is my own view that my profession and indeed the larger culture has elevated the lack of single-mindedness to a kind of virtue, when sometimes it is, but often it is not, and this has occurred on conceptual and empirical bases that are, at the least, debatable.

In his book *The Social Conquest of Earth*, E. O. Wilson wrote, "An unavoidable and perpetual war exists between honor, virtue, and duty, the products of group selection, on one side, and selfishness, cowardice, and hypocrisy, the products of individual selection, on the other side . . . The worst in our nature coexists with the best, and so it will ever be."[2] Wilson's is a rich, wise, and biologically based view of human nature, and the partial solutions that I propose in this chapter are, in large part, an attempt to heed the inevitable tension in human affairs between things like honor and things like hypocrisy and self-indulgence.

I have already alluded to the fact that I think one promising direction in terms of a solution to mindlessness involves an emphasis on virtue and also on stoicism. But those are no fun! So let's start instead with a pair of observations, both of which have the potential to harness self-interest and redirect it. First, navel-gazing is not a good look. Research on people with prominent narcissistic traits shows that although they tend to make a fairly good first impression, they also tend to erode that positive impression over time via their self-absorption. But one hardly needs a research study to understand that excessive self-focus becomes tedious, and that its opposite, which might be characterized as joint attention to the external features of the interpersonal or natural worlds, can contain some of life's most pleasant, memorable, and occasionally even precious moments. Try as I might, I come up empty when I try to recall instances in which my or someone else's self-focused ramblings represented anything close to a precious moment. So much of the modern sensibility I decry in these pages is tied up with the notion of looking good in the eyes of others. I would submit, given our creaturely, primate natures, that moments of emotional attunement with others leave a relatively deep and lasting impression on others. Want to look good? Then more caring, less preening.

Second, still on the topic of potential solutions that harness the energy of desultory cultural trends, there may never have been an era in human history with more emphasis on "just having fun" than ours. What are duty, honor, and obligation compared to fun? Fine, then let's ask, "What's fun?" or, to turn the question around, "What's boring?" A possible answer has to do with variety and its absence. A repetitive, recursive focus on the self is tedious for any number of reasons, but a prominent one involves the lack of variety. If novelty and variety are "just having fun," then it follows that repetitive self-concern is not. Indeed, in light of the vastness and variety of the universe, it truly beggars the imagination that our often lint-filled navels so frequently capture our gaze.

"Just having fun"—that is, seeking novelty in the endless external environs—and doing so with attention to others' observations and ideas, themselves sources of variety, are self-serving but in a way that is not self-focused. They are self-serving because they look good in the eyes of others and are enjoyable. They lack self-focus because their orientation toward the outer world breaks the loop of recursion.

Sticking with the martial arts–like strategy of turning an opponent's momentum against the opponent, "just having fun" and seeking novelty and variety can be seen as youthful activities. They thus not only look good to others because they seem relatively selfless, but also because they fit well within an age of maturity fears. Indeed, it is conceivable that delayed maturity might, via processes related to creativity and play, foster innovation and thus push cultural and other progress. Perhaps, but not all innovations are culturally generative; I would nominate self-marriage as an exemplar of this truth.

A focus on youthfulness may or may not be helpful, but a focus on today's *youth* may very well be, in the sense that they are after all our posterity and also that seeing youthful people and faces tends to bring everyone out of their self-absorptions. This can be seen everywhere as people interact joyfully with strangers' babies, but it can be seen especially in people who have not seen a young

person in a while. A visit to Antarctica, for example, tends to pro-
voke this reaction (as one to Mars will one day soon). In a memorable example, author Mary Roach described in her book *Packing
for Mars* an episode in which a half dozen or so adult men had just
landed in Australia from Antarctica, after a stay of several months.
They spotted a mother pushing her infant in a stroller, and rushed
over to her, so exuberant to see a baby's face after months of de-
privation that the mother was momentarily scared for her and her
baby's safety. In the May 23, 2016 issue of the *New Yorker*, Jonathan
Franzen described a similar feeling after returning to Argentina following 3 weeks in Antarctica: "... I discovered that three weeks on
[an Antarctica cruise ship], looking at the same faces every day, had
made me intensely receptive to any face that hadn't been on [the
ship], especially to the younger ones. I felt like throwing my arms
around every young Argentine I saw."[3] We are evolved to orient to
babies and youth, and because we co-evolved with canines, they can
stimulate similar reactions, as can readily be observed in settings like
parks, where dogs and certainly puppies can be even more popular
than their human counterparts.

Indeed, dogs are a part of nature, and even brief immersions
in nature have been shown to be health-inducing. In the psychotherapy of depression, the clinic I direct regularly dispenses advice
to sufferers to increase their exposure to nature, including pets
and other animals, sunlight (which has been shown to be an effective antidepressant in its own right, especially morning sunlight),
trees and plants (including tending to them in gardens), and bodies
of water (including the activities our ancestors did on and in them,
like swim, fish, canoe, kayak, sail, etc.). These are not big asks, in
part because people are naturally disposed to do them. We have
already seen regarding interacting with dogs that an above-zero
percentage of people, if given a choice between the death of their
own grandmother and that of a random dog, spare the dog. The
reason things like playing with dogs and gardening help mitigate
depression is multi-determined, but one likely mechanism is the
reorientation from internal to external, a guardrail against the
cultural plummet into recursion and solipsism.

To my own sensibilities, solutions like this, or like novelty-seeking
and an emphasis on fun, can strike a chord of vapidity, and thus I reference them not because of their gravity—they mostly have none,

though interactions with babies and nature can have their profound moments—but because of their ease and feasibility. I advocate for being clear-eyed about one's place in the cosmos and all it contains. I understand that my own preferences for things like true hardiness and genuine seriousness of mind place me squarely in a small minority. This minority has much to teach, and I intend to draw out some of its lessons next, but realism forces a reminder that these lessons are not for most; for most, the best counsel possible may be to see if you can lose yourself, at least from time to time, in new and fun activities.

An additional benefit of this counsel is its realism regarding self-interest, which not only exists and not only is powerful, but can be seen as a pillar if not the pillar of biological life. Earlier in the book, I noted Wittgenstein's view that ". . . solipsism . . . coincides with pure realism. The self of solipsism shrinks to a point without extension." Anything that shrinks the self, even if it is selfish, is compatible with the agenda of this book. This philosophical vantage point, when combined with simple things like fun- and novelty-seeking may aid in facing and embracing self-concern and thereby take a step toward moving beyond it. Human nature, I have argued in the preceding pages, is largely reflexive and emotional, whereas in some accounts of mindfulness, it is refined and meditative. "Wittgenstein's solution" can be thought of as taking a refined and meditative approach to thinking about reality, and in this construal of reality, along with things like the infinitude of the universe and the triviality of Earth in both time and space, belong the pull of the self and the view that humans share with the rest of biological life its creatureliness and reflexiveness.

Turning now to solutions that ask somewhat more of us, it is interesting to ponder as a starting point the tension in 20th-century thought in psychology between behaviorism and cognitivism. Behaviorism in its strict form lost the battle of ideas, and it lost because of ideas; that is, to argue for the exclusion of ideas and other aspects mental life in behavioral science, and instead to advocate a sole focus on contingencies and behavioral output, struck most of idea-having humanity as wrong on its face. One of its virtues, however, was a relentless emphasis on results, and another was the side-stepping of mental recursion and solipsism. Notice, in this context, the vast intellectual chasm between 20th-century behaviorism and the self-celebratory versions of mindfulness decried in these pages. Can behaviorism's virtues be salvaged in a post-behaviorism 21st century?

I have a nominee for a psychotherapy that may do just that. It goes by the somewhat unwieldy name of cognitive behavioral analysis system of psychotherapy, or CBASP for short. We have encountered the therapy before, as I pointed out in Chapter 1 that CBASP appeared more helpful than a mindfulness-based treatment in a clinical trial on chronic major depressive disorder. The essence of the approach is to focus on bits of one's experience, and within those bits, decide on and pursue what in CBASP-speak are termed "desired outcomes." Interestingly, CBASP places constraints on what counts as a "desired outcome," avoiding the obvious pitfall of pining after that which is simply not possible and that which is hopelessly solipsistic. Specifically, a "desired outcome" must be desirable in the sense that both patient and therapist immediately and intuitively can see its desirability. If this criterion strikes you as tautological to the point of unnecessity, I would counter that you must not have spent much time in a chronic episode of major depressive disorder, or much time with those in such episodes. One of the many pernicious aspects of the condition is that it can rob one of desire; in this state, the question "What would be desirable to have happen in this situation?" can seem perplexing and unanswerable.

Not only must the outcome be desirable, according to the principles of CBASP, it must also be realistic (i.e., obeys the laws of physics) and attainable (i.e., realistic given any local or personal constraints). Moreover, optimal desired outcomes are focused on behavior more than on emotion, and specifically on one's *own* behavior as opposed to the behaviors and emotions of others.

As described thus far, CBASP may seem a candidate for spurring the very kinds of self-absorption for which I criticized derided forms of mindfulness. After all, a good desired outcome according to CBASP is focused on one's own behavior, and in that sense, is of course self-focused. A key point, however, is that this self-focus is meant as a strategic means to a more important end, namely the end of obtaining, more times than not, desirable results within sliver after sliver of day-to-day experience. These results, it is true, could themselves also be self-focused, but a folk-philosophical insight from CBASP principles is that desirable outcomes need not be, indeed tend not to be. Instead, successful slivers tend to pursue and more often than not produce various forms of interpersonal harmony. The therapeutic essence of CBASP is to edit, tweak, or replace thoughts and behaviors that interfere with desired outcomes with thoughts and behaviors that foster them.

This is a very brief and somewhat superficial primer on CBASP, possibly leading to the objection that something so simple would have no hope of remedying much of anything, certainly not something as complex and grave as chronic forms of major depressive disorder. Indeed, even the much more extended treatments of CBASP tend to produce this kind of skepticism, to which I have two responses. The first is that CBASP is simple in one sense but not in another. The sense in which it is simple—and I can attest that this simplicity comes as a relief both to neophyte therapists as well as to those who train them—is conceptual; the principles, philosophy, and ideas underlying the approach are down-to-earth and accessible. Nevertheless, some things that are simple in concept can be more difficult in practice, and CBASP is no exception to this rule. My other answer to CBASP skepticism is the better answer, and it boils down to "the proof is in the pudding" (or for the purists, "the proof of the pudding is in the eating"). The therapy's clinical trial track record is impressive, and includes one of the more impressive studies I have encountered.[4] In this work, published in the *New England Journal of Medicine*, the authors showed that not only did CBASP by itself achieve favorable results, and not only did it do the more so in concert with an adjunctive antidepressant, but it did so among a patient population selected to be hard to treat (i.e., those with highly chronic forms of mood disorders).

When people master CBASP, they are pulled out of the mire of their own particular thoughts and feelings, and focus instead on what is happening outside their own head; indeed, a common refrain in CBASP thought is to report on events as would a "fly on the wall." The "fly on the wall" has no access to one's subjectivity and can only see things that are concrete and observable by everyone. Like fun- and novelty-seeking, CBASP has potential to harness self-interest (e.g., getting desired outcomes) in the service of an outer orientation toward the larger interpersonal world, thus disrupting problematic and isolating recursive processes.

It is worth noting in passing that CBASP and authentic mindfulness share at least two characteristics. First, just as true mindfulness counsels moment-to-moment awareness, CBASP advises immersion in situation-to-situation awareness, taking each sliver-like situation as the current alpha and omega, and dedicating one's thoughts and behaviors to the attainment of desired outcomes within each sliver. Second, just as genuine mindfulness advocates for a nonjudgmental stance, CBASP is among the least judgmental of all the members of the larger cognitive-behavioral family of treatments. That is, many forms of cognitive-behavioral therapy (CBT) take as their goal the correction of distorted thinking. Some patients react to the emphasis on the need for correction and the presence of distortion as critical and blaming (when done by a sensitive therapist, CBT need not be critical or blaming, it should be noted). CBASP makes an end run around this potential problem, by de-emphasizing the idea that thoughts and behaviors are good or bad, right or wrong, distorted versus not, and instead simply asserts that if a thought or behavior is preventing a desired outcome, tweak that thought or behavior. Granted, there is still some judgment inherent in this approach, in that the distinction between thoughts and behaviors that do versus do not facilitate desired outcomes requires discernment. Still, the difference in judgment between "your thinking is distorted" versus "that thought or behavior isn't working, let's try some different ones" is noticeable, particularly to patients who are criticism- or rejection-sensitive. Furthermore, "your thinking is distorted" turns one's gaze inward, whereas "that's not working for you" requires attention to what might work in the outer world.

I do not propose that strategies like CBASP, along with the encouragement of fun- and novelty-seeking, represent ways toward profound societal change (although the clinical changes wrought by CBASP can be quite profound). Rather, they may be "thumbs on the scale," small things that may tip the social balance away from its current focus and toward "our better angels," virtues like dignity, clear-eyed humility, oneness, and, dare it be said, even service and self-sacrifice. At the outset of this book, I compared distorted versions of mindfulness to a lit match dropped in the kerosene bucket of larger cultural processes like egoism, leading to a conflagration of self-glorification. That worry is real, but on a more sanguine note, it takes just a drop or two of water to douse a lit match.

Are there strategies, however, that operate more like a fire hose than like a couple of drops of water? Debatable, but to fuel that debate, I offer some possibilities. I have referred a few times, often with admiration, to military settings. In robust military cultures, an essential implicit ethos is not "you're an expendable piece of a larger machine" but rather "you're an essential part of our mission." In the latter phrase, the word "essential" could lead to overestimation of the importance of the individual, were it not leavened by the word "part" and also subsumed by the larger mission. Thriving military cultures tend not to view service members as expendable cogs but rather as an important part (but just a part), resisting going so far into self-sacrifice and stoicism that people become expendable. Feeling expendable is a documented risk factor for suicidal thinking and behavior,[5] and it is interesting to ponder whether military subcultures that have lost their way regarding the "expendable" versus "essential" continuum played a role in the rise in military suicide over the last decade or so.

In the same *Los Angeles Times* piece on military dogs, which was mentioned in the Introduction, one soldier said of his German shepherd, "He saved my life several times; he had my back. Some guys talk to their dogs more than they do to their fellow soldiers." The soldier added, "They're definitely not equipment." The reference to "equipment" may seem somewhat of a puzzling non sequitur, but it is not; it is a reference to the theme of expendability. As the article pointed out, "equipment is a kind of dirty word among dog handlers," which stems from the fact that in the Vietnam War, hundreds of working dogs were left behind, deemed to be excess equipment. (The soldier's German shepherd, by the way, survived the war and returned home to the United States.) It is an interesting aside that it is a convention in the U.S. military that dogs outrank their handlers by one rank.

One need not be a dog-lover to sympathize and to see that the word "equipment" has an unfeeling character and "excess equipment," the more so. But, upon reflection, is it really so bad to be "equipment," is it really such a bad word? What, then, of the word "instrument," as in "Lord, make me an instrument of your peace" (the opening line of a popular version of the Prayer of St. Francis)? I doubt I am alone in preferring "instrument" to "equipment," perhaps because "instrument" occurs in the positive context of the aforementioned prayer (which continues "... Where there is hatred, let me sow love. Where there is injury, pardon ..."). In another version of the prayer, the opening line is rendered "... make me a channel of your peace," rather than say a "container." "Instrument" is a nicer term than "equipment;" "channel," nicer than "container."

Why? Both equipment and instruments are used and then put away. It is *how* they are used and put away that is often different. The sentence "The worker lovingly put away her equipment" sounds odd, whereas the sentence "The worker lovingly put away her instruments," less so, and "the musician lovingly put away her instrument" much less so. Similarly, it makes some sense to refer to a "mere" piece of equipment, and less apt (though not nonsensical) to refer to a "mere" instrument.

Instruments and equipment are used; dogs and service members are deployed and optimally are an essential part of the mission. In a real sense, however, being deployed *is* being used ... for a mission; being used is thus not necessarily a problem in itself. But being used carelessly or disrespectfully is a different matter. Much of our modern ethos has lost distinctions like this, so that now we all want to be ends and not means.

Except in genuine service settings, an exemplar of which is the military, and other examples of which include numerous volunteer activities, public school teaching in general and especially in distressed communities, law enforcement, the Peace Corps, firefighting, and Doctors Without Borders, to name a few. In a time of deep political division, it is interesting to reflect upon which of these are generally admired, which less so, and why. If it were possible to separate out the question of service provision per se from the question of to whom services are being provided, most if not all of these vocations and avocations would be viewed with admiration. The military, law enforcement, and firefighting serve and protect all, and thus tend to stir at least some appreciation in all. In public school teaching and the Peace Corps, to take two examples, the "otherness" of who is served can distract from the selflessness of the service per se, alas. None of this need detract from the reality that all these are fundamentally admirable, and furthermore, that their being mandatory for everyone, at least for a brief time, might stem the tide of egoism and foster some of the attitudes promoted in this book.

Some may be inclined to insist that service be limited to the military, a sentiment with which I sympathize, but there are reasons that doing so may not be best. For one, it is at least conceivable that a policy like that could encourage excessive militarism. Second, and more to the point of this book, I asked a leading researcher on cross-cultural differences in personality, Bradley University's David Schmitt, to run a relevant analysis, to which he generously agreed. Specifically, Professor Schmitt had in hand the average score on a narcissism scale in samples from 58 countries around the world, ranging from Austria to Zimbabwe. From the Central Intelligence Agency (CIA)'s website, I obtained information per each country on whether or not military service is compulsory, and provided this information to Schmitt. He computed the correlation between a country's average narcissism score and whether that country mandated military service. The correlation was nonsignificant, but just barely so ($p = .054$). Importantly, its direction was such that countries that mandated military service tended to have higher narcissism scores. There are numerous explanations for a result like this, but the result is not especially encouraging of the notion that military service would mitigate cultural trends involving egoism . . . but service more generally still might.

In context of service provision, the 2016 presidential election—more specifically, Secretary Hillary Clinton's selection of Senator Tim Kaine as her running mate—yet again brought to my attention just how profoundly political leanings can affect different people's perception of the same indisputable fact pattern. After graduation from Harvard Law, Kaine served on the city council of Richmond, Virginia, before becoming the city's mayor. Subsequently, he served as Virginia's lieutenant governor and then its governor. He chaired the Democratic National Committee. As I write, he is a U.S. senator. I had naively assumed that a record of achievement like this would be viewed with admiration, even it were begrudging from one side of the aisle. What to me reads like a respectable record of success and service was quickly branded by some as that of a "career politician," a view immune to the fact that Kaine practiced law for well over 15 years. "A lifetime of public service" versus "career politician;" same fact pattern, wildly different conclusions. Notice, incidentally, that even if someone is providing public service for purely selfish motives, it can nonetheless be salutary for that individual as well as contributory to the common good. I offer a small local example: My family and I live on a stretch of road that contains a substantial amount of natural beauty, a kind that is unique to northern Florida. As I drive through that stretch, it is a regular irritant to see trash strewn along it, the juxtaposition between it and the local flora jarring enough to remind me of the Narcissi posting about first-class travel amid people grieving a fallen scholar or the victims of an earthquake. As I jog along that stretch of road, I carry a trash bag and pick up the trash myself, and my entire motivation is selfish, in that I would like to experience that particular irritation of seeing trash as I drive as infrequently as possible. The activity, however, happens also to be to the common good (e.g., it is better for the environment, my neighbors appreciate it), and furthermore, as long as I am careful about snakes, poison ivy, and the kind of trash that should be left to a professional, it is personally salutary in that it motivates me to jog and it brings me into closer contact both with nature and with my neighbors (who sometimes stop to chat). There are moments of solemnity: I occasionally pause for a moment of respect at one of the two small, primitive Baptist church cemeteries along that stretch of road. There are moments of humor: I found a six-word note, written, I inferred from the medium—paper and crayon—and from the handwriting, by a girl of approximately seven years of age. The first two words were "Go Dawgs"—it was football season and "Dawgs" is an intentional misspelling of "Dogs" and a reference to the University of Georgia football team, the Bulldogs. The final four words suggested that a certain "Lisa" did not share the young writer's allegiance, for the missive concluded "Lisa is a poop."

Call me a "minor public servant" or a "self-serving amateur trash collector"—and I admit that the latter is more accurate—either way, the activity pulls one's gaze outward and facilitates social contact, reflection, physical activity, and humor. One could practice mindfulness while doing it, but the benefits of the activity would accrue even if one did it mindlessly (as I do). Related to the activity's encouragement of socializing with neighbors, I noted earlier that one promising aspect of self-compassion is its emphasis on common humanity (as long as it is not construed as an excuse for self-indulgence, as in "I gave in to temptation, I'm flesh and blood, I'm only human"). My little trash-collecting hobby, though selfishly motivated, has increased my connection to humanity, at least that part of it that lives along the same stretch of road as I do, as well as to non-neighbor friends with whom I occasionally converse about my hobby. The latter not infrequently use terms like "admirable" to characterize the activity, and when I correct them that it is actually quite selfish, they seem unpersuaded. Here too, then, the unquenchable demand of self-interest has been answered in a way that has both selfless and selfish reverberations and benefits.

Returning to Schmitt's data on narcissism in different countries, in asking him to run the correlation between a country's average narcissism and whether that country mandated military service, a glaring and unmistakable fact leapt out. Putting aside military service, the narcissism score in males clearly exceeded that in females within each country, and in some countries (e.g., Canada, Israel, United States), the difference is very large. In this context, efforts to empower girls and women are interesting to consider. First Lady Michelle Obama is leading one such effort, focusing on educational access for girls in Africa and Southern Europe. The First Lady has taken to social media not just to promote this effort but also to allow American girls and boys to follow the effort and in so doing, absorb the message that their educational access is a privilege and a blessing that not all countries' children have, and that therefore it should not be taken for granted. Also to promote the initiative, the First Lady made an appearance on "carpool karaoke" with James Corden from *The Late Late Show*, an appearance which, unless forced through same refractory process that reduces Kaine's record to that of a mere "career politician," is hard to see as anything other than very charming. One basis for the First Lady's effort is that increased educational access for girls is likely to make numerous societal problems at least somewhat better, and my own intuition, for what it is worth, is that she is right. It is conceivable, however, that a consequence of empowering girls and women would be a rise in female narcissism levels, perhaps even to a degree to rival male levels, the results of which could be truly dispiriting. This eventuality seems dubious, because it presumes a close association between power and narcissism, when in actuality that connection tends to be modest. Moreover, there are various discrete aspects to narcissism, such as exploitativeness, entitlement, exhibitionism, and proneness to lead, and the largest male–female differences tend to emerge regarding the more malignant facets like exploitativeness and entitlement.[6] Generally speaking then, girls and women are less exploitative than men and boys, but approximately as ready to lead as boys and men . . . if given access and opportunity, that is.

Another set of potential solutions stems from current work in various domains on attentional retraining, cognitive bias modification, and evaluative conditioning approaches to problems like marital dissatisfaction and suicide risk. In the work on marital dissatisfaction, social psychologist Jim McNulty's research, funded in part by the Department of Defense–supported Military Suicide Research Consortium (https://msrc.fsu.edu), has shown that simple pairings of images of one's spouse with positively valenced images like ice cream, babies' faces, and puppies have a detectable, nontrivial, and lasting effect on marital satisfaction. This is the case regardless of whether participants are aware that they were seeing such pairings. The military's interest in this kind of work derives from the facts that marital conflict is a regularly observed precursor in military suicide and that aspects of military life like deployments can stress marriages. Regarding this book's emphases, one can envision a repurposing of McNulty's conditioning technique to improve people's views of selflessness. For instance, imagine an online gaming experience that, in the periphery, pairs images of selflessness with game success. Granted, this has a little bit of "Big Brother" to it, but interventions like this can be done with effectiveness under conditions of full consent and awareness. Moreover, I don't recall signing a consent form for fluoride to be in my family's drinking water, but I am glad it is there. I imagine that substantial chunks of the American public do not know what fluoride is or that it is in their water or why, but if they did, most would also be glad it's there. Just as adding fluoride to the water supply reduces cavities, evidence suggests that so would adding small amounts of lithium reduce deaths by suicide.[7]

Speaking of which, psychologist Joe Franklin paired aversive images (e.g., tarantulas, snakes) with images of self-injury (e.g., a blade pressed against the skin) and across three separate trials, obtained evidence of reduced suicide-proneness.[8] Importantly in context of mention earlier of embedding an intervention in a gaming experience, the invention by Franklin and colleagues *is* a game, and they showed that participants enjoyed the intervention like they would a game. The logic in force here suggests that minds are movable or at least nudgable across many domains, such as marital satisfaction, reduced suicide risk, and many more. If these things are nudgable, it is likely that orientations toward egoism may be as well. Interestingly, McNulty's intervention on marital satisfaction uses reward, Franklin's on suicide-proneness, punishment. Interventions that reward selflessness and punish egoism thus have potential. These kinds of findings harken back, incidentally, to research mentioned in Chapter 1 on the ordering of images and words, and how something as simple as photos of trees being in the right seasonal order made a difference in participants' meaning in life. Here again, a small tweak is nudging a mountain-like psychological process.

If the goal is not so much to diminish egoism as to encourage authentic mindfulness, recall the research using an implicit method in which participants are instructed to form three-word sentences from a string of four words such as "awareness play hockey kids." The answer, "kids play hockey," leaves out the mindfulness-related word ("awareness") and yet nevertheless improved participants' mindfulness. I wrote of this approach approvingly in a previous chapter because it manages to use a simple nudge-like task to affect a not-so-simple target (i.e., mindfulness), and crucially, it does so without the common faux mindfulness pitfall of navel-gazing.

Throughout much of the book, I have extolled the virtues of mundane attitudes and activities like keeping to a daily routine and frequent walking. (Speaking of the latter, and in connection with embedding effective interventions within gaming platforms, I was delighted to learn that the 2016 gaming phenomenon of Pokémon Go directly incentivizes walking—actual physical walking, not virtual walking. Though less directly, it also incentivizes social connection, in that players are directed toward the same physical location and often end up in conversation with one another about the game and other topics once there. In the psychotherapy clinic I direct, we have begun recommending the game as a supplement to the psychotherapy of depression and also as a way for those with isolating video game addictions to transition out of addiction.) Unlike much of the hyperbolic praise that is heaped on mindfulness, the empirical support for these kinds of things as health-promoting is utterly convincing. Absent considerable and repeatedly confirmed evidence, to promote alternatives to these is an unethical menace to public health and to other aspects of the public good. Advocates of mindfulness and allied approaches suggest that such approaches are completely compatible with more down-to-earth strategies, a claim that is true in a literal sense. However, what is also true is that in much of the mindfulness literature and also in workshops and retreats, one can come away with the impression that mindfulness is the alpha and the omega to health, serenity, wisdom, and so on. This book has attempted to show that not only is that a wild exaggeration, but it can be an unfortunate distraction from things that really do work.

Similarly, self-care, self-forgiveness, and self-compassion over-emphasize the self and thus distract people from their most useful insights, especially that the goal of readiness to serve is subserved by the means on tending to one's own basic physical and mental health. It is reasonable to prioritize self-care as long as it is done not as an end in itself, but as a way to stay "mission-ready," as the astronauts and others at National Aeronautics and Space Administration (NASA) do. To see self-care and so forth as otherwise is a distraction from the nobility and togetherness of a shared mission, whatever that mission may be.

I admire attitudes, philosophies of life, and activities that pull us out of ourselves, that redirect our gaze from the trivial and fleeting concern of ourselves outward to the eternal and infinite cosmos. The trajectory of the redirection from inward to outward is fully consistent with authentic mindfulness; indeed, it at least in part defines it. It is furthermore consistent with stoicism. As with mindfulness and its degraded versions, stoicism is often misunderstood; in stoicism's case, misunderstood for a glum, unemotional, and overly serious mindset—a mindset, mind you, that I would choose over that of the Narcissi unhesitatingly. However, authentic stoicism is nothing like this; the stoic philosophers like Cato and Epictetus advised us to live a virtuous life, and for them, virtue largely meant being true to our nature. They took it as self-evident that our nature included the ability to reason, and thus we should strive moment to moment to be reasonable. And our nature included the instinct toward gregariousness with our fellows, and thus we should prioritize our duty to others and deploy our reason in so doing. There is nothing despondent here. On the contrary, considerable room is left for things like joy and delight, things not often associated with stoicism but which the stoics explicitly encouraged, the only constraints being reason and duty to others.

Entire academic careers can be and have been spent on the issue, but allow me a brief attempt to say more about what the stoics viewed as reasonable. I see two main pillars to stoic reason, one of which might be termed *true control,* the other, *ephemerality.* Regarding true control, the stoics simply advised that we deploy our attention and efforts only toward those situations, things, and people over which we have at least some influence, and as for everything and everyone else, pay no mind. Modern readers may have a reaction along the lines of "hey the stoics stole that from the Serenity Prayer." The prayer in question goes ". . . grant me the serenity to accept the things I cannot change, courage to change the things I can, and wisdom to know the difference." Other readers will find this prayer lacking in substance and somewhat trite. But I think both sets of readers miss something. Those who feel the stoics robbed from the Serenity Prayer have overlooked or never knew that the stoics were thinking about this theme around 2,000 years ago, whereas by most accounts, the Serenity Prayer is a product of the 20th century. Those who see the prayer as superficial perhaps have forgotten or never knew that the prayer's whole point was a major emphasis and preoccupation of stoic thought 2,000 years ago.

Interestingly, though I do not believe the Serenity Prayer or stoic philosophy are mentioned in writings on it, CBASP, described earlier, very much endorses this same notion. Indeed, an acceptable desired outcome is one over which one can realistically exert influence via one's own behavior (which is under one's control or can be), with no mind paid to things extrinsic to this. As with stoicism, there is nothing glum or dispiriting in CBASP's philosophical underpinnings; on the contrary, the system's entire point is to alleviate the despondency of chronic forms of depression (it works for much else too), and as we have seen, there is reasonable evidence that it is effective in this.

One pillar of stoic reason, at least in my understanding of it, is thus a disciplined focus on what is within one's sphere of influence. This discipline of mind has similarities to authentic mindfulness' emphases on paying attention on purpose and on "choicefulness." One thing that is not within one's present sphere of influence is the past; though it is perhaps more arguable, much the same can be said of the future, at least in the sense that it is not here yet. Thus, very similar to mindfulness, one can find repeated reference in stoic philosophy to the present moment, which brings us to a second pillar of stoic reason, ephemerality. Like the bubbles blown into the air by a child, really even more ephemeral than that, the present moment is there for an instant and then it is instantly gone. To focus on the present moment thus means an acceptance, an embrace really, of the fleeting, ephemeral nature of all things, to include one's thoughts, feelings, biases, passions, and fears, but also to include one's life, others' lives, everything that you see around you—all, in the scale of the infinitude of the cosmos, ephemeral. "Generations come and generations go, but the earth remains forever," the author (probably Solomon) tells us in the first chapter of Ecclesiastes. The stoic philosophers would knowingly smile on this verse, and it is here that I believe stoicism is misunderstood as glum and unfeeling. We love each other; some love themselves. To face the reality that all that one loves will return to dust can certainly be seen as upsetting or even as unnatural immersion in the pessimistic or the macabre. Stoic philosophers would respond that this is a mistake in reason; they would insist that the undeniable fact of the ephemerality of everything encourages living now, taking joy in the present moment, cherishing others (and oneself if one insists) now, before it is too late—and it eventually will be too late. To vex oneself over the fleeting nature of everything, to immerse oneself in the wish or fantasy that it were not so, is to violate the other pillar of stoic reason, true control. The very nature of the cosmos dictates ephemerality, and to imagine one has influence on the cosmos is a feat of egoism that even this culture of narcissism would struggle to endorse.

The writings of 18th-century American revolutionists promote with unrivaled eloquence individual liberty and equality, but just as prominently, they advocated for duty to others. The U.S. Constitution's preamble—which, the father of a fallen American soldier memorably reminded us in the summer of 2016, not everyone seems to have read—is actually mostly about duty to and harmony with others, from the opening words, "We the people" through to "domestic tranquility," "common defense," and "the general welfare." The signatories to the Declaration of Independence closed it with a mutual pledge to one another of their lives, their fortunes, and their honor. In all this, the American Founders benefited from stoic thought, because the stoics, too, believed in human reason and saw as one of its main functions the taming and relegation of impulse and passion in the larger service of a well-functioning society.

Designers of middle-school, high-school, and college curricula thus may benefit from a second look at what is included, or at least at what is prioritized, in reading lists and other course materials. A great irony is that Jefferson and Cato had a profound understanding of the diversity of ideas centuries before the current version of intellectual diversity, which often can seem neither intellectual nor diverse. The American Founders and the stoics were imperfect creatures of their time, just as you are, just as I am; their ideas are nevertheless timeless and a needed antidote to cultural trends in which a member of the House of Representatives feels free to yell to the President, "You lie!" during a joint session of Congress, or in which, during a college lecture on the stoics or a speech by the President himself, some audience members stare glassy-eyed and slack-jawed at their personal devices, seeing all while seeing nothing.

Near the beginning of the book in my reflections on penguins and professors, I stated that the penguins represented a third way, in addition to the two of authentic mindfulness and self-satisfied professorliness, and in this context, I compared the penguins to the stoics. The comparison works in some ways, for example, the penguins and the stoics are fully living in the moment, unconcerned with that which they cannot control, like the past or like the ephemeral nature of everything. And furthermore, in their way, both the penguins and the stoics embody duty to others. The penguins are stunningly self-sacrificial—or more accurately, endure extreme hardship on behalf on their progeny and their genes—and the stoics directly extolled duty to others as a virtue as well as indirectly via their emphasis on the ephemeral and trivial nature of passions and impulses involving self-concern. It is certainly the case that the lampooned professor exhibits little of this, so much so that it has become very rewarding to chance upon the few who still do, akin I imagine to finding a Vaporeon in Pokémon Go (a rare and valuable character I am told, the appearance of which in July 2016 in Central Park in New York City caused a near-stampede). However, it is worth pointing out not only how much the stoics would have agreed with my derision of the (alas not always) fictional professor, but also how much they would endorse the tenets of authentic mindfulness. Thus, instead of three ways, there are really only two. On the one hand, we have the self-preoccupation and self-satisfaction of the professor and also of enthusiasts for various forms of corrupted mindfulness; on the other hand, we have the doggedness, attentiveness, calm, and humility of the penguins, the stoics, and the practitioners of authentic mindfulness. Bad being stronger than good,[9] when I began this book, the corruption of mindfulness caught my attention more than did its authenticity, and the corrupting trends at work remain a focus. But this focus should not distract us from authentic mindfulness' humility, nobility, and promise. As with the stoics and the Founding Fathers, so with the collection of ideas that constitute authentic mindfulness, in that imperfection can exist along with ideas of considerable reach, profundity, and utility.

Moments before his death, Goliath said to David, "Am I a dog, that thou comest to me with staves?"[10] Sheathed in bronze and towering over all, Goliath was boastfully offended that a mere shepherd would confront him, particularly with just a sling, some stones, and a staff ... then he perished. Like Goliath, mindless mindfulness is big, shiny, and boastful, and ironically, heedless of its weaknesses. Mindfulness need not perish, but faux mindlessness should, and this book pleads for a return to a selfless and authentic mindfulness, combined with a selfless stoicism gazing outwardly intently enough on virtue that the reign of the Narcissi ends, overcome by mindlessness toward self-concern and its myriad entrapments.

We have been infected with a set of ideas that has weakened us. The ideas take various forms, but they share a view of the importance of the individual self as compared to things like principle, posterity, and the greater good. They celebrate individual rights and entitlements but neglect individuals' responsibility and duty, and they assume that whatever occurs to a particular mind has value and importance in its own right (mindfulness gone mindless), when in reality, the usual thought or feeling in the mind of any given human is so lacking in profundity that ironically, it staggers the mind. From whence this infection? The source is multi-determined, but there is a strand of thought within psychology that tends to encourage it: Namely, the flight of fancy that goes under the name of mindfulness. (However, as this book asserts, that is a misnomer because the original concept of mindfulness, although imperfect, is down to earth and sensible. I have argued here that it is where the field has taken this original idea that is problematic.)

Is there any hope for a return to authentic mindfulness and a virtuous stoicism? The stoics thought so, so did American colonists, and so did David with his slingshot. And so do babies: When infants see a puppet play involving a virtuous puppet and a selfish one and can thereafter choose which puppet to play with, babies reach for virtue. Goodness, indeed selflessness, written into our very cells and souls, is within our grasp.

Notes

Introduction

1. See Williams & Kabat-Zinn, 2011.
2. See Mental Health Foundation, *Nearly one in three people are regularly stressed, survey for mental health awareness week reveals*, May 10, 2015. Retrieved from www.mentalhealth. org.uk/news/nearly-one-three-people-are-regularly-stressed-survey-mental-health-awareness-week-reveals.
3. Jonathan Franzen, The end of the end of the world, *New Yorker*, May 23, 2016, p. 50.
4. The quote is from Shakespeare, *Coriolanus*, act II, scene 1.
5. Quoted from the *Los Angeles Times*, March 30, 2013.
6. Teper, Segal, & Inzlicht, 2013.
7. Kabat-Zinn, 2012, p. 104.
8. Kelly April Tyrrell, *UW, Madison schools team up to train mindfulness muscles, University of Wisconsin-Madison*, July 1, 2014. Retrieved from http://news.wisc.edu/uw-madison-schools-team-up-to-train-mindfulness-muscles.
9. See Hart, Ivtzan, & Hart, 2013.
10. Wilson, 2012, location 172 of 5093 in the ebook version.
11. Kabat-Zinn, p. 60.

12. Isabell, 2010.
13. Hames, 2015.
14. Anestis et al., 2015.
15. See Burnaby, 1955.
16. Thompson, 2011, p. 31.
17. Beilock, Carr, MacMahon, & Starkes, 2002.
18. Brown & Ryan, 2003.
19. Stanley et al., 2006.
20. Wilson Mickes, Stolarz-Fantino, Evrard, & Fantino, 2015.
21. Sheldon et al., 2014.
22. Hafenbrack & Vohs, 2016.
23. Baumeister, Vohs, Aaker, & Garbinsky, 2013.
24. Bergeron & Dandeneau, 2016.
25. This last point assumes that the participants in the mindfulness condition of Wilson et al.'s (2015) study were mostly gazing inward. The results fit well with that assumption, but I acknowledge it is only an assumption.
26. Bechara, 2004.
27. Franzen, 2016, p. 48.
28. Described on the National Public Radio (NPR) radio show *Fresh Air*, which aired on September 11, 2012.
29. T. Perry, Military's dogs of war also suffer post-traumatic stress disorder, *Los Angeles Times*, November 26, 2012.

Chapter 1

1. Lin et al., 2016.
2. Meehl, 1973.
3. Wilson, 2014, Kindle locations 365–368.
4. Wilson, 2014, Kindle location 374.
5. Marsha Linehan has made similar points in her seminal work on dialectical-behavior therapy (e.g., Linehan, 1993).
6. The distinction between brooding and reflecting was important in the late psychologist Susan Nolen-Hoeksema's theorizing on rumination and its consequences, e.g., Miranda & Nolen-Hoeksema, 2007.
7. Kabat-Zinn, 2012, p. 37.
8. Jammer, 2002.
9. Pope, n.d., electronic mailing list message.

10. cf. Teper, Segal, & Inzlicht, 2013.

11. Mrazek, Franklin, Phillips, Baird, & Schooler, 2013.

12. Mrazek et al., 2013, p. 777.

13. Mrazek et al., 2013.

14. Hafenbrack, Kinias, & Barsade, 2014.

15. Purser & Loy, Beyond McMindfulness [blog post], *Huffington Post*, July 1, 2013. Retrieved from www.huffingtonpost.com/ron-purser/beyond-mcmindfulness_b_3519289.html.

16. David DeSteno, The morality of meditation, *New York Times Sunday Review*, July 5, 2013. Retrieved from www.nytimes.com/2013/07/07/opinion/sunday/the-morality-of-meditation.html.

17. Raes, Griffith, Van der Gucht, & Williams, 2014.

18. Leonard et al., 2013.

19. Kenny & Williams, 2007.

20. e.g., Tang, Hölzel, & Posner, 2015.

21. e.g., Hughes et al., 2013.

22. See Kuyken et al., 2016, for a compatible analysis.

23. Wells et al., 2013.

24. Davidson et al., 2003.

25. Tang et al., 2015.

26. Garland et al., 2011.

27. Kuyken et al., 2015.

28. Michalak, Schultze, Heidenreich, & Schramm, 2015.

29. Segal, Williams, & Teasdale, 2012.

30. Williams et al., 2014; Kuyken et al., 2015; Michalak et al., 2015.

31. Bowen et al., 2014.

32. See www.davidlynchfoundation.org/message.html.

33. R. Purser & A. Cooper, Mindfulness' "truthiness" problem: Sam Harris, science and the truth about Buddhist tradition, *Salon*, December 6, 2014. Retrieved from www.salon.com/2014/12/06/mindfulness_truthiness_problem_sam_harris_science_and_the_truth_about_buddhist_tradition.

34. Erickson et al., 2011.

35. MacLean, Surviving Whole Foods [blog post], *Huffington Post*, September 16, 2013. Retrieved from www.huffingtonpost.com/kelly-maclean/surviving-whole-foods_b_3895583.html.

36. ten Brinke et al., 2015.

37. Brown, Pavey, & Bauman, 2014.

38. e.g., Chu et al., 2016.
39. Carlson et al., 2015.
40. Carlson et al., 2015, p. 483.
41. Shaku, Tsutsumi, Goto, & Arnoult, 2014.
42. Dalrymple, 2009.
43. Aldrin, p. 146.
44. Described by Thomas Wehr in a lecture at Florida State University in the Rushton Neuroscience Lecture Series, circa 2002. See also Wehr et al., 1998.
45. Heintzelman, Trent, & King, 2013.
46. Khoury, Lecomte, Gaudiano, & Paquin, 2013.
47. Sundquist et al., 2015.
48. Strauss, Cavanagh, Oliver, & Pettman, 2014.
49. Foster's *Guardian* article is titled "Is mindfulness making us ill?"
50. Shapiro, 1992.

Chapter 2

1. Max, 2013.
2. *George Stroumboulopoulos Tonight*, 2011. Retrieved from www.cbc.ca/strombo/videos/guest-interview/jeff-tweedy.
3. Thomas H. Maugh II, *Los Angeles Times*, September 17, 2012.
4. Cf. Goldstein, 1980.
5. Lieberman, p. 113.
6. Lieberman, p. 113.
7. *Congressman Tim Ryan announces mindfulness based stress reduction (MBSR) grant award for Kent State University and the University of Pennsylvania* [press release], September 4, 2014. Retrieved from https://timryan.house.gov/press-release/congressman-tim-ryan-announces-mindfulness-based-stress-reduction-mbsr-grant-award.
8. Molly Ball, Congressman Moonbeam: Can Representative Tim Ryan teach Washington to mediate? *Atlantic Monthly*, September 2013. Retrieved from www.theatlantic.com/magazine/archive/2014/09/congressman-moonbeam/375065/.
9. Ruth Fowler, The trouble with trigger warnings, *Al Jazeera America*, June 1, 2014. Retrieved from http://america.aljazeera.com/opinions/2014/6/trigger-warningsbooksptsdhighereducation.html.

10. Rebecca Mead, Comment: Literature and life, *New Yorker*, June 9/16, 2014, p. 40.
11. Todd Gitlin, Please be disturbed: Triggering can be good for you, kids, *Tablet*, March 13, 2015. Retrieved from www.tabletmag.com/jewish-news-and-politics/189543/trigger-warnings-on-campus.
12. Niederkrotenthaler et al., 2012.
13. Jobes, Berman, O'Carroll, Eastgard, & Knickmeyer, 1996.
14. Anestis et al., 2015.
15. Meehl, 1973, p. 253.
16. Eccl. 11:5.
17. Purser & Loy, Beyond McMindfulness [blog post], 2013.

Chapter 3

1. See Tara Isabella Burton, Keep smiling, *Paris Review*, February 20, 2014. Retrieved from www.theparisreview.org/blog/2014/02/20/keep-smiling.
2. Rosie Scammell, US tourists caught carving names into Rome's Colosseum, *Guardian*, March 8, 2015. Retrieved from www.theguardian.com/world/2015/mar/08/us-tourists-caught-carving-names-into-colosseum-rome.
3. Jennifer O'Connell, Selfie, word of 2013, sums up our age of narcissism, *Irish Times*, December 11, 2013. Retrieved from www.irishtimes.com/life-and-style/selfie-word-of-2013-sums-up-our-age-of-narcissism-1.1623385.
4. From a 1950 reprint of Simmel's work.
5. Durkheim, 1897, p. 299.
6. The title of Bawer's article in the September online issue of the New Criterion is "Ore or ordure?" See www.newcriterion.com/articles.cfm/Ore-or-ordure--7696.
7. See Twenge, Campbell, & Gentile, 2012.
8. See, for example, www.selfmarriageceremonies.com/unveiled.
9. Ehrenreich, The selfish side of gratitude, *New York Times*, December 31, 2015. Retrieved from www.nytimes.com/2016/01/03/opinion/sunday/the-selfish-side-of-gratitude.html?_r=0.
10. e.g., Graham, Gouick, Krahé, & Gilanders, 2016.

11. Jacob Gershman, Lawyers go Zen, with few objections, *Wall Street Journal*, June 18, 2015. Retrieved from www.wsj.com/articles/lawyers-go-zen-with-few-objections-1434586250.

12. Cleckley, 1941.

13. This appears at location 1725 of 5149 in the e-book (Dalrymple, 2012).

14. May 8, 2015.

15. Dean, 2015.

16. *Tom Brokaw's "Space race" Olympic special airs tomorrow* [press release], February 14, 2014. Retrieved from http://nbcsportsgrouppressbox.com/2014/02/14/tom-brokaws-space-race-olympic-special-airs-tomorrow.

17. Aldrin, 2009.

18. Paul Gallagher, Neil Armstrong's last interview: Rare glimpse of man and moon mission, *The Guardian*, August 25, 2012. Retrieved from www.theguardian.com/science/2012/aug/25/neil-armstrong-last-interview.

19. Aldrin, 2009, p. 10.

20. Margaret Kane, Say what? 'Young people are just smarter,' CNET, March 28, 2007. Retrieved from www.cnet.com/news/say-what-young-people-are-just-smarter.

21. Barbara J. King, Why do 202,586 people want to leave our planet for Mars? *Cosmos & Culture*, April 10, 2014. Retrieved from www.npr.org/sections/13.7/2014/04/10/300601241/why-do-202-586-people-want-to-leave-our-planet.

22. As also shown by Twenge and colleagues, 2014.

23. From a 2013 paper presented at the 1st International Conference on Human-Agent Interaction by Bartneck and colleagues.

24. Topolski, Weaver, Martin, & McCoy, 2013.

25. The team included Daryl Cameron, Michael Inzlicht, and William Cunningham.

26. Cameron & Payne, 2011.

27. Twenge et al., 2008.

28. Arnett, 2013.

29. Twenge & Kasser, 2013.

30. Bianchi, 2014.

31. Brummelman et al., 2015.

32. From the April 23, 2014 issue of *Princeton Alumni Weekly*, pp. 8–9.

33. The quote is from the book *The Memory Chalet* (Judt, 2012).

Chapter 4

1. Gershman, Lawyers go with Zen, June 18, 2015.
2. Gawande, 2014, p. 18.
3. Described in an article in the *International Journal of Behavioral Development* by April Smith et al., 2016.
4. Bohannon, Goldstein, & Herschkowitsch, 2009.
5. 1 Cor. 6:19.
6. Gawande, 2014, p. 22.
7. Joiner, Hom, Hagan, & Silva, 2016.
8. Fischer et al., 2008; Kim, De Vries, & Peteet, 2016.
9. Ganzini, Silveira, & Johnston, 2002; Ganzini et al., 2003.
10. Elgot, 2015.
11. Pakenham, 2015.
12. e.g., Germer & Neff, 2013.
13. The title of Wright's article is "Why can't we all just get along? The uncertain biological basis of morality" (p. 110).

Chapter 5

1. Haidt & Joseph, 2008.
2. Wilson, 2012, Kindle locations 808–815 of 5093.
3. Franzen, The end of the end of the world, p. 55.
4. Keller et al., 2000.
5. Woznica & Shapiro, 1990; Joiner, Hom, Hagan, & Silva, 2016.
6. e.g., Grijalva et al., 2015.
7. Blüml et al., 2012.
8. Franklin, Puzia, Lee, & Prinstein, 2016.
9. Baumeister, Bratslavsky, Finkenauer, & Vohs, 2001.
10. 1 Sam. 17:43.

References

Aldrin, B. (2009). Magnificent desolation: The long journey home from the moon. New York: Harmony Books.

Anestis, M., Bryan, C., May, A., Law, K., Hagan, C., Bryan, A., ... Joiner, T. (2015). Dangerous words? An experimental investigation of the impact of detailed reporting about suicide on subsequent risk. *Journal of Clinical Psychology, 71,* 1031–1041.

Arnett, J. J. (2013). The evidence for generation we and against generation me. *Emerging Adulthood, 1*(1), 5–10.

Bailey, B. (2014). The splendid things we planned: A family portrait. New York: Norton.

Bailey, M. (2003). *The man who would be queen.* Washington, DC: Joseph Henry Press.

Bartneck, C., Obaid, M., & Zawieska, K. (2013). *Agents with faces— what can we learn from Lego minfigures?* Proceedings of the 1st International Conference on Human-Agent Interaction, Sapporo, Hokkaido, Japan, pp. III-2-1. Retrieved from http://bartneck.de/publications/2013/agentsWithFaces/bartneckLEGOAgent.pdf

Baumeister, R. F., Bratslavsky, E., Finkenauer, C., & Vohs, K. D. (2001). Bad is stronger than good. *Review of General Psychology, 5*(4), 323–370.

Baumeister, R. F., Vohs, K. D., Aaker, J. L., & Garbinsky, E. N. (2013). Some key differences between a happy life and a meaningful life. *The Journal of Positive Psychology, 8*(6), 505–516.

Bechara, A. (2004). The role of emotion in decision-making: Evidence from neurological patients with orbitofrontal damage. *Brain and Cognition, 55*(1), 30–40.

Beilock, S. L., Carr, T. H., MacMahon, C., & Starkes, J. L. (2002). When paying attention becomes counterproductive: Impact of divided versus skill-focused attention on novice and experienced performance of sensorimotor skills. *Journal of Experimental Psychology: Applied, 8*(1), 6–16.

Bergeron, C. M., & Dandeneau S. (2016). Implicitly activating mindfulness promotes positive responses following an ego threat. *Journal of Social and Clinical Psychology, 35*(7), 551–570.

Bianchi, E. C. (2014). Entering adulthood in a recession tempers later narcissism. *Psychological Science, 25*(7), 1429–1437.

Bloom, T., & Friedman, H. (2013). Classifying dogs' (Canis familiaris) facial expressions from photographs. *Behavioral Processes, 96*, 1–10.

Blüml, V., Regier, M. D., Hlavin, G., Rockett, I. R., König, F., Vyssoki, B., ... Kapusta, N. D. (2013). Lithium in the public water supply and suicide mortality in Texas. *Journal of Psychiatric Research, 47*(3), 407–411.

Bohannon, J., Goldstein, R., & Herschkowitsch, A. (2009). *Can people distinguish pâté from dog food?* (Working Paper No. 36). New York: American Association of Wine Economists. Retrieved from http://www.wine-economics.org/aawe/wp-content/uploads/2012/10/AAWE_WP36.pdf

Bowen, S., Witkiewitz, K., Clifasefi, S. L., Grow, J., Chawla, N., Hsu, S. H., ... Larimer, M. E. (2014). Relative efficacy of mindfulness-based relapse prevention, standard relapse prevention, and treatment as usual for substance use disorders: A randomized clinical trial. *JAMA Psychiatry, 71*(5), 547–556.

Brown, K. W., & Ryan, R. M. (2003). The benefits of being present: Mindfulness and its role in psychological well-being. *Journal of Personality and Social Psychology, 84*(4), 822–848.

Brown, W. J., Pavey, T., & Bauman, A. E. (2014). Comparing population attributable risks for heart disease across the adult lifespan in women. *British Journal of Sports Medicine*, 1–8. doi:10.1136/bjsports-2013-093090

Brummelman, E., Thomaes, S., Nelemans, S. A., De Castro, B. O., Overbeek, G., & Bushman, B. J. (2015). Origins of narcissism in children. *Proceedings of the National Academy of Sciences, 112*(12), 3659–3662.

Burnaby, J. (Ed.). (1955). *Augustine: Later works*. Library of Christian Classics: Vol. VIII. Philadelphia, PA: Westminster John Knox Press.

Cameron, C. D., & Payne, B. K. (2011). Escaping affect: How motivated emotion regulation creates insensitivity to mass suffering. *Journal of Personality and Social Psychology, 100*(1), 1–15.

Carlson, L. E., Beattie, T. L., Giese-Davis, J., Faris, P., & Tamagawa, R. (2015). Mindfulness-based cancer recovery and supportive-expressive therapy maintain telomere length relative to controls in distressed breast cancer survivors. *Cancer, 121*(3):476–484.

Chu, C., Hom, M., Rogers, M., Moberg, F., Hames, J., Suh, S., & Joiner, T. (2016). Is insomnia lonely? Exploring thwarted belongingness as an explanatory link between insomnia and suicidal ideation in a sample of South Korean university students. *Journal of Clinical Sleep Medicine, 12*(5), 647–652.

Cleckley, H. (1941). *The mask of sanity*. St Louis, MO: Mosby.

Dalrymple, T. (2009). *Second opinion*. Cheltenham, UK: Monday Books.

Dalrymple, T. (2012). *Farewell fear*. London: New English Review Press.

Davidson, R. J., Kabat-Zinn, J., Schumacher, J., Rosenkranz, M., Muller, D., Santorelli, S. F., . . . Sheridan, J. F. (2003). Alterations in brain and immune function produced by mindfulness meditation. *Psychosomatic Medicine, 65*(4), 564–570.

Dean, M. L. (2015). *Leaving orbit: Notes from the last days of American spaceflight*. Minneapolis, MN: Graywolf Press.

Dreger, A. (2015). *Galileo's middle finger*. New York: Penguin.

Dufrene, T., & Wilson, K. (2012). *The wisdom to know the difference*. San Francisco: New Harbinger.

Durkheim, E. (1897). *Le suicide: Etude de sociologie*. Paris: F. Alcan.

Elgot, J. (2015, June 3). Stephen Hawking: "I would consider assisted suicide." *Guardian*. Retrieved from https://www.theguardian.com/science/2015/jun/03/stephen-hawking-i-would-consider-assisted-suicide

Erickson, K. I., Voss, M. W., Prakash, R. S., Basak, C., Szabo, A., Chaddock, L., . . . Wojcicki, T. R. (2011). Exercise training increases size of hippocampus and improves memory. *Proceedings of the National Academy of Sciences, 108*(7), 3017–3022.

Faulkner, W. (1932). *Light in August.* New York: Smith & Hass.

Ferguson, C. J. (2015). "Everybody knows psychology is not a real science": Public perceptions of psychology and how we can improve our relationship with policymakers, the scientific community, and the general public. *American Psychologist, 70*(6), 527–542.

Fitzgerald, F. S. (1925). *The great Gatsby.* New York: Scribner's.

Fischer, S., Huber, C. A., Imhof, L., Imhof, R. M., Furter, M., Ziegler, S. J., & Bosshard, G. (2008). Suicide assisted by two Swiss right-to-die organisations. *Journal of Medical Ethics, 34*(11), 810–814.

Franklin, J. C., Puzia, M. E., Lee, K. M., & Prinstein, M. J. (2016). A brief mobile app reduces nonsuicidal and suicidal self-injury: Evidence from three randomized controlled trials. *Journal of Consulting and Clinical Psychology, 84*(6), 544–557.

Ganzini, L., Goy, E. R., Miller, L., Harvath, T. A., Jackson, A., & Delorit, M. A. (2003). Nurses' experiences with hospice patients who refuse food and fluids to hasten death. *New England Journal of Medicine, 349,* 359–365.

Ganzini, L., Silveira, M. J., & Johnston, W. S. (2002). Predictors and correlates of interest in assisted suicide in the final month of life among ALS patients in Oregon and Washington. *Journal of Pain and Symptom Management, 24,* 312–317.

Garland, E. L., Gaylord, S. A., & Frederickson, B. L. (2011). Positive reappraisal mediates the stress-reductive effects of mindfulness: An upward spiral process. *Mindfulness, 2*(1): 59–67. doi:10.1007/s12671-011-0043-8

Gawande, A. 2014. *Being mortal.* New York: Macmillan.

Germer, C. K., & Neff, K. D. (2013). Self-compassion in clinical practice. *Journal of Clinical Psychology, 69*(8), 856–867.

Graham, C. D., Gouick, J., Krahé, C., & Gilanders, D. (2016). A systematic review of the use of acceptance and commitment therapy (ACT) in chronic disease and long-term conditions. *Clinical Psychology Review, 46,* 46–58.

Grijalva, E., Newman, D. A., Tay, L., Donnellan, M. B., Harms, P. D., Robins, R. W., & Yan, T. (2015). Gender differences in narcissism: A meta-analytic review. *Psychological Bulletin, 141*(2), 261–310.

Goldstein, M. (1980). The politics of Thomas Szasz: A sociological view. *Social Problems, 27(5)*, 570–583.

Hafenbrack, A. C., Kinias, Z., & Barsade, S. G. (2014). Debiasing the mind through meditation mindfulness and the sunk-cost bias. *Psychological Science, 25(2)*, 369–376.

Hafenbrack, A. C., & Vohs, K. (2016). Mindfulness meditation impairs task motivation but not performance. Manuscript under editorial review.

Haidt, J. (2008). Morality. *Perspectives on Psychological Science, 3(1)*, 65–72.

Haidt, J., & Joseph, C. (2008). Evolution and cognition. In P. Carruthers, S. Laurence, & S. Stitch (Eds.), *The innate mind: Vol. 3. Foundations and the future.* (pp. 367–391). New York: Oxford University Press.

Hames, J. (2015). *Testing the efficacy of two prevention interventions for individuals at risk for suicide and depression* (Doctoral dissertation). Florida State University, Tallahassee, FL.

Hart, R., Ivtzan, I., & Hart, D. (2013). Mind the gap in mindfulness research: A comparative account of the leading schools of thought. *Review of General Psychology, 17(4)*, 453–466.

Hecht, J. M. (2013). *Stay: A history of suicide and the philosophies against it.* New Haven, CT: Yale University Press.

Heintzelman, S., Trent, J., & King, L. (2013). Encounters with objective coherence and the experience of meaning in life. *Psychological Science, 24(6)*,991–998.

Hendin, H. (1998). *Seduced by death: Doctors, patients, and assisted suicide.* New York: Norton.

Howe, N. (2000). *Millennials rising: the next great generation.* New York: Penguin.

Hughes, J. W., Fresco, D. M., Myerscough, R., van Dulmen, M., Carlson, L. E., & Josephson, R. (2013). Randomized controlled trial of mindfulness-based stress reduction for prehypertension. *Psychosomatic Medicine, 75(8)*. doi:10.1097/PSY.0b013e3182a3e4e5

Isbell, L. (2009). *The fruit, the tree, and the serpent: Why we see so well.* Cambridge, MA: Harvard University Press.

Jammer, M. (2002). *Einstein on religion.* Princeton, NJ: Princeton University Press.

Jobes, D. A., Berman, A. L., O'Carroll, P. W., Eastgard, S., & Knickmeyer, S. (1996). The Kurt Cobain suicide crisis: Perspectives from research, public health, and the news media. *Suicide and Life-Threatening Behavior, 26*(3), 260–271.

Joiner, T. (2014). *The perversion of virtue: Understanding murder-suicide.* New York: Oxford University Press.

Joiner, T. E., Hom, M. A., Hagan, C. R., & Silva, C. (2016). Suicide as a derangement of the self-sacrificial aspect of eusociality. *Psychological Review, 123,* 235–254.

Judt, T. (2012). *The memory chalet.* New York: Penguin.

Kabat-Zinn, J. (2012). *Mindfulness for beginners: Reclaiming the present moment—and your life.* Louisville, CO: Sounds True.

Keller, M. B., McCullough, J. P., Klein, D. N., Arnow, B., Dunner, D. L., Gelenberg, A. J., ... Trivedi, M. H. (2000). A comparison of nefazodone, the cognitive behavioral-analysis system of psychotherapy, and their combination for the treatment of chronic depression. *New England Journal of Medicine, 342*(20), 1462–1470.

Kenny, M. A., & Williams, J. M. G. (2007). Treatment-resistant depressed patients show a good response to mindfulness-based cognitive therapy. *Behaviour Therapy and Research, 45,* 617–625.

Khoury, B., Lecomte, T., Gaudiano, B. A., & Paquin, K. (2013). Mindfulness interventions for psychosis: A meta-analysis. *Schizophrenia Research, 150*(1), 176–184.

Kim, S. Y., De Vries, R. G., & Peteet, J. R. (2016). Euthanasia and assisted suicide of patients with psychiatric disorders in the Netherlands 2011 to 2014. *JAMA Psychiatry, 73*(4), 362–368.

Kirp, D. L. (2014, January 12). Meditation transforms roughest San Francisco schools. *SFGate.* Retrieved from http://www.sfgate.com/opinion/openforum/article/Meditation-transforms-roughest-San-Francisco-5136942.php

Kuyken, W., Hayes, R., Barrett, B., Byng, R., Dalgleish, T., Kessler, D., ... Causley, A. (2015). Effectiveness and cost-effectiveness of mindfulness-based cognitive therapy compared with maintenance antidepressant treatment in the prevention of depressive relapse or recurrence (PREVENT): A randomised controlled trial. *The Lancet, 386*(9988), 63–73.

Kuyken, W., Warren, F., Taylor, R., Whalley, B., Crane, C., ... Dalgleish, T. (2016). Efficacy of mindfulness-based cognitive therapy in prevention of depressive relapse: An individual patient data meta-analysis from randomized trials. *JAMA Psychiatry,* 73(6): 565–574.

Leonard, N. R., Jha, A. P., Casarjian, B., Goolsarran, M., Garcia, C., Cleland, C. M., ... Massey, Z. (2013). Mindfulness training improves attentional task performance in incarcerated youth: A group randomized controlled intervention trial. *Frontiers in Psychology, 4,* 792.

Lieberman, J. (2015). *Shrinks: The untold history of psychiatry.* New York: Little, Brown.

Lin, Y., Fisher, M. E., Roberts, S. M. M., & Moser, J. S. (2016). Deconstructing the emotion regulatory properties of mindfulness: An electrophysiological investigation. *Frontiers in Human Neuroscience, 10.* doi:10.3389/fnhum.2016.00451

Linehan, M. M. (1993). *Cognitive-behavioral treatment of borderline personality disorder.* New York: Guilford Press.

Max, D. T. (2013). *Every love story is a ghost story: A life of David Foster Wallace.* New York: Penguin.

Meehl, P. E. (1973). Why I don't attend case conferences. In P. E. Meehl, *Psychodiagnosis: Selected papers.* New York: Norton.

Michalak, J., Schultze, M., Heidenreich, T., & Schramm, E. (2015). A randomized controlled trial on the efficacy of mindfulness-based cognitive therapy and a group version of cognitive behavioral analysis system of psychotherapy for chronically depressed patients. *Journal of Consulting and Clinical Psychology, 83*(5), 951–963.

Miranda, R., & Nolen-Hoeksema, S. (2007). Brooding and reflection: Rumination predicts suicidal ideation at 1-year follow-up in a community sample. *Behaviour Research and Therapy, 45(12),* 3088–3095.

Mrazek, M. D., Franklin, M. S., Phillips, D. T., Baird, B., & Schooler, J. W. (2013). Mindfulness training improves working memory capacity and GRE performance while reducing mind wandering. *Psychological Science, 24*(5), 776–781.

Niederkrotenthaler, T., Fu, K. W., Yip, P. S., Fong, D. Y., Stack, S., Cheng, Q., & Pirkis, J. (2012). Changes in suicide rates following media reports on celebrity suicide: A meta-analysis. *Journal of Epidemiology and Community Health, 66*(11), 1037–1042.

Pakenham, K. I. (2015). Training in acceptance and commitment therapy fosters self-care in clinical psychology trainees. *Clinical Psychologist, 18*(3), 1–9.

Raes, F., Griffith, J. W., Van der Gucht, K., & Williams, J. M. G. (2014). School-based prevention and reduction of depression in adolescents: A cluster-randomized controlled trial of a mindfulness group program. *Mindfulness, 5*(5), 477–486.

Segal, Z., Williams, J. M. G., & Teasdale, J. (2012). *Mindfulness-based cognitive therapy for depression*. New York: Guilford.

Seijo-Martinez, M., Carral, J. M. C., & Carlos, A. P. (2014). Aerobic physical exercise stabilizes cognitive status in non-demented elderly: An in-patient pilot study. *Neurology, 82*(10), suppl. P1.004.

Shaku, F., Tsutsumi, M., Goto, H., & Arnoult, D. S. (2014). Measuring the effects of Zen training on quality of life and mental health among Japanese monk trainees: A cross-sectional study. *Journal of Alternative and Complementary Medicine, 20*(5), 406–410.

Shapiro, D. H. (1992). A preliminary study of long-term meditators: Goals, effects, religious orientation, cognitions. *Journal of Transpersonal Psychology, 24*(1), 23–39.

Sheldon, K. M., Prentice, M., & Halusic, M. (2014). The experiential incompatibility of mindfulness and flow absorption. *Social Psychological and Personality Science, 6*(3), 276–283.

Simmel, G. (1950). *The sociology of Georg Simmel* (Vol. 92892). K. H. Wolff. (Ed.). New York: The Free Press.

Smith, A., Keel, P., Bodell, L., Holm-Denoma, J., Gordon, K., Perez, M., & Joiner, T. (2016, June 21). "I don't want to grow up, I'm a [Gen X, Y, Me] kid:" Increasing maturity fears across the decades. *International Journal of Behavioral Development*. Advance online publication. doi:10.1177/0165025416654302

Smith, J. C., Nielson, K. A., Woodard, J. L., Seidenberg, M., Durgerian, S., Hazlett, K. E., . . . Rao, S. M. (2014). Physical activity reduces hippocampal atrophy in elders at genetic risk for Alzheimer's disease. *Frontiers in Aging Neuroscience, 6*, 61.

Stanley, S., Reitzel, L., Wingate, L., Cukrowicz, K., Lima, E., & Joiner, T. (2006). Mindfulness: A primrose path for therapists using manualized treatments? *Journal of Cognitive Psychotherapy, 20*, 327–335.

Strauss, C., Cavanagh, K., Oliver, A., & Pettman, D. (2014). Mindfulness-based interventions for people diagnosed with a current episode of an anxiety or depressive disorder: A meta-analysis of randomised controlled trials. *PLoS One, 9*(4), e96110.

Sundquist, J., Lilja, Å., Palmér, K., Memon, A. A., Wang, X., Johansson, L. M., & Sundquist, K. (2015). Mindfulness group therapy in primary care patients with depression, anxiety and stress and adjustment disorders: randomised controlled trial. *British Journal of Psychiatry, 206*(2), 128–135.

Tang, Y-Y., Hölzel, B., & Posner, M. (2015). The neuroscience of mindfulness meditation. *Nature Reviews Neuroscience, 16,* 213–225.

ten Brinke, L. F., Bolandzadeh, N., Nagamatsu, L. S., Hsu, C. L., Davis, J. C., Miran-Khan, K., & Liu-Ambrose, T. (2015). Aerobic exercise increases hippocampal volume in older women with probable mild cognitive impairment: A 6-month randomised controlled trial. *British Journal of Sports Medicine, 49*(4), 248–254. doi:10.1136/bjsports-2013-093184

Teper, R., Segal, Z. V., & Inzlicht, M. (2013). Inside the mindful mind how mindfulness enhances emotion regulation through improvements in executive control. *Current Directions in Psychological Science, 22*(6), 449–454.

Thompson, J. A. (2011). *Why we believe in god(s): A concise guide to the science of faith.* Charlottesville, VA: Pitchstone.

Topolski, R., Weaver, J. N., Martin, Z., & McCoy, J. (2013). Choosing between the emotional dog and the rational pal: A moral dilemma with a tail. *Anthrozoös, 26*(2), 253–263.

Twenge, J. M., Campbell, W. K., & Carter, N. T. (2014). Declines in trust in others and confidence in institutions among American adults and late adolescents, 1972–2012. *Psychological Science, 25,* 1914–1923.

Twenge, J. M., Campbell, W. K., & Gentile, C. (2012). Generational increases in agentic self-evaluations among American college students, 1966–2009. *Self and Identity, 11,* 409-427.

Twenge, J. M., & Kasser, T. (2013). Generational changes in materialism and work centrality, 1976–2007 associations with temporal changes in societal insecurity and materialistic role modeling. *Personality and Social Psychology Bulletin, 39*(7), 883–897.

Twenge, J. M., Konrath, S., Foster, J. D., Keith Campbell, W., & Bushman, B. J. (2008). Egos inflating over time: A cross-temporal meta-analysis of the Narcissistic Personality Inventory. *Journal of Personality, 76*(4), 875–902.

Wells, R. E., Yeh, G. Y., Kerr, C. E., Wolkin, J., Davis, R. B., Tan, Y., . . . Press, D. (2013). Meditation's impact on default mode network and hippocampus in mild cognitive impairment: A pilot study. *Neuroscience Letters, 556,* 15–19.

Wehr, T., Turner, E., Shimada, J., Lowe, C., Barker, C., & Leibenluft, E. (1998). Treatment of a rapidly cycling bipolar patient by using extended bed rest and darkness to stabilize the timing and duration of sleep. *Biological Psychiatry, 43*(11), 822–828.

Weir, A. (2014). *The martian.* New York: Crown.

Williams, J. M. G., Crane, C., Barnhofer, T., Brennan, K., Duggan, D. S., Fennell, M. J., ... Shah, D. (2014). Mindfulness-based cognitive therapy for preventing relapse in recurrent depression: A randomized dismantling trial. *Journal of Consulting and Clinical Psychology, 82*(2), 275–286.

Williams, J. M. G., & Kabat-Zinn, J. (2011). Mindfulness: Diverse perspectives on its meaning, origins, and multiple applications at the intersection of science and dharma. *Contemporary Buddhism, 12,* 1–18.

Wilson, B. M., Mickes, L., Stolarz-Fantino, S., Evrard, M., & Fantino, E. (2015). Increased false-memory susceptibility after mindfulness meditation. *Psychological Science, 26*(10), 1567–1573.

Wilson, E. O. (2012). *The social conquest of the earth.* New York: Liverwright/Norton.

Wilson, E. O. (2014). *The meaning of human existence.* New York: Liverwright/Norton .

Wittgenstein, L. (1922). *Tractatus logico-philosophicus.* New York: Harcourt, Brace.

Woznica, J. G., & Shapiro, J. R. (1990). An analysis of adolescent suicide attempts: The expendable child. *Journal of Pediatric Psychology, 15*(6), 789–796.

About the Author

THOMAS JOINER grew up in Georgia, went to college at Princeton University, and received his PhD in Clinical Psychology from the University of Texas at Austin. He is the Robert O. Lawton Distinguished Professor in the Department of Psychology at Florida State University (FSU), Tallahassee, Florida. Dr. Joiner's work is on the psychology, neurobiology, and treatment of suicidal behavior and related conditions. Author of more than 580 peer-reviewed publications, Dr. Joiner is the Editor-in-Chief of the journal *Suicide and Life-Threatening Behavior* and was awarded the Guggenheim Fellowship and the Rockefeller Foundation's Bellagio Residency Fellowship. He received the Young Investigator Award from the National Alliance for Research on Schizophrenia and Depression, the Shakow Award for Early Career Achievement from the Division of Clinical Psychology of the American Psychological Association, the Shneidman Award for excellence in suicide research, the Dublin Award for career achievement in suicide research from the American Association of Suicidology, and the Award for Distinguished Scientific Early Career Contributions from the American Psychological Association, as well as research grants from the National Institute of Mental Health, Department of Defense (DoD) and various foundations. The Lawton Professorship and the Dublin Award are the single highest honors bestowed, respectively, by FSU and the American Association of Suicidology.

He was a consultant to the National Aeronautics and Space Administration (NASA)'s Human Research Program and is the Director, with Pete Gutierrez, PhD, of the DoD-funded Military Suicide Research Consortium, which is a $30 million project. The effort was recently extended for a second 5-year phase at a similar funding level.

Dr. Joiner has authored or edited 17 books, including *Why People Die by Suicide* (published in 2005) and *Myths About Suicide* (published in 2010). The book *Lonely at the Top: The High Cost of Men's Success* was published in 2011, and the book *The Perversion of Virtue: Understanding Murder-Suicide* was published in 2014. Largely in connection with *Why People Die by Suicide*, he has made numerous radio, print, and television appearances, including write-ups in *The Wall Street Journal* and *The Times* of London, a radio interview on NPR's *Talk of the Nation*, and two appearances on the *Dr. Phil Show*. He runs a part-time clinical and consulting practice specializing in suicidal behavior, including legal consultation on suits involving death by suicide. He lives in Tallahassee, Florida, with his wife and two sons, the elder of whom is an FSU junior.

Index